Karen Bartlett is a writer and journalist, contributing to *The Times*, *WIRED*, *Newsweek*, *TIME* and the BBC. Karen was formerly the director of a leading campaign group for democracy and human rights, and is the author of five other non-fiction books: *The Health of Nations*, *The Diary That Changed the World: The Remarkable Story of Otto Frank and The Diary of Anne Frank*, *After Auschwitz* with Eva Schloss, *Architects of Death: The Family Who Engineered the Holocaust* and *Dusty: An Intimate Portrait of a Musical Legend*. She lives in London.

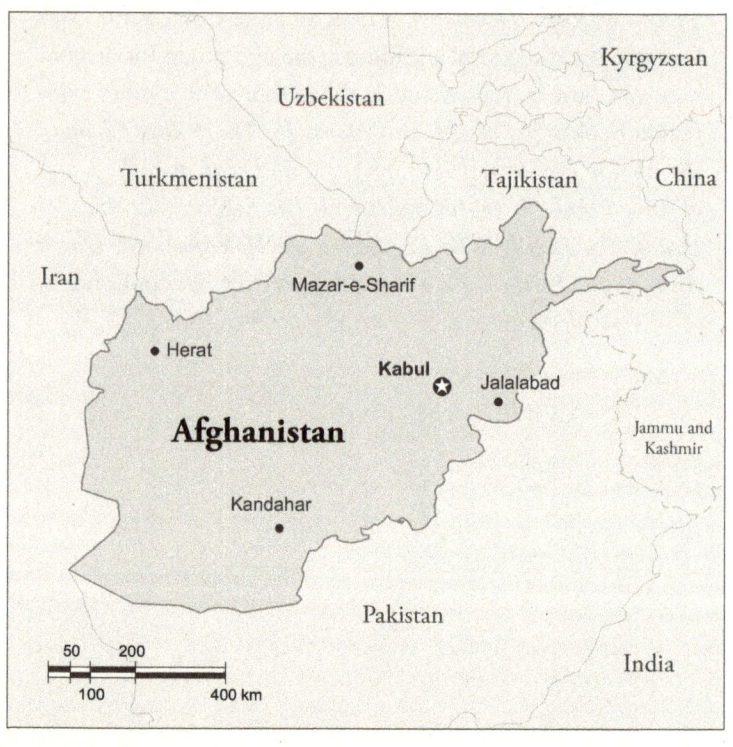

Karen Bartlett

The Escape from Kabul

A True Story of Sisterhood and Defiance

Published in the United Kingdom by Duckworth in 2025
First published in the United States by The New Press, New York, 2025

Duckworth, an imprint of Duckworth Books Ltd
1 Golden Court, Richmond, TW9 1EU, United Kingdom
www.duckworthbooks.co.uk

Copyright © Karen Bartlett, 2025

All rights reserved. No part of this publication may be reproduced, stored in a retrieval system, or transmitted, in any form or by any means electronic, mechanical, photocopying, recording or otherwise, without the prior permission of the publisher.

The right of Karen Bartlett to be identified as the Author of this Work has been asserted by her in accordance with the Copyright, Designs and Patents Act 1988.

A catalogue record for this book is available from the British Library

Composition by Bookbright Media

Printed and bound in Great Britain by Clays Ltd, Elcograf S.p.A.

The authorised representative in the EEA is Easy Access System Europe, Mustamäe tee 50, 10621 Tallinn, Estonia.

Paperback ISBN: 9781914613937
eISBN: 9781914613944

Contents

Map of Afghanistan — ii
Prologue — 1
Introduction — 5

Part One: Escape

1. A Death in Kabul 15
2. The Last Day in Afghanistan 33
3. Tayeba's Escape 49
4. The Last Flight Out 59
5. No Way Out 71

Part Two: Building Justice

6. A Sisterhood Formed in Vermont 87
7. An American in Kabul 105
8. Nafisa: A Pioneer 113
9. Anisa: The Advocate 123
10. Anisa: A Supreme Court Nomination 129
11. Nafisa: Tackling the Narcotics Trade 139
12. Raihana: The Next Generation 147
13. Raihana: The Right to See the Sky 171
14. Tayeba: The Promise of Return 193

Part Three: Judges in Exile

15. Somebody Else's Shoes 211
16. Year Zero 221
17. Buddies.. 231
18. A Tree Transplanted Takes Time to Grow 245
19. The Conscience of the Nation................... 255

Epilogue   263
Notes   266
Acknowledgments   266

Prologue

August 2021: Women's Night

IMAGINE IF THE BEST NIGHT OF YOUR LIFE IS THE ONE YOU spend in the dark. It's hot—very hot, because all the power has gone out. There are no breezes to cool you, and no lights to see by. You are a woman in Nangarhar, Afghanistan, and for the first and only time in your life you can creep outside and sit and talk to other women. For hours you can talk together about your lives, your family—your dreams. You can laugh and be free. Then as the sky lightens you have to slip back into the shadows, alone, silent, smothered. Into the true darkness. If only the power would go out every night, you say. If only we could have this night of freedom again.

This is the night Raihana Attaee remembers. These were the voices of the women she heard every day in her courtroom, where she sat as a judge and passed judgment on the men who attacked them, oppressed them—and often, easily, killed them.

"On the back of the Nangarhar court building, a small door opened to the driveway of the Nangarhar court family houses. There were six houses on the driveway, three on each side. Six judges' families occupied those houses." The houses were old and in poor condition, but the judges were happy to live there, Raihana says, because it was too dangerous to live outside the court compound. Five of the homes belonged to men judges; one belonged to Raihana, a Hazara woman judge with a small family who had moved there from Kabul.

"In the year I lived in the Nangarhar court's house, I could not see a woman's face," Raihana says. "When I had the chadari on, I could not breathe normally. I could not see where I was walking. My eyes became tired and dizzy. When it was hot, I sweated and felt smelly. I felt sorry for those women who had to wear the chadari each time they left home." The women were at home all day, and rarely went farther than the driveway.

"In summer Nangarhar becomes very hot; it goes above 104 Fahrenheit. People use large water coolers to cool their houses. The electricity was not stable, and sometimes it cut off. On one of those days in the middle of summer, the electricity disconnected. We waited for a while, and it did not come back on. When there was no electricity, no one could stay inside the houses, as they became too hot. Everyone had to come to the yard to find a shadow and wait for the electricity. After hours of sitting in the yard, the sky darkened, and there were no stars or moon." Raihana's husband, Maqsood, received a phone call from a friend telling him that all the men had gathered in front of the court building, so Maqsood took their young son, Arsam, and joined them. Raihana stayed in the yard with Humira, a young girl who looked after their son. "A few minutes later there was a knock on the door. It was a twelve-year-old girl named Shukria. 'Judge Attaee,' she said, 'all the women are out on the driveway, and all the men have gone to the court building. Mom said you might like to join us. It is dark, so the men can't see us.'"

Raihana says, "I couldn't believe it. I had never seen so many women together on that driveway, and they were not wearing the chadari. The women's eyes shone under the dark sky, and they seemed very happy. They wanted to be together. They seemed so at ease, and welcomed me. That night women of different ages joined together and had a happy time. Women talked and laughed loudly. Girls danced and played together. One of the girls sang a sweet Pashto song, and we all enjoyed it. Her mother called on her to stop singing. She replied, 'Mom, it is too dark, no man can recognize the singer or dancers. There are no boys to take the message to my father or brothers. It is women's night.' The mother laughed, and she continued singing. The moon—and electricity—did not return until midnight. The darkness allowed women to breathe freely, talk, and laugh loudly. They allowed women to be unsupervised, not watched and judged by men."

It was almost midnight when the lights came back on. "Suddenly, those noisy girls became silent. Women said goodbye to each other. Everyone went quickly back to their own houses. Then the men came back to the courtyard, and life was normal again. The driveway became silent once more. When I put my head on the pillow, I thought about the women's free and happy moments on the driveway. Women would choose a different life if they had freedom. They would prefer a happy, free, noisy, and friendly life. Women in my country never have a choice about how to live. When we come into this world, men, culture, religion, and values decide for us. I thought about those women, some of whom were first wives, and some of whom were second wives, and how hard it must be to be the second choice."

The next day some girls from the courtyard came to Raihana's house. "One of them said, 'I hope the electricity goes off again tonight, and we can meet on the driveway. We love dancing and playing.'" Raihana turned on the television for them and left them alone to listen to music. When they eventually went home they were laughing and teasing each other about who had the best dance moves.

"Only a few days later the Taliban took over again. Now women in all parts of Afghanistan live as women in Nangarhar. They must wear the chadari and try to see the world from those tiny holes in the front," Raihana says.

Her dream is simple but fundamental: "I hope on one sunny, bright day, women can sit together on that driveway in Nangarhar court with no chadari. I hope the blue-eyed singing girl can sing again." Now Raihana lives in New Zealand on a street with six houses, like in Nangarhar. From her new driveway she can see a neighbor in her eighties who drives to the swimming pool every day, and another middle-aged woman who rides her bike with her family. "Who knows, maybe one day a woman in her eighties can drive up that driveway in Nangarhar and enjoy being independent. Maybe one day a woman in her forties can ride her bike there. Afghan women must fight for that day."

Introduction

LATER, ANISA RASOOLI'S GREATEST FEAR WAS THAT PEOPLE would watch the footage from August 2021 and think that the Afghans clinging desperately, fatally, to the outside of the planes taking off from Kabul were naïve. "They were not stupid. They knew that they were going to die. They chose that rather than what life under the Taliban would bring—the extinguishing of hope."

Anisa understands everything about hope and its ending. For twenty years, from 2001, when the Taliban were toppled by the U.S.-led invasion, until 2021, when the chaotic withdrawal of U.S. and international forces led to the triumphant return of the Taliban to power, she had been one of the great hopes for her nation—a leader among the 270 women judges who were not just professional pioneers but also at the very forefront of building a new justice system in Afghanistan.

Afghanistan appointed its first woman judge, Jameela Farooq Rooshna, in 1969—late in the reign of Afghanistan's last king, Mohammad Zahir Shah, and during the prime ministership of pro-Soviet general Mohammed Daoud Khan.[1] A few years later, in 1973, Daoud Khan overthrew the king in a coup and made himself president, introducing a number of social reforms, including encouraging more women to join the workforce and improving women's rights.

The late 1960s and 1970s were a time when other Islamic countries, including Egypt and Pakistan, were appointing women to the judiciary. European countries, including Italy and France, also began appointing women during this period—but while women in

Europe and the United States faced inequality and sexism, women in Islamic countries were subject to a different debate. Opponents argued that, according to Islamic rules, women could not sit in judgment of men. In *Women Judges in the Muslim World*, Nadia Sonneveld and Monika Lindbekk write: "In many countries the appointment of women as judges remains a controversial issue, due to a general perception that such appointments might not be in conformity with the *shari'a*." Women should be "disqualified as judges based upon an interpretation of *sura* an-Nisa' 4:34, that men are *qawwamuna* (protectors) over women."[2] Iran banned women judges after the establishment of the Islamic Republic in 1979 for this reason, and to this day there are no women judges in Saudi Arabia.

In Afghanistan the decades following the appointment of the first women judges were turbulent. President Mohammed Daoud Khan was overthrown and murdered in 1978 by the Afghan Communist Party, whose leadership then fought among itself to hold on to power. At the same time, ethnic and religious leaders who were opposed to social reform and granting women more rights began an armed resistance in the countryside, forming a force known as the mujahideen. As the power struggle in Kabul intensified, the Soviet Union invaded Afghanistan on December 24, 1979, in an effort to shore up the communist regime. War between the mujahideen—now backed by the United States—and the Soviet forces raged for ten years, until Soviet troops withdrew in 1989, leading to a further period of war and instability as rebel groups fought for power.

Anisa Rasooli, her colleague and friend Nafisa Kabuli, and other senior women judges in this book trained and began working as judges in this period.

By the mid-1990s, however, one group had gained dominance: the Taliban, supported by Pakistan. The name Taliban meant literally "the students" but referred to religious students in particular. After years of war, the Taliban claimed that they would bring peace to Afghanistan under a strict Islamic regime that brutally cracked down on women's rights. In 1994 the Taliban captured Kandahar, then Herat in 1995, and the capital city, Kabul, in 1996.

To the outside world the Taliban seemed extreme. Inside Afghanistan the group imposed a merciless and brutal regime for five years. Everyone suffered: music was banned, children were not allowed toys or stuffed animals, men were forced to grow long beards. Undoubtedly, women suffered the most. The atrocities and hardships were unspeakable. Girls were barred from going to school; women were not allowed to work or even leave the house without a male chaperone. They could not show their skin in public, wear noisy shoes, or wear white socks (as white was the color of the Taliban flag).[3] The Taliban believed that women should be silent in the world and should not speak in public. Since female doctors were not allowed to work, women could not get health care. A woman found walking on the street with a man who was not a relative was subject to one hundred lashes. The world became accustomed to the sight of the women of Afghanistan confined to their smothering blue burqas, long garments that covered every inch of their bodies, including their faces. Grainy smuggled videos broadcast on Western news showed women stoned to death in public stadiums. No crime against the Taliban was too small to be punished: one woman had her thumb cut off for wearing nail polish.[4]

The careers of the women judges of Afghanistan abruptly stopped when the Taliban took power in 1995, and they were banned from working as judges for six years. Some left the country; others stayed and taught girls in secret. Then, unexpectedly, everything changed.

The attacks of 9/11 led the United States to demand that the Taliban hand over the attacks' mastermind, Osama Bin Laden, who was living and operating in Taliban Afghanistan in the Tora Bora Mountains. When the Taliban refused, U.S. air strikes against Taliban targets began on October 7, 2001. After weeks of intense fighting, the Taliban abandoned province after province until they gave up control of a final province, Zabul, on December 7, 2001, and their reign was officially pronounced over. Later that month Hamid Karzai was sworn in as the leader of an interim government and, backed by the United States and other international allies including the UK, Australia and New Zealand, the country embarked upon twenty years of democratic government.

For the small number of women judges, the change was immediate and profound: they were called back to work and picked up the daunting task of rebuilding a justice system while trying to institute wide-ranging reforms and recognition of international human rights laws. Although they were poorly paid at first and had almost no modern equipment or even law texts, they diligently set about their work, and in time their careers blossomed. Soon a new generation of young women followed them and entered the judiciary.

In Afghanistan students graduate from high school and then take a university entrance exam called the Kankor. They can enter the judicial system through two routes: by studying civil law in law school, or by studying Islamic law, *shari'a*. After completing one of those courses of study, the most successful graduates can then apply to take a one-year course in the judiciary and qualify as judges. Young judges are appointed and then begin their career, although for several years they will be under the supervision of more-senior judges.

The Supreme Court is the highest judicial authority in Afghanistan; it consists of nine members appointed by the president and confirmed by the parliament. The chief justice of the Supreme Court is appointed by the president from among the nine members of the Supreme Court. The Afghan judiciary is composed of the Supreme Court itself, the courts of appeal, and the primary courts, whose powers and operations are regulated by a specific law (the Law on the Formation and Jurisdiction of Courts). Prior to 2001, the judiciary encompassed criminal courts, civil courts, public security courts, commercial courts, administrative courts, and courts that handled crimes against national and international security. Additional courts were created between 2001 and 2021 with the support of the international community, including courts for addressing crimes related to violence against women, courts for addressing major narcotics crimes (Judicial Center for Combating Narcotics), courts for addressing serious corruption cases (Judicial Center for Combating Major Corruption), courts that addressed land-grab issues, family courts, and juvenile courts.

In Afghanistan, cases are handled by a judicial panel consisting of three judges (the chief judge, the investigating judge, and the associate judge). When a case is received by the court, the chief judge reviews it first and appoints one judge as the investigating judge and another as the associate judge. These judges then examine the case. If all documents and evidence are complete and there are no issues or ambiguities, they coordinate with the chief judge to schedule a hearing and instruct the court office to notify all parties involved of the date and time.

The court session is then held, and after hearing all presenters (prosecutor, defendant, victim, defense lawyer, witnesses, and other involved parties), the chief judge asks the defendant for any final requests or statements. The judicial panel then retreats to the deliberation room to discuss and decide the case. Each judge has equal voting power and can offer a dissenting opinion. The decision is written up by the investigating judge, but all three judges sign it, and responsibility is shared equally among them. The decision is then announced publicly by the chief judge.

The women judges of Afghanistan operated within this system, but although their numbers grew significantly between 2001 and 2021, they faced deep discrimination, corruption, and constant security threats (often being sent to work in remote provinces where fighting with the Taliban was ongoing), and they were often assigned to courts that were at the forefront of changing deeply entrenched Afghan customs and society, including family court, narcotics court, the court for crimes against national and international security, and the court that heard cases of violence against women. The Taliban and their many supporters bitterly opposed these changes, and thus the courts and judges that implemented them. Because so many of these courts, and the new laws they applied, were created and supported by the United States, the United Kingdom, and international allies, the women judges were frequently accused of being nothing more than foreign stooges. The threats to their safety and lives were real, and, as their stories show, their day-to-day existence became more perilous as the Taliban and other groups fought back against U.S. and allied forces and suicide bombings became more frequent.

The fate of the women judges was sealed when the Taliban and the United States signed the Doha Accord in 2020—ignoring the ruling Afghan government. The Doha Accord included provision for the withdrawal of U.S. and NATO troops and for talks to begin between the Taliban and the Afghan government. As a result, the Taliban increased their attacks, and NATO troops scaled down their defense.

Under that agreement, the Trump administration agreed to reduce U.S. forces from 13,000 to 8,600 troops by July 2020, followed by a complete withdrawal by May 1, 2021. When President Joe Biden took office in January 2021, 2,500 U.S. troops were stationed in Afghanistan, and in April President Biden stated that these remaining forces would be withdrawn between May 1 and

September 11, 2021. The Taliban began a final offensive on May 1, however, and soon province after province fell under Taliban control. On July 8 President Biden moved the timetable for troop withdrawal forward to August 31, 2021.

The speed of the Taliban's advance and the collapse of Afghan government forces shocked the women judges—as well as U.S. intelligence, which had estimated that it would take months for the Taliban to reach Kabul.

Afghan women judges symbolized everything the Taliban despised and feared. Without help, the judges knew, the Taliban would hunt them down and kill them. Over the course of twenty years they had transformed the judiciary of their country—tackling endemic corruption, challenging traditional ideas of what a woman could do, and overseeing new laws aimed at reducing horrifying levels of violence against women and children. Supported by the United States and NATO, the women judges were at the very heart of the mission to build Afghanistan as a modern, democratic country that respected the rule of law and human rights. Surely, the judges believed, they would be evacuated to safety. But in August 2021 it seemed like no government would intervene to help them. There was no plan for their evacuation, and no seats for them on planes to fly out of the country.

The women judges felt betrayed and abandoned. As the horror of the Taliban takeover unfolded, one group came to their aid and stayed by their side—a handful of women judges from around the world who were part of a membership organization called the International Association of Women Judges (IAWJ). These international women were senior figures in their profession, but they were completely inexperienced in evacuating people from conflict zones. Few of them had ever been to Afghanistan. Yet they knew that the lives of the Afghan women judges depended on them, and when called upon to help they immediately agreed, bringing together a hastily organized coalition of supporters and throwing themselves into a round-the-clock rescue operation in a country that was quickly descending into chaos.

This is the story of the women judges of Afghanistan and the courageous role they played as pioneers of justice. It is also the story of their terrifying escape and the women who helped them. As many of the women judges of Afghanistan start new lives abroad they remember their friends and colleagues who did not make it out—those who were murdered, and those who are still living in Afghanistan—and all of the women in their country who are now unable to work or leave their homes. Together with the women judges of the IAWJ they have pledged to continue their work until every woman judge is safe—and every woman in Afghanistan can be free.

PART ONE

Escape

1.
A Death in Kabul

Dear Mother! From the first time that we opened our eyes to this world we witnessed your self-sacrifice for us. We cannot compensate you for what you have done, but we hope that, in this moment, this card will make you happy. Thank you for being with us! Happy Mother's Day!

When Qadria Yasini was murdered on her way to work, the physical possessions left strewn around her were meager and mundane. On the backseat of the car, beside her body, was a black leather handbag from Homme+Femme, a mobile phone, a plastic bottle of water, and a well-read law book. Among these ordinary mementos of life, there was also a single piece of white paper, folded and refolded along well-worn creases. This piece of paper contained a Mother's Day message from her sons, Abdullwahab, nineteen at the time the message was written, and Wali, then eighteen. In the eight months since they had given it to her, she had looked at its words of love every day.

Wali was still in bed that cold Sunday morning in January 2021 when his mother was getting ready for work. Before leaving their home she told him she had put some money for food in a drawer. Then she pulled on a new coat, closed the door behind her, and climbed into the car that picked her up every day for the drive to the Supreme Court in Kabul. They had a regular routine: every day the driver stopped and collected another one of Qadria's female colleagues, Zakia Herawi. Somewhere en route that morning they agreed to pick up another acquaintance. The third woman was a teacher, not a judge, but Qadria was often helpful and generous, and she knew that getting a ride in a government car made an otherwise often long and difficult commute much easier.

None of the women realized that they were being followed by a man on a motorbike, the same man who had been watching Qadria since she left her house.

"There were three of them," Wali says. "They followed her from our house and they waited until both judges were in the car because they wanted to make sure that they had both of them. Once Zakia Herawi approached the car, they attacked. One man was just waiting there; the other one came on the motorbike, looked in, made sure that both of them were there, and then went back and made a phone call. Another man came—and the three of them shot from three sides."

Qadria clutched her leather handbag to her chest in a futile effort to protect herself, but she was gunned down where she sat. Both fifty-three-year-old Qadria and her forty-seven-year-old colleague Zakia were murdered that morning. Their third friend, the teacher, was not attacked and survived. When Qadria's possessions were returned to her sons they unfolded her Mother's Day greeting and found it riddled with bullet holes. Later when they watched CCTV footage they saw a young man, hardly older than them, riding away after killing their mother, waving his gun in the air.

Tragically, Qadria Yasini had recently been offered a pistol for protection—but she had turned it down. She didn't believe she needed a gun.

Qadria was unusual among the women judges. Unlike many, she did not come from a distinguished or well-known family. Her father was a mechanic in Kabul, and her mother was a housewife. Above all, though, the family valued education—even for girls. Qadria was clever, and by studying hard she became one of only a small number of students who were admitted to the prestigious French-Afghan school Lycée Malalai, which her sons remembered "introduced her into the whole world." When the time came to sit for the Kankor alongside a hundred thousand other students across the country, Qadria became one of only a thousand to get admitted to Kabul University to study law. She studied for a further four years and was accepted into the judicial law program.

Once qualified as a judge, she began work. With her background from the Lycée Malalai, Qadria was particularly interested in French law and the Napoleonic Code, which were fundamental to Afghan law. It was an auspicious start to what should have been a highly successful career, but soon it was brought to a horrible halt when the Taliban came to power in 1996.

Like so many other Afghans, Qadria Yasini fled over the border and began a new life in exile. In Pakistan, Qadria married her husband, who was a doctor, and retrained as a physician's assistant so that she could work alongside him. She gave birth to two sons, Abdullwahab and Wali. When the Taliban were ousted from power in 2001, the family returned to Afghanistan, working for an NGO and traveling together across remote areas to provide medical care to local villages. As the years passed, the new government and an influx of Western aid brought about a visible transformation. Abdullwahab and Wali noticed smooth highways replacing the single tracks across the mountains that they had once had to travel on foot or on horseback.

Eventually, however, the family decided to settle in Kabul, where the boys could receive an education and Qadria could finally resume her career as a judge. After resubmitting her qualifications, Qadria began work for the Supreme Court of Afghanistan in 2010 and wrote a groundbreaking book about inheritance law. It was a complicated and often thorny issue among Afghan families, and until she wrote her book, information had been only passed on by memory from the Quran.

Life was still far from easy, however. In 2015, when Wali was twelve, his father announced that he would like to marry a second wife—something that appalled and upset the family. Although men in Afghanistan are permitted to take several wives, most modern Afghans, like Qadria, Abdullwahab, and Wali, considered it an embarrassing and outdated custom that usually made the man's first family very unhappy. In law, women were permitted to request a divorce, but in practice that usually meant having to give their husbands full custody of their children, regardless of the circumstances. Qadria told her husband that if she could keep her children, she would give him all of her money and her home. He agreed, and Qadria, Abdullwahab, and Wali left with nothing to start a new life living with Qadria's brother, the kids' uncle.

As a single mother, Qadria continued to work for the Supreme Court and write law books, turning down lucrative and high-profile judicial positions, which she believed placed her in too much danger. Tragically, that decision did not save her life.

The murders of Qadria Yasini and Zakia Herawi devastated their families and sent a shock wave through the community of Afghan women judges. Nafisa Kabuli, one of Afghanistan's most senior women judges, shakes her head when she remembers that day. "Everyone went quiet," she says. "We couldn't stop crying. We all knew Qadria so well. And Zakia had her career ahead of her." Nafisa had lived through the murder of her boss, the chief judge of the narcotics court, a few years before, as well as an attempt on her own life. In the lead-up to the killing of Qadria and Zakia, the women judges of Afghanistan had been warned by the government to increase their security. Now they were not only horrified and sad but also deeply afraid.

News of the assassinations rippled uneasily through the wider international community, too. For several years, the women judges of Afghanistan had been working in close partnership with peers who were members of the International Association of Women Judges (IAWJ). Over many summers, a handful of Afghan judges had visited the United States for three-week-long trips to Washington, D.C., and Vermont. Zakia Herawi had been one of those judges. "She was just a fun young woman," says Farah Bayat, an Iranian translator who had fled persecution in her homeland and lived in the United States for many years, befriending and working with many of the Afghan and American women judges.

Judge Vanessa Ruiz, senior judge of the District of Columbia Court of Appeals, remembers Zakia as a "small, delicate, winsome-looking judge, [who was] very curious." Later, the enormity of what happened to the women judges of Afghanistan would hit Vanessa when she was looking at an old photo of herself with an Afghan judge named Kamila Noori, who had escaped and resettled in Washington, D.C. "[Kamila] and I are seated next to each other on a sofa in my chambers, and the person to the other side of me was Zakia Herawi. That just reminded me, if I ever needed reminding, how very personal this was to all of us helping them get out of the country, because they truly were at terrible risk. You could see in that one picture a person who was assassinated and one who made it out."

Now, in 2021, the IAWJ was helping the judges revive the Afghan Association of Women Judges, a professional organization that would allow them to increase their skills and experience and to advocate for women in the judiciary. In January 2021 the women serving on the board of the IAWJ were in the process of organizing the participation of the Afghan women in their biannual conference, due to take place that summer in New Zealand.

"We supported their Afghan Women Judges Association," says New Zealand Supreme Court justice Susan Glazebrook, who served as president of the IAWJ from 2021 to 2023. "They had been through some ups and downs." The Afghan Women Judges Association had been set up by Nafisa Kabuli and Anisa Rasooli against all odds, as male judges in Afghanistan did not support the idea of an association just for women, and at one stage the Afghan Supreme Court had even tried to shut the association down.

After the Taliban was ousted in 2001, the number of Afghan women judges grew significantly, to almost 270—and were a more established group, with members who held different opinions. By 2021, they were at a turning point about how the organization would be run. A split had emerged between the older women judges, who had begun work in the 1990s, and the new generation, who had only experienced life in post-9/11 Afghanistan. The older judges wanted to advocate more generally for the rights of women and children in Afghanistan. For them, the association was more than a professional network; it was a platform for promoting a shared, progressive, feminist agenda. The younger women judges, by comparison, saw themselves primarily as professionals, and were concerned more about salary, benefits, and promotions. For them, the Afghan Women Judges Association was like a union, which should work to benefit its members. The same thing happened everywhere when feminism advanced, their American friends observed ruefully. It was like the Gloria Steinems and Susan Brownmillers of 1970s New York clashing with *LA Law*.

By 2021, the Afghan women judges had already visited some international conferences, including one in New Zealand where Susan Glazebrook had hastily pulled together a program of events for the women to attend. "It's a two-way exchange. We learn from each other; we learn about different situations, and we learn about what you have in common."

The international women judges were shocked when Qadria Yasini and Zakia Herawi were assassinated.

"We felt very strongly that it was part of a general intimidation of women. It was making a big statement about women in public life. The terrorists were targeting men as well, but they were particularly targeting women, and it was clear that it was a message to say, 'Don't put your head above the parapet.' Not just for women who were going to be in positions of power, but for all women," Susan Glazebrook says. "We learned afterwards that this was just the tip of the iceberg. Many of the women judges had very near misses; many of them had family members who'd either been killed or beaten up by the Taliban. One husband of a judge was in a wheelchair. The Taliban had beaten him so badly he'd had a stroke."

A handful of women judges who were members of the IAWJ quickly formed a group to help—even though at that stage it was impossible to imagine what that effort would involve and how much it would bind them together with each other and with the women of Afghanistan.

Susan Glazebrook was joined by an Australian colleague, Judge Robyn Tupman of the District Court of New South Wales. Judge Anisa Dhanji, of the United Kingdom, played a big role, as did Nova Scotia Supreme Court justice Mona Lynch, from Canada; Judge Gloria Poyatos Matas, of the High Court of the Canary Islands, in Spain; and, from the United States, Judge Vanessa Ruiz, of the District of Columbia, and Judge Patricia (Patti) Whalen, who had served both as a judge in the state of Vermont and as an international judge for the War Crimes Chamber at the Court of Bosnia and Herzegovina.

The international women never presumed to know what Afghan

women were going through, but they came from a variety of backgrounds themselves, and understood what it was like for women in different countries to establish themselves as lawyers and judges.

Susan Glazebrook had grown up in what is known as "The King Country," a farming and rugby area on the North Island of New Zealand which had undergone English colonization like the rest of the country, but was also the home of the Māori king, King Tawhiao, who took refuge there after the New Zealand Wars in 1865 and had remained largely immune to European influence until the late 1800s. "It was quite a different sort of upbringing, really, to the sort of upbringing that you had in the cities. We had chickens in the backyard, and often in the house as well. We had lambs and a goat. It was a sort of place where if you had to put shoes on you had to wear them all day, which we didn't want to do, so we went to school barefoot. Māori culture was very strong in the community, and I learned Māori as a child."

In Spain, Gloria Poyatos Matas grew up in a working-class family in Barcelona and worked to pay her way through university and law school before becoming a labor lawyer for a Spanish trade union federation, Comisiones Obreras, and founding the Association of Women Judges in Spain with eleven others. Gloria says she was among the first to promote an equality-in-the-law program with Spanish children. She has promoted equal justice between men and women, and holds a doctorate in justice from a gender perspective.

Mona Lynch came from Cape Breton in Canada, also a working-class area formerly reliant on coal mining, steel, and fishing. There, "strong people have overcome a lot of hardship. They always kind of just get done what has to be done. That's the kind of the culture here," Mona says. As a young woman, Mona was studying to become a legal secretary when she discovered she was pregnant; at that point she dropped out of her program of study to work and bring up her daughter. As a single mother, she returned to Dalhousie Law School in the 1980s and won a prestigious prize in commercial law before deciding to devote her career to working in legal aid and in defense of young people instead. "I worked for Nova Scotia Legal Aid for about fifteen years, representing young people who were charged with criminal offenses and young people who were involved in the child protection and child welfare system. I was then seconded by the province of Nova Scotia to coordinate the implementation of new legislation coming into effect for young people charged with criminal offenses, and I was in the process of doing that when I got the call that appointed me to the Supreme Court of Nova Scotia."

Anisa Dhanji grew up in Kenya. While they were never refugees, her family had emigrated from the Indian subcontinent to East Africa, and then Anisa emigrated twice, first with her family to Canada in her teens, and then to the United Kingdom as an adult. She says she understands from her lived experience what it takes to restart your life in a new country. It can take a generation or more before you feel you belong. Overcoming race-related obstacles is also part of her DNA. "In Kenya, my grandparents ran a business supplying premium crockery and cutlery to the English clubs during the colonial era, but as Asians, they were not allowed to go inside the clubs, except sometimes through the back door. At school, my mother was the only Asian allowed to take lessons with the white girls because she was very bright and it was thought she would be a good influence. Like the Afghan judges, I understood from early on that a good education would be essential. I 'get' how determined and resilient they must have been to succeed as women judges in Afghanistan, and also how much they will need to draw on these qualities to rebuild their lives now. Interestingly, several of the judges have asked me about what it is like to start over. They also know from my name that I am a Muslim," Anisa says, "and there is an unspoken understanding and trust with the Afghan women from this shared faith as well."

Vanessa Ruiz is a senior associate judge on the District of Columbia Court of Appeals and an immediate past president of the IAWJ. Born in San Juan, Puerto Rico, Ruiz says she was "propelled into law" by seeing the immense changes the courts could make during the social upheavals of the 1960s and 1970s.[5] Five years after graduating from Georgetown University she successfully argued an important civil rights case before the U.S. Supreme Court. In *Havens Realty Corp. v. Coleman* she represented an African American renter and a nonprofit housing group that used testers to identify and fight discrimination in housing practices.

"What's interesting about all of us is that none of us came from a 'privileged' background," Robyn Tupman says. "We do not have the sort of 'silver spoon' background that people in the U.K., U.S., and Australia expect when they think about people who are judges."

Tupman became a judge of the District Court of New South Wales in Australia in January 1996—one of the first women to be appointed to that court. "I grew up in the western suburbs of Sydney, a mainly working-class area, where neither of my parents had much education. I was the first person in my extended family ever to go to university. My father left school at thirteen to help his family on their dairy farm in northern New South Wales but ended up as a detective inspector of the New South Wales Police Force, and the first head of the New South Wales Homicide Squad. My mother was amongst the first women to become a police officer there. They were both extremely committed to education for my sister and me and I ended up with scholarships to attend university and law school. I was drawn to the law because I grew up in the 1970s at the time of social revolution and change and I wanted to use the law to help make a better life for women and children in particular but also to try to help end discrimination across the board."

At first this diverse IAWJ group made small plans: they wanted to give posthumous awards to the assassinated women judges at the their Asia-Pacific regional conference in May 2021 in Auckland, and ask two Afghan women judges to speak at the conference, remotely from Afghanistan, to discuss their security issues.

"Originally the committee was just going to work on what we had pledged to do at the conference, but during the conference itself, on May 10, there was a bomb attack on a school targeting girls." More than eighty-five people, including many girls, were killed in the attack on Sayed ul-Shuhada High School in Kabul. Susan Glazebrook says, "As a result, we passed two resolutions: a resolution pledging our ongoing support for the [Afghan] women judges in the wake of the two assassinations, and another one about girls' education. We wanted to do whatever we could to help. The Afghan women judges desperately wanted us to bring their plight to the attention of the world. We said we'd do that."

That summer the Taliban were advancing province by province across Afghanistan, seemingly with ease. Women judges in outlying provinces were starting to move back to Kabul for their safety, because most still thought the capital would hold.

Thirty-year-old Tayeba Parsa was one such judge. "Two months before Afghanistan fell, I bought a car and started to practice driving. I couldn't drive to work because traditionally it is not acceptable for women to drive, so I used to drive part of the way to work in the courts, and then when I got near I changed places with my driver. The people who worked in the courts were traditional, too, and I didn't want my colleagues to see that I was driving and accuse me of not being a religious person."

The car Tayeba had bought was a 2012 Toyota Corolla, old by American standards—but a good car in Afghanistan in 2021. The car cost $10,000, a huge amount for an ordinary Afghan, but still cheap for a foreign car. "Buying that car came with a warning,"

Tayeba says. According to the salesman, "the prices were low because there were rumors that the Americans were going to leave Afghanistan and the Taliban would come."

Tayeba refused to believe it. "Car salesmen used every scandal, every rumor, to get more money. Afghanistan wasn't very safe anyway. There were always attacks and bomb explosions. Even in Kabul I'd pass a road and then get a call from someone saying, 'Are you alive? Are you OK? A bomb just exploded on that road.' I faced this news every day, so I didn't believe the car salesman at all.

"When the Taliban did come, it was a huge shock," Tayeba says. "The Taliban had changed their way of attack. They started to attack a specific target directly, like a judge or a minister or a staff car of a special court. They placed bombs under governmental officers' cars."

After Qadria Yasini and Zakia Herawi were assassinated, the women judges felt an immense threat. Tayeba says, "It was very risky for us and we didn't feel safe. The judiciary started to distribute guns to women judges and told us we would have to protect ourselves. It seemed unbelievable. Everyone was scared. I had a colleague who cried every day—what if the Taliban return? I didn't understand much about the Taliban because I had never lived under their rule, but the older women were so worried."

Tayeba had an American mentor named Gayle Zilber who was helping her learn English. Every week they would discuss matters in Afghanistan, including the deteriorating security situation. Tayeba also discussed the increasing number of attacks and the worrying "peace negotiations" between the Taliban and the United States, with the involvement of the British Foreign, Commonwealth and Development Office. The United Kingdom had given financial and logistical support to some Afghan courts, including the antiterrorism courts, and the British Foreign, Commonwealth and Development Office's Roger Coventry, based in Kabul, was looking for an Afghan woman judge who could speak English. Coventry offered to put Tayeba in touch with Anisa Dhanji, a U.K. judge and member of the IAWJ, whom Coventry knew from other international work. Tayeba emailed Anisa, mentioning the security problems the women were facing and the fact that if some sort of deal was reached with the Taliban it was likely that the first consequence would be that all of the women judges would be fired.

Anisa Dhanji and Tayeba began speaking by phone and on the messaging app WhatsApp, building a relationship that, unbeknownst to them then, would become critical within just a few weeks. The IAWJ issued a statement of support and asked Tayeba to share it with the Afghan Supreme Court.

"I went to the chief justice in person and shared that statement, and he agreed to publish it on the official website of the Supreme Court," Tayeba says.

As Tayeba busied herself with all of these issues, however, the Taliban left the Doha negotiations and began to take the provinces by force.

"It happened very quickly. Several provinces collapsed and we realized that, yes, they are coming, it's possible. Still, I couldn't believe it. I didn't really believe it until Kabul collapsed and Gayle gave me the news. She said that the CIA predicted Afghanistan's collapse within six months. When I woke up the next day and thought about it I was overwhelmed with sadness—I'd just bought a car. I was engaged to be married."

At first Tayeba wasn't interested in joining the new incarnation of the Afghan Women Judges Association, but the president and one of Afghanistan's most senior women judges, Nafisa Kabuli, asked Tayeba to take on the role of communications officer.

Tayeba was asked to give one of the speeches at the IAWJ conference, alongside judges Anisa Rasooli and Nafisa Kabuli. Roger Coventry had made complicated arrangements for the women to speak first from the British embassy and then from the Serena Hotel, a luxury hotel that was popular with foreigners and wealthy Afghans and had a good internet connection and security.

"I was very nervous about that speech," Tayeba says. "It was so important to us to make other countries and judges aware of our situation." After Tayeba and the judges shared their problems, they invited the IAWJ women to work with the Afghan women to help them advocate and reform their association effectively.

"Our concerns were changing. At the beginning we were worried that we would not be allowed to work, but soon we realized that the Taliban were coming—and we had antiterrorism judges who put the Taliban's members in jail for their terrorism activities, and had even sentenced them to death. It was incredibly dangerous for those judges."

As the IAWJ women judges attended the virtual meetings, they heard the change. "Some of them wanted to leave, but most of them were saying, 'Look, I love my country, I love my job, I think it's really important. I'm very committed to the rule of law; I'm committed especially to the courts like those for the elimination of violence against women. I really want to make sure that gender equality and the rule of law is upheld. All I want is to know that I'm going to be able to go home in the evening in safety,'" Susan Glazebrook says.

"It became evident in the meetings that they were just scared to death," Vanessa Ruiz adds. "The Afghan women judges also were torn about what they should do. They were scared for themselves and for their families—and in that sense they wanted to get out of there. But they were very committed to their country and didn't want to leave, they didn't want to give up."

Tayeba remembers the sadness of those conversations. "Some of the Afghan judges cried. We were bewildered. What would happen to us? Why were all the countries who had supported us leaving?

We didn't want to leave our country. We wanted to stay. 'Help us,' we said. 'Advocate for us. Do not leave us.'"

Over the course of less than a month, the situation had deteriorated drastically, first with the collapse of the provinces. "Herat, Jalalabad, Ghazni. Ghazni was our neighboring province, where my fiancé lived," Tayeba says. "He was working in the capital city of the province and wanted to visit his parents in his village, but he couldn't reach them. He escaped to Kabul. We thought that Kabul was safe, but within two days Kabul collapsed, too."

Tayeba had been working closely with Anisa Dhanji and other U.K. judges to set up a mentoring group, pairing one Afghan woman judge with one U.K. judge. The plan was to start with ten pairings and expand from there. The first five Afghan judges who signed up could not speak English, however, so Tayeba quickly identified ten who could speak English. At the U.K. end, the judges met to agree upon the parameters of the mentoring program. The mood was strangely sober as it became clear how much the landscape had changed since the U.K. judges had first expressed an interest in partnering with Afghan judges. This would be no ordinary mentoring. The U.K. judges, too, would need guidance and support. They would need to keep abreast of changing circumstances on the ground so that their interactions with their Afghan colleagues were relevant and meaningful. The burden of explaining what was going on in Afghanistan should not fall to the Afghan judges. Security was also an immediate concern. The U.K. judges needed to be aware, for example, that the Afghan judges might not always be free to speak but might not be able to say so. Family members and neighbors were not necessarily allies, and conversations with unknown people overseas in English could inadvertently put the judges at risk. Over the coming weeks the members of the U.K. group were in regular contact with one another, and Anisa Dhanji kept them closely apprised of the changing situation on the ground, sharing information—sometimes several times a day—as it came in from various sources and was vetted as being reliable. Often they also turned to Roger Coventry, who by then was back in the United Kingdom but in contact with colleagues in Kabul and was committed to helping not only the women judges but also the prosecutors and other public defenders he had worked with.

In their initial contacts, Anisa and Tayeba had explored whether the Afghan women judges needed a physical space away from the courts where they could meet so that they could more easily keep in touch. Tayeba had started to look for quotes for spaces and negotiate with companies for contracts. Nothing they could do, however, could keep pace with events. "One moment we were talking about a contract for office space, and the next we were reaching out to experts to find out how we could keep in contact if the internet was cut off," Anisa recalls.

The IAWJ team also identified other priorities, and work began with urgency, often starting right after the court day ended and continuing well into the night and weekends. How would the Afghan judges access money if they were locked out of their bank accounts? It was going to be essential to have reliable identification and location information on all the judges, and to be able to reach each of them directly if necessary. Most important was to identify who would be immediately at risk. "Suddenly one day Anisa Dhanji called and said, 'If the Taliban come, which judges do we need to try to get out first?'" recalls Tayeba. They knew that the judges who had been working in the courts supported by allied forces or funded by the United Kingdom, like the antiterrorism court and the anti-corruption court, would likely be the first ones targeted. People from the ethnic Hazara population had been persecuted by the Taliban when they were last in power, so Hazara judges, like Tayeba herself, were also likely to be at risk.

Together, Anisa and Tayeba went back and forth, looking at documents and checking on whether it was still possible to get visas from any of the embassies, all of which seemed to be planning their own evacuations. As the press in Afghanistan began to self-censor, the judges outside Afghanistan often had more current and reliable information than the judges in Afghanistan, so sharing information became an important daily task, though under the shadow of the risks that such communications now carried. "We were also trying to work out how the Afghan women would stay in touch with each other on the ground in Kabul. In the last days, Anisa Dhanji asked me for the contact details of my fiancé and also my sister who lived in Denmark in case we lost contact," says Tayeba. Nobody put into words the circumstances in which contact might be lost, but it was understood that they were not talking only about a drained phone battery.

Hurriedly, the IAWJ arranged a series of interviews with the international media, including the BBC, to highlight the terrifying situation the women judges found themselves in. Nafisa Kabuli, Anisa Rasooli, and Tayeba tried to explain their desperate situation. "Women judges were in danger," Tayeba explained. If the Taliban came, they would be executed.

The next day Tayeba was asked to do another interview, but by then there was no electricity because the Taliban were so close. "They cut the power to Kabul—and I remember in that interview I recorded the interview using the light from my cellphone."

It was the last night—as well as the last light. The Taliban had reached Kabul, and for the Afghan women judges, life as they knew it was over.

2.

The Last Day in Afghanistan

FOR DAYS NAFISA KABULI AND HER CLOSE FRIEND AND COLleague Anisa Rasooli had heard the rumors: *The Taliban are coming.* As two of the most experienced women judges in Afghanistan, they had presided over notorious cases, sending Taliban members to prison, overseeing high-reaching narcotics trials, and navigating the endless and byzantine institutional corruption. If the Taliban retook Kabul, Anisa and Nafisa knew, they would be ruthlessly hunted down, tortured, and murdered.

"Everybody was saying, 'They are coming, they are coming,' but we didn't think that they were coming that quickly," says Nafisa.

On the evening of August 14, 2021, Nafisa and Anisa spoke on the phone with Patti Whalen and their longtime translator, Farah Bayat. Patti had been watching the U.S. news that was still reporting it could be months before a complete Taliban takeover—but Anisa told her they were at the entrance to the city. But still, no one knew quite where to go or how to react. Could it even be real?

Nafisa says, "The next day I woke up and looked out of the window. I only lived one block away from the Supreme Court, and the streets were usually packed and busy. That day everything was quiet.

"I didn't know what to do—so I went to court. There were a few judges and some other employees there, and all anyone could talk about was that the Taliban were coming. 'The Taliban are coming . . . the Taliban are coming . . . They are getting very close.' Then someone came and told us that the chief justice was saying, 'Leave now, don't stay in the court!'"

Nafisa stepped outside into a scene of total chaos. "Everything was out of control. People were milling around everywhere, and the traffic was so bad no one could move. It was horrible."

The closest safe place she could think of was her brother's home. When Nafisa rang her family she could hear the panic in their voices. "Just come and stay here. Don't move!" they told her. The whole family was very worried—and the main reason for their worry was Nafisa.

Ominously, the Taliban had arrived at the gates of Kabul's notorious Pul-e-Charkhi prison and thrown them open. Many of those imprisoned were murderers and criminals who had been sent there by women judges—including Nafisa. Now they were out on the streets of the city, determined to hunt down those they blamed for their imprisonment.

Soon Nafisa and the other women judges began searching for any means of escape they could find. Nafisa had heard of a woman working with a nongovernmental organization (NGO) and the U.S. State Department who was trying to coordinate a way out of the country for women at risk.

"I sat down with my niece Samira and another judge, Kamila Noori, and we wrote a letter in English to the woman at the NGO," Nafisa says. "I was the one who was most at risk because I was one of the ones who had judged cases and given out sentences against the Taliban."

That night Nafisa and Samira sat up hour after hour trying to send and resend the email, but all they got was an automated response saying the mailbox was full. At 4:00 a.m. they gave up.

Nafisa's only other connection to the outside world was through her translator, Farah, who was desperately trying to collect information and coordinate any possible means of help with the women judges from the IAWJ.

The IAWJ had been communicating on WhatsApp for weeks, discussing, organizing, and reacting to the unfolding events. As the situation became urgent, they began a twenty-four-hour-a-day Zoom meeting. In Canada, Mona Lynch was spending the month in a rustic summer cabin in Cape Breton overlooking Bras d'Or Lake. When she sat down and opened her laptop, it was hard for her to believe she was going to be playing a key role in trying to evacuate women to safety from Afghanistan. Her partner, Chris, would later tell her that she had met her soulmates—especially Robyn Tupman, who was, he said, the only person he'd ever heard curse like her. A little farther south, in rural Vermont, and farther south still, in Washington, D.C., Patti Whalen and Vanessa Ruiz were also deeply involved, while from Australia and New Zealand, respectively, Robyn Tupman and Susan Glazebrook joined the call bleary-eyed in their pajamas. As New Zealand was eighteen hours ahead of New York, Susan's husband eventually opted to sleep in the spare bedroom as the sound of messages and calls continued all night, while Robyn's husband would often be awakened by Patti Whalen's voice booming in the darkness and would say to Robyn, "America calling!" U.K. judge Anisa Dhanji was on holiday in Iceland, where she was sharing a hotel room with her family. She remembers spending half the night in the bathroom, joining the Zoom calls from there, so as not to disturb them.

"We very naïvely, as it turns out, thought that it would be obvious to anybody that these women should get seats on planes out of Afghanistan," Susan Glazebrook says. "They were women who had been judges in terrorism courts. They were also people who'd been incredibly important to the democracy-building work in Afghanistan. We thought it would be easy to get them included in evacuation plans, but that couldn't have been further from the truth."

In the United States, Patti Whalen, Vanessa Ruiz, and Farah Bayat were working to pull together a spreadsheet of all the Afghan judges attempting to escape and their geographic locations.

Farah says: "I felt called to do this work. I was persecuted in Iran, and fled to the U.S., so I knew what the women were going through. Vanessa Ruiz told me we should have the names, details, and passport numbers of all the judges. So Tayeba and I made an Excel form, but the Excel form wasn't dynamic and we needed to update it and see the changes instantly—so Patti's son built us a bespoke database. Vanessa asked me how much time I would need to spend on this, and I told her about two hundred hours. She said, 'Two hundred hours, that's a lot!' It turned out it was more like two thousand hours. Soon I was getting more than one hundred and twenty messages a day from the judges, and I could only sleep for two hours a night."

The IAWJ judges compiled endless lists of the names and personal details of the judges and their families and filled out countless forms, without which the Afghan judges would never be allowed to board planes or be considered for asylum. As soon as they completed one form, another government official would ask for slightly different information, and the process would have to begin again. It was often a thankless task. "We got told that finally we were talking to the right person, and it turned out to be not the right person. We had a whole lot of people who were offering to undertake Rambo-style missions, at great expense, which sounded like boys' own fantasy adventures," Susan Glazebrook says.

Anisa Dhanji says, "It was pretty fluid—there was no top-down management. There was nobody saying, 'You will do this' and 'You will do that.' It was whoever was awake, dealing with a particular crisis, dealing with a particular moment, who then became the person closest to that particular issue [and] would end up knowing about it and would follow it through—and then other people would pick up." She shakes her head. "There was no project plan for any of this, no flow charts, and no risk assessment, just a bunch of women judges determined to do whatever we could."

Using the best information they had, the IAWJ judges told Nafisa to try to go to the North Gate of the airport.

"It's so strange, looking back," Nafisa says. "My sister and I got ready as if it was just an ordinary trip, flying out of Afghanistan. I took one big suitcase and my sister took another big suitcase and we carried them down to the street. When we got outside people started laughing at us and saying, 'Hey, don't you know what's going on? No one can get out—and you are trying to take these big suitcases with you?'

"We started to make our way to the airport, but the chaos and confusion and fear were so bad that it looked like the last day of the world. We were in the apocalypse.

"Everybody was out on the street. It was a world of chaos."

The Taliban were everywhere, and, unprovoked, they would start shooting in the air or even shooting at people. Nafisa's niece Samira took a picture of the scene, but a Taliban fighter saw her and said, "Are you taking a picture? Give me your phone!" Samira quickly said, "Oh, no, no, I'm not taking any pictures. Somebody just sent me a picture." Nafisa's sister fainted from the fear and the heat, and they desperately searched for water for her.

"Everybody was pressed close together; no one could move or go anywhere because everyone wanted to go to the airport. Suddenly we got a message from Farah Bayat and the IAWJ that told us not to go to the North Gate but to go to another gate, so we tried to get a car to take us there. There was artillery fire all around us, and people were catching fire and their faces were burning up in front of our eyes. We were desperately trying to hold on to our documents and belongings. All we could hear was gunfire, and people shouting and screaming and trying to save their own lives."

Samira was staying in contact, minute by minute, with Farah, who was also talking to Anisa Rasooli and her family as they, too, made a desperate attempt to get to the airport. By now Nafisa, her sister and brother-in-law, and her niece Samira were exhausted. Samira told Farah, "I can't do it. I can't go any further."

In the chaos of the day Nafisa and Anisa couldn't contact each other directly, but Farah stayed in touch with both, trying to guide the two together. "I can't even move," Nafisa's niece Samira told Farah. "I can't even hear you."

"Look in front of you," Farah urged her, "look in front, and walk diagonally."

Patched together on Zoom across the world, Farah and the judges from the IAWJ were trying to figure out where Anisa and Nafisa were and how on earth they could get them to the airport. Frantically they studied maps of Kabul and different entrance gates to the airport in a city that none of them knew.

Nafisa was starting to fear that she would never get out of Afghanistan. In desperation, the family flagged down a small minibus and climbed in the back. But three young men jumped in beside them. The men said, "Sister, don't worry, come to our house with us. You'll be safe there." Nafisa realized immediately that something was wrong, so she stopped the van and the family got out. "I said, 'If I'm going to be killed, then I'm going to be killed—but not by you. I'm going to my own home.'"

At that moment Anisa called Nafisa and told her that they were waiting on the street for her. Nafisa found another taxi, and the family tracked down Anisa's location. When they saw Anisa's nephews waving at them, they were flooded with relief. Now Anisa's and Nafisa's families could make their escape together.

"I was living in the south of Afghanistan when we started to hear about the Taliban advancing across the country," Anisa says, picking up her part of the story. "My family was very worried that I would be cut off and captured, so I decided that the best thing was to get to Kabul. I left my house on August 13 and traveled to my brother's home. The Taliban took over on the fifteenth of August, and two days later I received a call from one of the neighbors to tell me that some men from the Taliban had already been to my house searching for me. They had guns and were saying, 'Where is the judge? We want to see her.' It was a horrifying moment. I realized that there was no place for me in Afghanistan anymore."

Anisa had been talking anxiously with the women from the IAWJ, too, particularly her close friend Patti Whalen. They talked about what the future held in store, and Patti urged Anisa to try to leave the country. For the next four days Anisa hid out in her brother's house, cut off from the outside world. She believed that the Taliban did not know where the house was, but even so, everyone was terrified. On August 17 Anisa realized it was time to try to escape. "It was impossible to stay in hiding at my brother's home for a long time. Eventually the Taliban would find me, and there was no way for me to survive there forever. I made the decision, packed one set of clothes, and left."

The problems they faced seemed overwhelming. "Two months earlier the Taliban had assassinated my youngest brother, who was a doctor and a government official in charge of delivering basic health services in three provinces, Parwan, Kapisa, and Panjshir. He was only forty-seven, and he was murdered on his way to work," Anisa recalls. "It was really painful for me. His children were with me, and they were obviously very scared. I wasn't scared for myself because I had experienced the Taliban the first time during the 1990s, but I was very scared for them because it was the first time that they were experiencing such a thing. It was really hard for them.

"When we received the signal from the IAWJ and Patti Whalen to leave the house, the whole family crowded into two cars and headed for the airport. On the way to the airport the crowd was enormous. When I saw the kind of things that people were doing just to get out of Afghanistan, I was horrified. I didn't believe that I would ever be able to get out, especially with young children."

Although Anisa and Nafisa were relieved to be reunited, the path to leaving the country still seemed impossible. The women and their families had spent hours struggling to make their way through packed streets. It was now the middle of the night, and everyone was caked in dirt and sweat.

"We had been fighting to make our way through the crowds all day. We were on unpaved roads, and it was dusty and muddy—it was like we were carried on a sea of people and chaos. We were swamped in filth," Nafisa says.

The two judges and their families took a car to Nafisa's brother's house, where they rested, showered, and ate. In the morning they left again to try to reach the North Gate of the airport. This time the situation was even worse. When Nafisa and Anisa emerged from the car, hordes of waiting people swarmed them and started hitting them, desperate to stop anyone from getting in front of them in the crowd.

Nafisa became overwhelmed, and they quickly returned to her brother's house to try to devise another plan. The family had now made two attempts to get to the airport and the situation seemed hopeless, but Farah called again and said that they should return to the airport, this time to an entry point known as the Blue Gate. She told them that a Polish lawyer named Anna Kruszewska was working with the IAWJ judges and the Polish Ministry of Foreign Affairs to let the women through the security cordon, then onto a flight out of the country.

Only a few weeks earlier Anna had been working as an intellectual property lawyer in Warsaw, with no involvement in international affairs or any idea that she would play a crucial part in the escape of hundreds of people from Afghanistan. A little burned out by work, she'd taken a month off to recharge and travel when she read Tayeba's anguished interview shortly before the fall of Kabul. When she saw the footage of people fleeing Afghanistan and falling off airplanes, her restful holiday never happened. "I remembered the first Taliban regime and I could not believe it was happening again. Then I saw a tweet that led me to Tayeba's interview and when I looked at her photo, and read that she thought she would be killed, it struck me, and I thought—not on my watch. As a lawyer, I have no rational explanation for how I felt, but I believed I could do something for these women."

Poland was part of the NATO forces in Afghanistan and in the midst of conducting its own evacuation. In a flurry of calls Anna first contacted a Romanian judge involved in the interview she'd seen, and then Susan Glazebrook at the IAWJ. Although Anna had no contacts with the Polish government, she rang friends, and then friends of friends, until she tracked down the person responsible for the Polish evacuation mission.

"I asked him if we could find some space for the Afghan women judges on the Polish planes and he said, 'Sure, but you need to organize the list,'" Anna says. "It was a very brief conversation. Incredibly brief. I was shocked that he agreed immediately. There were no ifs or buts. He understood the situation, and he connected me with his team in Afghanistan and in Poland. I was in touch with the prime minister's office, the Polish Ministry of Foreign Affairs, and teams of special forces soldiers. But I didn't realize what that would mean. It meant I was going to have to be responsible for getting these women out."

Anna was now on call twenty-four hours a day and responsible for liaising with everyone. Sleeping for no more than three hours at a time, she would wake to find hundreds of new messages. For days she remained shut up in her apartment, glued to her phone and laptop, surviving on a few groceries dropped off by her mother.

Communications flew back and forth via WhatsApp. "This is really a story of modern technology," Anna says—but everything was confused. Polish soldiers were guarding the entrance to the Blue Gate at the airport, and Anna was told that if the judges could get there and mark their hands with a symbol the soldiers recognized, they would be allowed in.

"Sometimes they would have a sign with something written on it that we had agreed, like the word 'Krakow,' or the letter 'P' for 'Poland' or 'J' for 'judge' marked on their hand. We had to keep changing the words and letters to stay ahead of the Taliban and make sure that no one realized what we were doing and copied it. Once we changed it to 'L' for a famous Polish football club."

No one even knew if the Blue Gate was really the color blue or whether it was a gate that also was called the Abikav Gate, or the Abbey Gate. Farah Bayat explains, "I knew *abi* meant 'blue' in Farsi, but they kept saying 'A-B.' And there was no time for me to explain—this gate is really blue."

"Things changed from one moment to the next," Anisa Dhanji, from the IAWJ, says. "We'd be on WhatsApp to somebody, and we'd be on the phone to somebody else, and it would be, 'This gate is closed,' 'The Taliban are at that gate,' 'Somebody has got through another gate,' 'The Taliban go to dawn prayers at such-and-such times and then the gates are not fully manned.' The first time we heard of Abi Gate, we didn't know whether they were saying 'A-B Gate,' meaning the letters 'A' and 'B.' Amid the chaos and crowds, the Afghan judges didn't know what was happening elsewhere at the airport, and sometimes we did, but it was only when we got hold of a decent map of the airport and identified where the barriers and checkpoints were, and the distance from one gate to another, that we could work out where the various judges actually were, and could start to guide them."

Nafisa and Anisa marked their hands with a "P" for "Poland" and prepared to try to reach the airport again. Each time, they had to pass through three rings of security—a terrifying process. The outer ring was controlled by the Taliban. It was by far the most daunting, and the women covered themselves with old clothes and tried to look as inconspicuous as possible. The second ring was manned by security personnel from the previous regime and was easier to pass through. Farah says, "They didn't beat [the women judges]. They treated them professionally. They asked the women if they had any passports or visas, because if anybody had a foreign passport they would be ushered through." The final ring of security was controlled by the allied armed forces guarding the airport.

Once again Nafisa and Anisa arrived early, at around 8:00 a.m., but as it had been the day before, the gate was surrounded by throngs of people all pushing and shouting and trying to get through. This time, however, they were reunited with a larger group of Afghan women judges whom the IAWJ was also helping to get out.

Anisa Dhanji says, "People got to the airport, on the whole, by themselves. People drove, abandoned their cars; they took taxis; there were multiple checkpoints to get to the airport. The airport itself had rings of people many, many deep, and it seemed impossible to get from one gate to another. Sometimes we would know that there were other judges nearby, but those on the ground did not. We tried to connect them to each other, but then their phone batteries would die. So we lost contact with some people and we didn't know whether that was because something had happened to them or just because their phone had died. Eventually we would reconnect, sometimes through someone else's phone. Then, for just a moment, we could breathe again, until we heard that someone had been beaten, or someone else had given up and gone back home, which they had left hours before thinking they would never see it again. Some had even hurriedly given away their belongings."

On the ground the scene was desperate and chaotic. "Kabul airport has many gates," Anisa Rasooli says. "People would just keep telling us to go to the North Gate, to the South Gate, East Gate, the Northwest Gate, and we were just following the directions, but no one could get inside and the whole situation was terrible and all we could do was wait. We couldn't get too close because that was dangerous with the crush of the crowd. We were there for almost three days."

Everyone in the group marked their hands with the letter "P" and held them in the air, but none of the Polish soldiers seemed to see them or recognize the symbols. In desperation Nafisa called Farah, who called Susan Glazebrook or Patti Whalen, who would then contact Anna Kruszewska. But Anna could only get through to one commander at a time, and that commander would tell some soldiers, but then the soldiers would change shift, and the process would start again.

Anna recalls: "The Polish special forces would ask me, 'Where is this person?'" To add to the problem, so many people were trying to use their cellphones at the airport that it created a communications overload, and it was extremely difficult for messages and calls to get through.

"It was very stressful," Anna says. "The clock was ticking and we were sure it was only a matter of time before the executions started." It seemed impossible to connect the judges to the Polish soldiers, but all Anna and Farah could tell the women was to keep trying.

"No soldier came," Nafisa says. "Nobody saw us."

Anisa adds, "By the last night we were losing hope. I thought that it wouldn't happen. My niece had an asthma attack and couldn't breathe and we had to take her to the hospital for emergency treatment. When I was there I sent a message to the IAWJ members that it was impossible to get inside the airport. We tried and we couldn't do it. We wanted to give up."

Across the world, the judges of the IAWJ and Farah were working frantically to find any other way out. The women judges waited for another hour and a half, until finally Farah told them to leave the Blue Gate and make their way to the Pakistani embassy in Kabul. If they could reach the embassy, they could board a bus with other diplomats who were leaving the country, and the Polish military would escort them through the airport.

It was a desperate, last-ditch effort, and Anna used all her powers of persuasion. "I called the person who was the head of the Polish evacuation and said, 'I have two of the most prominent judges that cannot get through the crowd. They are older women, and more frail. Can we do something to help them?'"

Anna had heard that the special forces were mounting a mission to get people out, and asked for the women judges to be included. Her contact told her the mission was only for VIPs, like those who worked for the International Monetary Fund. Anna replied, "Yes, but these women are special, too!" Her contact said no. "I gave him another speech. He said no again." Finally, Anna made another plea. "Honestly, I've never been so proud of myself as a lawyer, because I thought I gave a pretty good speech. I was the most convincing I've ever been. He listened and he said, 'OK, you've made your point.' It was also a very expensive and dangerous mission—so I've also never been more proud of Poland for doing it." When she heard the good news, Anna broke down in tears. Finally Nafisa Kabuli and Anisa Rasooli were on the list.

"I still wonder how we got through all of that," Nafisa says—the endless hours, the heat, the dirt, the thirst, the hunger, and the exhaustion. "We saw people set on fire in front of our eyes. We stood next to a drain for hours that was full of raw sewage."

"It was disgusting—and terrible," Anisa says. "The Taliban and army kept throwing smoke bombs and grenades. There were thousands of people swarming at the gates. I was so afraid that something would happen to one of my nephews or nieces. I would never have forgiven myself for bringing them to the airport, thinking I was taking them to safety, but perhaps sending them to their death."

Around the globe, the judges from the IAWJ were doing everything they could to help, but they feared it would not be enough. "We were very depressed during that period. We had thirty hours with them on Zoom, hearing as they were walking through the checkpoints, then their disappointment when they had to turn back at various points. At one checkpoint, one of the judges' husbands had a gun pointed at his head. Another one was beaten, and she was in shock because this was something that had just never happened to her before and she couldn't believe it. And then somebody lost their child in the crush of people." Anisa Dhanji recalls with horror that "one of the judges told us that she stepped on a child who she thought was dead. When I heard that, I couldn't help the tears. People were starting to die. People went to the airport, and then left when they thought they couldn't do it—and then returned the next day and stayed all night."

Nafisa remembers, "We have a [Farsi] saying—a human being is softer than a rose petal and harder than a stone. At that moment we were harder than a stone. I don't know what happens to your spirit so that you get strength to go through all these situations." Although the hardships they faced were physical and the fear was tangible, what Nafisa dreaded most was losing her dignity. "I was thinking, 'I am a judge and I don't want to be treated as less than a human being.' I was afraid that if the Taliban got me, they might belittle me, they might strip me of my dignity, and they might make me feel that I was nobody and nothing."

Now Nafisa and Anisa seemed to have a way out, but it was the early hours of the morning, and traveling to the Pakistani embassy at that time would arouse suspicion. Once again the women returned home to wash and rest. No one could sleep, Nafisa says. And the women across the world who were helping them couldn't sleep, either.

Early the next morning the women left home for the final time and arrived outside the Pakistani embassy. The location was under heavy surveillance by the Taliban, and everyone's nerves were frayed. Nafisa could see someone suspicious coming down the street toward them and quickly messaged Farah. Farah replied, urging them to try to stay hidden. The man got closer and closer, but just as the women were starting to panic they heard footsteps on the other side of the embassy gate and a key turning in the lock. After agonizing seconds the gate to the embassy swung open, and they could step safely inside.

After days on the streets, walking into the embassy was like entering a world of safety and calm. For a few hours at least the families could relax, eat a little, and have a drink. When the time came to leave, they went into the courtyard to board one of the fifteen or so buses leaving for the airport with Polish diplomats. After days of crazy chaos on the streets of Kabul, it seemed surreal to now be swept so quickly through the crowds—although the threat of the Taliban was still ever-present.

"The final trip to the airport was terrifying because the Taliban stopped our buses a couple of times. I think it might have been because the Pakistani ambassador was on board. They didn't harm us in any way, but the Taliban asked the drivers, 'Where are you going and who are you?' Fortunately, we continued, and at around 1:30 p.m. we got inside the airport at last," Anisa says.

Inside the gate, another judge was waiting, too—their young colleague Tayeba Parsa.

3.
Tayeba's Escape

TAYEBA PARSA'S ESCAPE FROM THE TALIBAN WAS EQUALLY nerve-racking and torturous. Her mother and sister had been granted visas to travel to Iran, and Tayeba and her new husband (they had had the religious ceremony for their wedding, the nikah, just two days earlier) were driving them to the airport when Anisa Dhanji called to say that the Taliban had reached Kabul.

"On the way we sat in heavy traffic," Tayeba recalls. "I couldn't understand where everyone was going. Then suddenly my sister checked Facebook and said, 'The Taliban came!' Soon after, Judge Anisa Dhanji called me and said, 'Be careful—all the prisons have been opened, even Pul-e-Charkhi, and all the prisoners have been released.'"

"It was the only time she broke down," Anisa says. "She understood immediately that these were the criminals that the women judges had imprisoned. She was more afraid of that than she was of the Taliban being on the road, because these prisoners had personal vendettas, and they were seeking vengeance. She realized that she would have to leave."

On the road, traffic was totally gridlocked. Tayeba and her family waited in their car for hours, with a terrible feeling of tension. After a long time Tayeba's mother and sister suddenly jumped out of the car, abandoned their luggage, and started to run to the airport.

"I was shocked when my mother and sister got out of the car and left me," Tayeba says. "I kept insisting that I would take them to the airport—but they wouldn't listen and were determined to go by themselves. After I'd heard the news about the prisoners being released I understood how dangerous the situation now was for me. I called my sister and said, 'Why did you do that? Why did you leave without saying goodbye? What if that is the last time that I see my mother?'" Tayeba was traveling in her own car and couldn't leave it behind.

Another of her sisters rang from Australia and burst into tears. "She kept saying, 'What does it mean? I can't do anything to help you, I can only ask God to protect you.'" As Tayeba sat and watched, she saw soldiers from the Afghan military stripping off their uniforms so that they couldn't be identified by the Taliban. "Then I started to cry because I realized that there was no one to protect us, no one was going to fight for us." Tayeba and her husband sat on the road for nine hours, until 7:00 p.m.

During this time Tayeba spoke to her father, who told her not to be afraid, but to meet him as soon as possible. "He said, 'Don't drive, because it makes the Taliban angry, and be very careful at checkpoints.'"

Anisa Dhanji also called with a chilling update. The Taliban had entered the Supreme Court building and they now had the names, addresses, and phone numbers of the judges. They agreed Tayeba should not go to any location the Taliban might know about, so Tayeba arranged to go to a hotel owned by her uncle in the Hazara district of Kabul.

Later Tayeba's father arrived on foot and said that he had seen the Taliban at checkpoints in the district. Local people were taking photographs with them.

Tayeba was scared to leave the hotel because, in the mounting panic, people were looting shops and offices. She always carried gold jewelry in the car, and she knew that if she tried to leave by car, thieves walking past on the street could force open the doors, steal their possessions, and attack them. The family discussed the situation for a long time, but eventually Tayeba's father convinced her that going back to their own home was really the best option. The hotel was a temporary refuge, but they could not stay there forever.

"We got into the car. My father and my husband sat in the front and I climbed into the backseat. I tried to cover myself and hide to avoid being seized at the checkpoints. I was terrified of making eye contact with the Taliban—and two years later that terror is still with me. I had my identity documents with me because I had been planning to go to court to apply for my marriage certificate."

When they arrived home Tayeba set about immediately destroying all her case notes and anything else that might reveal her identity as a judge. She worried about what to do with the gun that the court had issued her for safety. If she hid it, the Taliban might find it. But if she gave it to her uncle, he would be in danger if it was later discovered by the Taliban.

For two long days she waited at home, working with the IAWJ to put together a list of all the Afghan women judges and to compile their identity documents.

Anisa Dhanji, in the United Kingdom, had served as a judge on many asylum cases and understood that two factors would be crucial in being able to ensure the women could apply for asylum wherever they might land. The first was whether they could prove they were in danger in their home country. That seemed evidently true for women judges in Afghanistan. The second was that they must be able to prove that they were indeed women judges—and some would have to prove that they had worked in certain courts, which is what gave rise to particular risks for them. Collecting all of this information was going to be a mammoth task, but they had to start somewhere.

"We had written a note to all the judges in Afghanistan earlier in the summer preparing them for what might happen," Anisa Dhanji says. "We didn't know it would happen as quickly as it did, but we had imagined a situation where they would have to leave and make asylum claims, and what they would need for that claim. We knew that if the Taliban took control it would be dangerous, and that they could not leave holding these different bits of paper. They had to copy and email the documents to somebody who could be trusted, and leave anything else in a safe place [from] where it could be sent afterward. They couldn't carry the original papers with them, but they needed some confirmation to get them through the rings of security."

Anisa, together with the U.K. partner judges, had been working out how to get judges like Tayeba, who had been part of the U.K. mentors scheme, "call-forward letters" that they hoped would help them through security and into the hands of British forces at the airport. Yet even though they were confronting life-and-death matters, the U.K. judges could not simply pick up the phone and request help from the British Foreign and Commonwealth Office. There were official lines they could not cross.

Farah Bayat, the IAWJ translator, told Tayeba that the IAWJ was also trying to get her evacuated to the United States, along with Anisa Rasooli and Nafisa Kabuli. The Afghan women had all made prominent appeals about their plight in many U.S. and international media interviews, and the IAWJ was trying to persuade the State Department that their lives were in imminent danger.

Before any help from the State Department was forthcoming, however, Tayeba received a call from Anna Kruszewska, who explained that she was a Polish lawyer who had read Tayeba's interview. "I didn't know where Poland was," Tayeba says "I hadn't even heard that name before, because we call it Lahestan."

Tayeba asked Anisa if Anna could be trusted. Anisa had in fact just finished speaking to Susan Glazebrook, who had received a message from Anna. It was late at night in New Zealand and Susan was exhausted. In Iceland, where Anisa was on holiday, the day was just beginning, so Susan handed over to Anisa the task of checking out who Anna was and following up on her offer to help. Anisa made inquiries and then spoke to Anna, quickly realizing that this was someone they could trust and work with. She was able to reassure Tayeba about Anna, but she also wanted Tayeba to be sure that leaving was the right decision for her. This was a message that the IAWJ judges would convey at different times to all the Afghan women judges they were in contact with. The decision to leave came with unknown risks. Even if they succeeded, they would be leaving Afghanistan as judges and arriving in a foreign country as refugees. They would be separated, perhaps permanently, from close family. If being a female judge in Afghanistan had been hard, this would be harder. Anna, too, told Tayeba, "I can't tell you to come to the airport. It's your decision. But if you decide that it is safe to come, we can help you."

"The judges were very brave," Anna says. "They trusted me, which was very stressful. Those were the most difficult phone calls of my life. I had to ring them and say, 'Are you ready to leave for the airport?' I didn't know if the road was safe. I didn't know if they were going to be killed. But I had to ask them if they were ready because the guards were there to escort them. And when they said yes, I had to guide them. That was the moment of trust, and of great solidarity, because now I was with them on every step of that road."

"So many of the judges were trying to get through to the airport," Anisa says. "We were constantly talking to and messaging them and each other. Where was X? Had she left home? Some were too scared to leave home. Some tried to get to the airport but the experience was so horrendous that they came back home. Some said they would try again the next day. Some said they would *not* try again the next day. Some said they would not try, and then they did try.

"We were trying to keep track of where the judges were, making sure we had contact with each one at least every few hours. We also had language barriers, but our interpreters were amazing, and they, too, worked through the nights. We were constantly assessing the risks. Over time, we learned certain things, but each day and night brought its own challenges. We didn't know whether going through the checkpoints was going to expose the judges to risk. We had to learn from those people who were trying a certain gate that tear gas was being used there, so we could alert others who might be heading to that gate. What we were getting from individuals actually at the airport was an important source of information, though some in our group, particularly Vanessa and Patti from the U.S., developed useful 'intelligence' channels because so many U.S. personnel were at the airport. Things on the ground changed constantly, though, so if at two o'clock in the afternoon it might be a good idea to go to the Abi Gate or to go to the Baron Hotel, it might be the very place not to go at six o'clock in the evening if the Taliban were then in the vicinity. We had to weigh up: Was it easier at night? Was it harder at night? We had to make these assessments on the spot, using the best information we had. A lot of prayers were said."

Back at home, Tayeba decided that she *was* ready. She packed a small bag and stepped outside with her father and husband, knowing that once they got to the airport they might not be allowed to board a plane. The risk was greater because they did not all have the correct documents: Tayeba's father's passport had expired, and her husband did not have a passport at all.

"I covered my face and hid in the backseat of the car again. On the way there was a huge crowd, and the Taliban was trying to scatter people by shooting. My father tried to approach the airport through the main gate, but when he got there the Taliban started to beat him. I jumped between them and said, 'OK, OK, we will leave the area and go home. Please do not beat him.'"

Tayeba got back into the car with her father and checked a WhatsApp group Anna had given her access to, which was for Afghans who had worked with the Polish military and were eligible for Polish evacuation. These people were gathering in a safe place, waiting for the right time to go to the gate. They told Tayeba a safe place to park near the airport, and she waited there from 1:00 p.m. to 10:00 p.m. "After I arrived there Anna asked for the other judges' WhatsApp numbers so that I could help them find parking. Five other judges joined me there with their family members. I asked two of my colleagues to bring a power bank for me because everybody's phone was dying. Anna tried to send soldiers to escort us, but they could not come outside. Finally at 11:00 p.m. we received the word that it was time to go to the gate again, and we went there and waited until 10:00 a.m. the next day. We stood behind the gate for twelve hours, without food or water. The crowd crushed us, and the Taliban was beating people. The worst moment was when I saw a Taliban soldier come within a heartbeat of shooting a man. He lifted his gun and pressed it to the man's chest. Luckily, the man was so shocked and terrified he fainted and collapsed on the ground before he could be shot," Tayeba says.

Anna asked Tayeba if she could see any Polish people there, and she confirmed that she had met a Polish woman journalist. The journalist, Jagoda Grondecka, was wearing a long black cloak and hijab, like the women judges, and was trying to approach the Polish soldiers on their behalf.

"She kept shouting at them in Polish, but they couldn't hear her, and they would shout back, 'Come to this wall—come closer.' But she couldn't get closer because the crowds wouldn't let her."

Eventually Jagoda told the crowd, "Let me go first and I will convince the soldiers to let us go through." As she passed by, Tayeba said, "I'm the judge." Grondecka beckoned Tayeba to follow her, and the crowd parted. Suddenly the two women reached the wall of the airport.

"We didn't know that the wall was moveable. It was a trick that the Polish soldiers used because they said, 'We cannot hear you, come to this wall,' and when the crowd let us through and we got there they suddenly opened that wall. It was actually a gate."

Tayeba and Jagoda slipped in together, and the wall closed behind them. Anna Kruszewska believes the Polish journalist played a truly heroic role in the evacuation. "She stayed in Afghanistan during those days. It was much easier for foreigners to leave, but she stayed and she used her leverage as a white woman to stay with Afghans and protect them with her presence. She stayed for hours in front of the gate and because of her our first group of women judges was let in. Tayeba went in basically holding her hand, and then Jagoda went back for other people."

Tayeba was now inside the airport, but her father and husband were still locked outside. She started crying. She didn't want to leave like that.

The soldiers took Tayeba to one side, and she explained that her father and husband did not have valid travel documents. Then Tayeba gave the soldiers the details of the other judges who were waiting to evacuate, including Nafisa and Anisa.

Half an hour later the soldiers returned and pointed out Tayeba's father and husband, who had now made it through the security gate but were still some way away, in a different group. "I saw my father in the distance, but I could only wave at him. I was relieved to see that he was eating because he has diabetes and needed food." The soldiers told Tayeba that she had to board a bus to get to the plane and that the bus had to drive back out through the gate and reenter through another. On the bus they closed all the windows so that people in the heaving crowds could not force their way onboard.

"When we got back inside the airport they took us to a safe, quiet, place—and I was so tired I just lay down on the stony ground. It was an open area with no shade, and we all lay there under the sun for hours. We were so hungry, but there was no food." At 5:00 p.m. the soldiers returned and told the women that it was time to board the plane.

Carrying only one small bag, Tayeba was bused to the runway, where a military aircraft would take them first to Uzbekistan before another plane would fly them on to Poland. But, looking around, Tayeba could see no sign of her father or husband—and with a terrible feeling she realized that she was alone.

Back in the United Kingdom, Anisa was in contact with Tayeba's sister Tahera, in Denmark, and with Anna in Poland. Vanessa Ruiz joined Anisa on the "Tayeba Exit" WhatsApp group, and together they monitored the situation through the night. "When I told Tahera that Tayeba was on a plane to Poland, I could almost hear her jaw drop," recalls Anisa. "It seemed extraordinary that they were going to Poland. At some point we had to tell her that her father and Tayeba's husband were not with Tayeba. Fortunately, we could later tell her they would be on another plane, also heading to Poland. Many hours later, though, there was still no news of Tayeba's arrival. Of course, this was a military flight, not a scheduled flight with public information about delays that we could check, and it took some time to establish that there had been a long refueling stop in Uzbekistan en route."

The military plane was loud and uncomfortable, Tayeba says. "It took off so fast and so steeply, I thought I would vomit." Outside she imagined her country falling away behind her, and felt the relief of safety mingled with intense anxiety about when and how she would be reunited with her family.

Anisa Rasooli left on one of the next flights. When it was their turn to take off she, too, sat silently on the plane, deep in reflection. Like the other judges, she had been sure that America would not abandon Afghanistan: "They had spent and done so much in twenty years. They had a huge army, they had rebuilt the education system, and day by day things were improving for women. For all of these reasons I was sure that America wouldn't leave Afghanistan alone." Now, Anisa realized, Afghanistan *was* alone, and she had seen her people risking their lives rather than live under a new Taliban regime. "They wanted to leave—at any cost."

Nafisa Kabuli says she also lost hope. "I felt like I had lost my life. I had lost everything. I remember how they came and frisked us before we got onto the bus to the airport that last time and it reminded me of how prisoners were treated—frisked and put on the bus and then taken to prison. That's how I felt. I thought my whole life became null. It was reduced to zero. And I didn't even know where they were going to take us. I didn't know what the future held." Nafisa starts crying when she remembers taking her seat on the plane. "We had a government in Afghanistan. We had a nation. We loved our people. From childhood I had been planning my future and how I could serve my people. Now everything had changed in front of my eyes."

When the plane took off, Nafisa wondered what and who she would become in her new life. "I was thinking that I had been working toward becoming somebody for my entire life, and building a future for my people—and now I was leaving everything behind, and with empty hands."

4.

The Last Flight Out

TAYEBA, ANISA, AND NAFISA HAD REACHED SAFETY IN POLAND, but so many judges were still left behind. By late August, the women judges of the IAWJ and their interpreter, Farah, were driven by a determination to save as many lives a possible, but hampered by chaos and confusion. And by now they were almost incoherent with exhaustion. Spanish judge Gloria Poyatos Mata wrote a record of her days spent on their Zoom call:

> It's 9:35 p.m. in the Canary Islands. I'm sitting at my dining room table converted into an improvised "evacuation war room"—and I've just realized that it is already night time.
>
> I've lost the sense of the day, the hour, and almost of life before August 2021. I realize that I have been connected to the IAWJ Zoom call since 5:30 in the morning. The Zoom never closes—it is an operations center to get our Afghan sisters out of hell.
>
> Members of our small group of judges enter and leave as if it were their living room. There are currently seven female judges and two Dari language interpreters online. The judges are part of a "diverse court." Our mission transcends holding trials and issuing sentences.

The lives of our Afghan colleagues now depend on our online deliberations.

None of us on the Zoom call wear robes—we're in comfortable T-shirts instead. Sometimes we eat at the keyboard, or comb our hair, or drink from our favorite mugs.

The two interpreters are much more than that. They also interpret the emotions of the judges who, from hidden places, remain crouched waiting for their opportunity to escape. They are full of fear, terror, and anguish. . . .

It's 10:35 p.m. Our group is working on a new evacuation. One colleague from Miami debates with Mona Lynch in Nova Scotia about some important detail. In Australia, Robyn Tupman, who has been working on this for hours, also has her opinion. Suddenly there is silence, and we see Susan Glazebrook typing. You can hear her sigh. She's been awake for twenty-six hours. . . .

In Vermont Patti Whalen is trying to get insulin for Asifa, Judge Amina's four-year-old diabetic daughter. To achieve this, she has already started contacting people in four countries and four different time zones. In the UK, Anisa Dhanji warns of receiving anonymous messages that offer help to judges and that they should never be answered. They are a trap. . . .

The group continues to verify data, investigate sources of possible ransoms, raise money, seek visas, negotiate with governments for aid, and face a vast array of bureaucratic and security problems. . . .

It's 5:35 am. The alarm sounds. I look at the group messages. Good news. Some judges and their families have managed to leave Afghanistan. In addition, Brazil has issued some visas that will allow other judges to leave. We have to find a way. I connect to Zoom, and we share in our collective joy that is always expressed with caution. Tomorrow things can change. . . .

An hour later there is more news. One of the young Afghan judges has given birth to a healthy baby girl. This little girl will grow up in a different country where women's human rights are respected. Her name is Liberty. On the Zoom call our group smiles, our morale reinforced. We continue. . . .

In the United States, Farah Bayat sat by her computer all day, updating the database with endless changes, listening to the Zoom call, and reading and answering hundreds of messages from desperate judges. "My computer was in my bedroom and all I did, all day long, was wake up, take two steps to the computer or five steps to the bathroom. When I was in the bathroom I would leave the door open because I wanted to hear if anything was happening."

Arrangements sometimes seemed impossible due to misunderstandings caused by differences in culture between Afghanistan and the West. On one occasion Vanessa Ruiz was desperately waiting for a photo for a visa application. "Everything was ready to go, but there was no photo," Farah says. No one could understand the delay, as taking a photo on a phone and sending it over seemed simple, but when Farah contacted the woman judge, she said she had been waiting to get an appointment at the photo studio. In Afghanistan, if you needed a photo, that was where you went—and to make matters worse, the photo studio did not have any electricity. The judge explained to Farah that she was trying to buy a canister of kerosene to power the photo studio's generator.

Even getting a home address to write on a form was difficult. Some judges did not know their street address and would send Farah long directions as if she were in Kabul and making her way to their house. Others couldn't get a handle on the iMap Farah had to send them so that they could pin their location for the special forces to come pick them up. Usually they sent it back with Farah's own address, which she had sent them only as a demonstration—and Farah would desperately ask: "Are there any young people in your family who can show you how to use a phone?"

The IAWJ had now formed partnerships with other organizations that wanted to help, including the International Bar Association and Jewish Humanitarian Response. Together, working against what seemed like insurmountable odds, so far they had successfully evacuated dozens of judges and their families to safe destinations across Europe and the Middle East—but many still remained in Afghanistan. One was Raihana Attaee.

Raihana was hiding in her mother-in-law's house in Kabul when she received a call from an anonymous number. When she answered she heard the threatening tone of a man speaking in Pashto, one of the main languages in Afghanistan and the language commonly spoken by the Taliban. "Do you recognize me?" he asked. Raihana said she did not. "I'm one of the prisoners that you put in jail," the man growled.

When he told her his name, Raihana remembered only too well who he was: a man who had killed his wife and whom she had sentenced to twenty years in prison. The "crime" his wife had paid for with her life was to have a secret phone. "When he found that phone, he brutally murdered her," Raihana says. The judge had sent him to prison for decades, but now he was free. "I asked him,

'How did you find my number?' The man laughed and said, 'I found your number—and now I am going to find you.'"

Raihana was still working in the courthouse in Nangarhar, nearly 125 miles to the east of Kabul, when the Taliban began to sweep across Afghanistan in the summer of 2021.

"The situation in Afghanistan was getting worse by the day. The negotiations for the Doha Accord were going in favor of the Taliban, and it seemed like many people were even saying favorable things about the Taliban to the international media. People thought that the Taliban had changed, that this time they were going to respect human rights and women's rights and would not be as conservative. But the people who knew the Taliban couldn't believe that. We were very afraid. We also couldn't believe that the Taliban would take total power in Afghanistan. We thought that they would perhaps form a coalition government. Even a coalition government was a very scary thought," Raihana says.

Raihana was stunned as the Taliban took over province after province in August. "It was unbelievable," she says. "Thirty-four provinces fell into the hands of the Taliban in only ten days."

The Taliban reached Nangarhar on a Friday night. "I was asleep in bed in my own home when a colleague rang me and said, 'Hurry up, get out of the house, the Taliban is in the city, they are going to come to the court next. They are close to your home—just flee.' I couldn't believe it because that day everything had been normal in Nangarhar. I also knew that Nangarhar was relatively close to Kabul, and when the Taliban took Nangarhar it meant they would also take Kabul."

It was the middle of the night, and Raihana had nowhere safe to go. But her colleague helped her to escape. "They sent a car, and I took my husband and son to their house—and from there we left for Kabul. I cried all the way. I saw the Taliban standing proudly on the streets with their guns, and ordinary people looked so afraid and worried—and hopeless. They didn't know where to go or what to do. I wore a burqa so that no one could recognize me. Kabul was already in the hands of the Taliban by the time we got there, and we went to my mother-in-law's house and hid inside for several days. I didn't dare to go out; only the men could go out to buy food. When they came home they told us that the Taliban were everywhere. No woman could be seen in the streets, and everyone was terrified. Many people were trying to get to the airport to leave the country—and everything about the situation seemed desperate. I didn't know what our future had in store for us."

Raihana had been staying at her mother-in-law's house for a few days when she received the threatening phone call. "I immediately changed my phone number, but now I was truly afraid for the safety of my family, especially my little boy. I left my mother-in-law's house and went to my father's house, and then went to my brother and sister's house. I didn't feel safe anywhere, and we kept moving from place to place."

Those days were very hard. Everyone Raihana talked to told her about the bad things the Taliban were doing. Some of the other women judges told her that the Taliban had been to their homes, searching for them. Others had been followed by prisoners who had been freed.

"We were prisoners now—in our own homes," Raihana recalls. She joined the IAWJ WhatsApp group and filled out countless applications for visas for different countries—the United States, Canada, Australia, Germany, and the United Kingdom. But none was successful.

Then, on the evening of August 26, a suicide bomber walked into the huge crowd of people waiting outside the Abi Gate at the Kabul airport and detonated his device. An ISIS-affiliated group that was fighting the Taliban, called the Islamic State–Khorasan

Province, claimed responsibility for the attack. At least 170 Afghans and 13 U.S. military personnel were killed, with hundreds of others injured. Eyewitnesses said they felt the ground pulled from under them in an enormous blast that tossed the bodies of countless victims up in the air. In response, the Taliban further tightened its rings of security around the airport, and on Saturday, August 28, the head of the U.K. armed forces, General Sir Nick Carter, announced that Britain had ended its evacuation mission, admitting they had "not been able to get everybody out." Two days later, on August 30, the last U.S. C-17 military cargo plane lifted off from Kabul, and President Biden announced that America's twenty-year military presence in Afghanistan had ended. General Kenneth McKenzie, commander of U.S. Central Command, thanked the Taliban for being "actually very helpful and useful to us as we closed down operations."

As everyone had feared, events had overtaken the evacuation efforts, and now escape for the Afghan women judges seemed virtually impossible. The IAWJ sent a letter over WhatsApp to their friends and colleagues that read:

Dear sisters:

Our hearts and prayers are with you and your respected families in these difficult days.

We have been working very hard to help you leave Afghanistan if you wish to do so. Unfortunately the bombing at the airport has meant that transfer out through the airport for Afghan nationals has now become impossible. That may change in a month or so possibly. And we are looking for other possibilities.

Be ready to leave: Have a small bag (grab bag) ready with absolute essentials in case we find an evacuation option for you and you have to leave quickly. Make sure you have food and water you can take with you easily.

Airport: No one else will be allowed into the airport by the U.S. forces. DO NOT go to or near the airport by yourselves. It would not only be dangerous because of a possible terrorist attack but also futile as you would not be given access.

Passports: Do not approach any embassies for visas as the Taliban are confiscating passports of Afghan nationals. Keep your passports and identity documents in an accessible place but as hidden as possible.

Stay safe: Each of you must focus ABOVE ALL on ensuring that you and your family stay safe during this dangerous time. This is your first priority. Trust your instincts. You know from your experience and knowledge what will keep you and your family safe.

Safe place: You need to find a safe place to hide. Try to have alternative places to move to if necessary. Keep a low profile. Be very careful who you trust. Never disclose where you are staying unless we tell you it is safe.

Hide the fact you are a judge: Destroy anything that indicates you are a judge. Please make sure that you have sent photos of your court ID to us and any other material proving you are a judge before destroying it.

Food and water: Keep reserves of water. Get as good a stock of lasting food (tinned, dried) as you can. The electricity and/or water might go off for even longer periods and possibly indefinitely.

Phones: Keep your phones fully charged. If you have more than one phone, only keep one on at a time.

Swap SIMs if needed. Make sure we have your email address and phone and WhatsApp numbers.

WhatsApp: We understand you have a WhatsApp group for all AWJA [Afghan Women Judges Association] judges. DELETE this group and do not use it anymore. It is unsafe. If one of you is compromised, then all of you are. Smaller groups are safer.

Electronic safety: Go through phones and computers and delete all contacts, photos, social media, messages, documents, etc. that might compromise you or identify you as a judge. Learn how to delete entire message logs on WhatsApp and other messaging apps and emails in advance so you can do it quickly if you are in trouble. Everything on your smart phone will be used against you if the Taliban takes your phone.

Phishing: The Taliban have started to send messages to some, pretending that they are Americans or Europeans and offering help to get you out. Never trust these messages. Always report them to us. We will check into it for you. Be careful.

Communications may be cut off: It is possible that mobile phones and internet might be turned off. If this happens seek safety, be patient, and afterwards, when services are restored, get back into communication with us again. If you do not remember our contact details, you can contact us through the IAWJ website: iawj.org. You may also like to send us contact details of relatives or friends outside Afghanistan so we can contact them if we cannot contact you.

Email contact: If you need to send anything to us email ****@gmail.com. Remember we will not abandon you. Keep safe and be strong. You are in our thoughts and our prayers.

> You are amazing women and we honour your courage.
> —Susan Glazebrook, Robyn Tupman, Anisa Dhanji, Gloria Matas Poyatos, Vanessa Ruiz, Patti Whalen, and Mona Lynch

"We were just waiting, day after day," Raihana says. "I started to get really afraid that the Taliban would search the house and find me, so I began talking to the media and asking for help. I told the journalists that I had to remain anonymous, but unfortunately someone published my real name and the court that I had worked in. That made the situation much worse.

"Soon after I got a phone call from a Talib who had been made a Taliban judge in the Nangarhar court. He said, 'You spoke out against us—and we will find you and punish you.'"

Raihana was terrified. "I didn't know what to do and I regretted everything—becoming a judge, doing the interviews, asking for help. Everything. I regretted being a mother, because I dreaded to think what would happen to my son if the Taliban arrested me. In the end I decided that all I could do was leave everything behind and go somewhere far away where no one knew me. But it was also somewhere where we had no means of survival. I was desperate, and I contacted Susan Glazebrook at the IAWJ and begged her to help. She said that she would try to help me—but I couldn't believe it, it seemed impossible."

Susan and the women of the IAWJ did help, though. A few hours later they arranged to move Raihana and her family to a safe house, where she remained in hiding for nearly three weeks. "When I reached the safe house with my husband and my son I felt like it was the happiest day of my life. After a month of running in secret from house to house we were finally secure and could relax. I was exhausted."

Eventually the IAWJ told Raihana that they had found a way out of Afghanistan, but she would have to travel to another city, Mazar-i-Sharif, and then from there fly to another country—although Raihana did not know what her final destination would be.

The bus from Kabul to Mazar-i-Sharif covers nearly 340 miles of what is considered one of Afghanistan's most beautiful highways. First it passes slowly through the outskirts of Kabul, with miles of street-side shops open to the road. Then it winds its way deep into the countryside, where rows of golden autumnal trees and tracts of farmland line the route, before rising into the mountains and crossing the snow-capped Salang Pass and then finally descending into the flat desert landscape of Mazar-i-Sharif.

"The Taliban stopped and searched us many times on the journey—but they didn't recognize that we were judges fleeing the country. When we reached Mazar we stayed for two days in a guesthouse with some of the other judges and their families. Getting to any airport at that point was very tough. The Taliban searched everything, and they even asked us to remove any jewelry that we had with us, including earrings. Then they weighed it and gave it back to us before—finally—they let us go to the plane."

The flight had been organized by the International Bar Association, which also had been working around the clock to evacuate judges, lawyers, and others who needed to flee. The $800,000 cost of chartering the plane had been paid for by donors, and the flight was filled with Afghan doctors, lawyers, judges, and all of their families.

"When I sat down on the plane I was overwhelmed with the strangest mixture of feelings I've ever experienced," Raihana says. "I've never felt that way before. I felt happy—because now I had a future. I was going to be free. I was also very sad for my country, and for my people. And I was *so* sad about the way that I was leaving my country. I was leaving my parents, my family, and my friends, and I couldn't even say goodbye. I felt like my life had been a struggle, but I had always believed it was worth it to help build a future for my people. Now I was leaving everything behind." The plane took off and flew into the darkness, landing hours later in the middle of the night. "We arrived in Greece, and I looked down onto the tarmac into the faces of the many strangers who had come to help us. Nothing was familiar, and I wondered what on earth I would do."

5.

No Way Out

RAIHANA DID NOT KNOW IT, BUT SHE WAS ONE OF THE LAST women judges to be evacuated from Afghanistan by air. The friends and colleagues she had left behind faced an even more precarious route to freedom—enabled and funded by a most unlikely mixture of people, faiths, and purpose.

"I think the idea of the rabbi, the judge, and the hijab is just like the craziest juxtaposition," Caroline Marks says. Marks was a lawyer and seasoned media executive who had scaled the heights of the New York business world before moving to an orange grove in Florida. There she led the efforts of Jewish Humanitarian Response in funding and coordinating the evacuation of the Afghan women judges, along with numerous other persecuted groups from Afghanistan. Jewish Humanitarian Response had evolved from the Aleph Institute, a chaplaincy and advocacy organization for criminal justice reform that originally had been founded to help Jewish men and women in isolated environments, such as U.S. jails and prisons and the military. That advocacy and humanitarian work had become international over time, but it was the vigorous leadership of Rabbi Zvi Boyarsky that had led to an offer of help and then an entire rescue program for the Afghan women judges.

"I think, as Jews, we don't do well with persecution and we don't do well when people are being driven underground. There's a biological need to respond, which we tend to do," Caroline says. After a call between Rabbi Boyarsky and Vanessa Ruiz and Susan Glazebrook from the IAWJ, Jewish Humanitarian Response started fundraising from its donors to pay for two full flights to the United Arab Emirates (UAE), a country that had agreed to become a "lily pad"—hosting the Afghans temporarily until they could move to their final destinations. As Jewish Humanitarian Response worked with the UAE on other programs, they would help negotiate landing rights for those evacuation flights.

"It started off very differently from where it ended up. There was no way of knowing exactly how the dots would end up being connected," says Yossi Levi, who works for Jewish Humanitarian Response. "What became apparent as this progressed is that the UAE, along with everyone else, was really disappointed that the international community didn't open up their doors as promised. Countries like the USA, U.K., and Canada, who had worked with these people, who knew them, and who had, in a way, contributed to their security concerns, then upped and left.

"There was a fundamental catch-22 to the whole situation. You had to be out of Afghanistan in order to be processed for any type of permanent resettlement. Countries did not want to take people from Afghanistan without knowing that there was some type of permanent resettlement plan and the Afghan person wasn't going to become their permanent refugee. And then, a little bit later, they wanted to know that somebody was vouching for these people, and that they were being vetted, because there were a lot of people that slipped in who were not who they purported to be.

"It was disappointing to see that the really large NGOs, who had the capacity and the funding to make a difference in a lot of ways, also said, 'We're out.' They basically took the position of the countries that had a military presence in Afghanistan and said, 'If they're out militarily, we're out.' Some of these organizations had field officers who were deeply embedded in the communities, and they just kind of rinsed their hands and walked away."

The team pulled together funding from a multitude of donors, including renowned author J.K. Rowling, Chicago businessman and fundraiser Jeff Adler, and attorney Gordon Caplan (who was sent to prison for his role in the 2019 Varsity Blues case when he and celebrities including actor Felicity Huffman were convicted of a scheme to pay for rigged tests and athletic records so that their children could get into top universities).

Now the combined efforts of Jewish Humanitarian Response, the IAWJ, and the International Bar Association were aimed at evacuating dozens of Afghan women judges and their families to safe countries. There was almost nothing they couldn't or wouldn't agree to—as long as it was legal. Yet despite all their efforts, the project was far from over. For all the women judges who had been flown to safety and were in temporary accommodations in Poland, Greece, Romania, or Spain, many others were still trapped in Afghanistan: hiding, afraid, uncertain about their future, and unsure if they would ever be free.

One of those judges was Tahera Karimi, an ethnic Tajik from Kabul with five children, including Mohammad Jan, a baby who suffered from a perforated heart, which required urgent treatment that was unavailable in Afghanistan.

Tahera's father was a judge who had been imprisoned by the Taliban during their rule in the 1990s, and she had been forced to wait until their overthrow in 2001 to complete her own education. By then Tahera was married with a baby daughter, and so she decided to begin her career in the administrative department of the Supreme Court, where she could access a kindergarten, before later becoming a judge in the commercial court and then joining the Public Security Court, investigating cases relating to the Taliban, kidnapping, counterfeiting money, treason, and drugs.

One day a week, Tahera went to the National Security Directorate to hear cases involving the most dangerous prisoners, including foreign nationals, like two Pakistani Taliban men who had infiltrated the Afghan national army and an Afghan who was an Iranian spy. "At that time security was relatively good, so I decided not to wear the niqab covering my face, which meant that the defendants could recognize me. Many of the defendants were opponents of the government, and when they saw me they turned their backs on me and said that seeing a woman is a sin."

After five years, in 2016, Tahera joined the family court, presiding over divorce cases, demands for dowry, custody of children, alimony, and cases involving termination of engagements. During this time, however, the security situation worsened. In the same year, Tahera's sister, an administrative officer, was tragically murdered in a suicide attack in front of the gate of the Supreme Court.

"It is the worst memory of my life. I left the Supreme Court an hour before the attack happened, and that was when I saw my sister alive for the last time. After the attack I rushed to the hospital and found her lifeless body. I washed my sister and cleaned off all the blood from her wounds."

After her sister's murder, life became extremely difficult. Tahera now had four children, and she feared for the future of her family and her country. "Day by day, the security situation worsened. Judges were targeted and killed in the provinces, and then in Kabul. Sometimes we were on duty when emergency situations arose and we were informed that there was going to be a suicide attack on the court. Our work stopped for hours and we were locked in our offices. The court took on the appearance of a military base."

On the August day that Kabul fell to the Taliban in 2021, Tahera was at work with her baby, then four months old.

"I felt trapped. By 1:00 p.m. the situation was chaotic. Everyone, including the chief of the Supreme Court, had left the court and gone home. They said that the Taliban had reached Pul-e-Charkhi prison and released all the prisoners. I was terrified and went home to get my children. We took a few essential things and then fled to the house of one of our relatives." As a soldier trained by the United States, and a member of the elite unit supporting the Afghan president, Tahera's husband was also a target. Later that night he joined them and told her that all the Americans had fled from the embassy, and that the Afghan president, Ashraf Ghani, had left the country.

"There was panic and chaos everywhere, and my husband and I were afraid that someone would find us. We turned off our phones and lived in secret for a few days until my brother-in-law, who had an American green card, sent us an emergency visa." Like so many others, Tahera and her family made their way to the airport and encountered the scenes of pandemonium and chaos.

"We stayed at the gates of Kabul airport for two days and nights. On the first night we went to Kasbah Gate, which was terrible. The guards were shooting in the air, which was terrifying and earsplitting, and when the crowds got out of control they shot at people to try and disperse them. One person was shot and was covered in blood. His family was hugging him and crying for help, but everyone was trying to run away and save themselves. My children were scared by all the screaming and crying."

By the second day Tahera's youngest child was gasping for breath, so she decided to take him to the hospital and then return to her relative's house. They were trapped. For months they lived in secret, staying in contact with the IAWJ, which was trying to help the next group of judges leave from the airport at Mazar-i-Sharif. To make the situation even more difficult, Tahera's family did not have passports, and the IAWJ was trying to arrange for them to travel with visas alone.

After endless delays and complications, on January 14, 2022, the

IAWJ contacted Tahera, told her that they had arranged for her evacuation, and introduced her to the local team of special operatives in Afghanistan who would help her reach Mazar-i-Sharif and board the plane there. Tahera and her family could leave Afghanistan within a week.

"We sold all the good things in our house in Kabul and moved to Mazar-i-Sharif on January 19 in the care of the evacuation team. We spent one night in a hotel, and on the second night we were told to be ready to fly out at 7:00 a.m. That night none of us slept. By 4:00 a.m. the weather was very stormy and cold and it was snowing heavily. It felt like eternity, but eventually the airport buses came and took us to Mazar-i-Sharif airport, and we went to the terminal with a sense of joy and hope, mixed with fear of the Taliban."

Twenty-six judges and their families, as well as defense lawyers and prosecutors, were waiting for the flight. As Tahera watched, some started to board the plane. Almost immediately, however, the Taliban came and said that the newly appointed head of airport security was coming—and boarding would stop for an hour or so. Tahera quickly sent a message to the evacuation group saying she feared that the Taliban would stop the flight. A message came back saying, "Don't worry, the flight will go ahead. We are negotiating with the Taliban."

Tahera and her family waited for hours, their anxiety rising. "All the children and women in the terminal were tired and disappointed, and the weather was so cold that my children's fingers were frozen. No one had eaten breakfast and it was now 1:00 p.m., so I bought a few biscuits and water with some Afghan money."

With a sense of looming disaster, Tahera eventually realized that the negotiations had failed—and the flight would not take off.

"There was a mess-up with the management of that flight," Caroline Marks from Jewish Humanitarian Response says. "They included a group of sixteen or so single women between the ages of nineteen and twenty-one who came from an orphanage for children from minority groups. When they turned up at the airport, the Taliban's response was that there was no way they were going to let those women fly anywhere. They made accusations like the women were going to be trafficked. They all had passage to Canada—they were not going to be trafficked. Everyone boarded and was ready to go, and the Taliban stormed the gate lounge and stopped the flight. It was a terrible moment, because no other flights went out after that."

Tahera Karimi says, "We did not have a passport, only a transit visa from Abu Dhabi to Canada. The airport security officers said those without passports had to go to a separate room. There were more than forty of us, and they angrily ordered us to turn off our phones and not to talk to anyone else. We were all so scared that we didn't speak a single word, but I could see the disappointment and tears in my children's eyes. My husband and I tried to remain calm, and I told my children that everything would be fine."

Tahera and her family were kept in the room at the airport for three hours. "They gave each of us a piece of paper to write down our information. They kept saying, 'Where are you going? What was your job? Who is Susan Glazebrook, who arranged your visa? Who sent you this visa?'" Tahera's husband said that he was a shopkeeper and his wife was a defense attorney who worked in a private office and did not have a government job.

At 4:00 p.m. the security guards herded everyone out of the room and into buses heading to the police headquarters for Balkh province. "Everyone was crying and we were very worried. The sixteen young and teenage girls from the Hazara tribe were among us, and none of their relatives were with them."

By the time the bus reached the police headquarters it was almost evening. "The head of airport security introduced himself as Miwand. We asked him, 'Why did you bring us here?' He said: 'You are traveling without a passport, and you are our guests for the night.' That only increased our fear. My husband said to Miwand, 'I have a wife and child. Leave them, and take the men.' He refused."

Tahera and the other women and children were taken to prison, where several rooms and a very dirty bathroom ran off a long corridor. The rooms had only a thin carpet and no heating or blankets.

"There were about fifteen women and children, and the room was so small that we could not even stretch our legs. There was no water or food, and the children were all hungry and crying." The men were transferred to another room, and a girl traveling with no family was taken to a separate room. At 10:00 p.m. the guards came and told everyone to hand over their money. They said it would be returned the next day when they were released. "The night was very dark, cold, and full of fear. My eldest son asked me, 'Mom, will they kill us tomorrow?'"

Tahera asked for blankets for her children but was refused and so ended up wrapping them in spare clothes. When the morning dawned, cold and clear, they were all feverish from cold and hunger and thirst. "A Taliban soldier brought a bag full of dry bread and he told us that there was nothing left to eat. My husband was very angry. He shouted that our children were dying of hunger and thirst, so the same soldier had to go and bring a jug full of water. That water was dirty, but we all had to drink it."

When Tahera asked when they would be freed, she was told, "If the mayor gives permission, you will be freed. If not, you are in prison." Finally, at noon, the head of airport security came and told everyone to stand in line and repeat whatever they were told to say—otherwise they would be killed. Then the guards started filming. Tahera's husband said, "I will do whatever you say, I will film the 'confession' that you want—but let women and girls go." After a long discussion, the guards agreed, and the men "confessed" on video. Tahera says that her family's "crime" was that they were traveling without a passport.

By now Tahera and her family had been in the prison for more than a day and a half. She too wrote out a confession for traveling without a passport and was fingerprinted along with her children. After they waited for three more hours, her phone and money were returned.

"Each family was released separately. My children each took their backpacks, I took my youngest child, and my husband carried our other bags. We left the headquarters on foot and walked for a mile and a half. Then we found a taxi, but we didn't know where to go."

The previous day Tahera's daughter had quickly deleted all their Signal and WhatsApp numbers and messages from the IAWJ and the evacuation group. "The taxi driver started the engine and we realized just how tired, hungry, and sick the children were. We told the driver to take us to the hospital, where the doctors said the children were suffering from pneumonia. After they examined us and gave us some medicine, we went to a hotel and booked a room. I didn't have the IAWJ contact numbers, but I remembered the phone number of a colleague who was traveling with us. I got in touch with her and she gave me the contact number of the evacuation group again."

Tahera and her family slept overnight in the hotel and then traveled to another hotel, where the evacuation group said other families from the failed flight were staying. Another message from the evacuation team followed to say that they were negotiating with the Taliban and that another flight would leave soon. But by the second night the situation was hopeless and Tahera was told to leave the guesthouse as soon as possible and get the bus from Mazar-i-Sharif to Kabul.

For Tahera and her family, the outcome seemed bleak, but for others on the failed flight the consequences were unspeakable—and fatal: "The young women from the Hazara orphanage were not released by the Taliban, and I heard that after we left the Taliban attacked the guesthouse where we had been staying and arrested more than forty people. I later learned that many of the women who were detained at Mazar-i-Sharif airport, and in the safe houses, were gang-raped by the Taliban, and that they were then killed by their families after being released."

Such an unimaginably horrible fate was not uncommon. In the lead-up to the 2021 Taliban takeover, judges were often kidnapped. One Afghan woman judge remembers, "If the judge was a man, his family wept and prayed for his safe return. If the judge was a woman, her family often said, 'We pray they kill you rather than send you home as a used woman.'"

Tahera and her family made their way back to Kabul, but there was nothing left for them to return to. "When we reached Kabul," Tahera says, "we had nothing left at home because we got rid of everything before traveling to Mazar-i-Sharif. We wandered from house to house among our relatives and friends. Then after twenty days the evacuation team sent us a message to say everyone should get a passport."

Neither the evacuation team nor the IAWJ could help secure Afghan passports, and Tahera and her husband discovered that the only way was to pay money to a broker. To make matters even more difficult, Tahera discovered that she would need papers to confirm that her youngest child was allowed to leave without treatment for the hole in his heart. Tahera and her husband scraped together $3,850 from their savings for the passports and gave their money to the broker.

"I took all the children, and we went to the passport office for the biometric checks. When we walked into the IT department the director asked us, 'Who took the order for you?' My husband said we received it so that we could take our children to Pakistan for treatment."

The director asked Tahera's husband to accompany him to the boss's office. When he did not return, Tahera asked another officer what had happened. "He said, 'The order you received is fake.'"

"I can't tell you how I felt. I sat on the chair, and we all became silent. A few minutes later, my husband came back with an armed Taliban soldier and told me it was true—the order was fake. The broker had deceived us and stolen our money."

The Taliban soldier told Tahera's husband that he must cooperate and find the broker. If he did so and they found the man, the family would be released. Tahera's husband agreed, but only on the condition that they let Tahera and the children go.

"I was relieved for me and my daughters, but I was very, very worried about my husband. We rushed home, and when we got there my husband called. He said they went to the broker's house, but only his mother was there. Then he said, 'I am now with the Taliban.' Then his phone was turned off."

For three days Tahera heard nothing about her husband's whereabouts or safety. She visited the passport office twice and asked for news, but they told her curtly that her husband was being held by intelligence officers.

"My children cried day and night and did not eat. I encouraged them and told them that their father would be released and return home. But I knew the Taliban was very cruel and did not respect any laws. They tortured people for no reason."

Tahera did everything in her power to find her husband, even asking Susan Glazebrook and Patti Whalen from the IAWJ for help.

"After thirteen days, my husband called me from an unknown number and said that he was in prison. Then he said that the phone he was ringing on belonged to a Taliban solider, and not to call him anymore. Then he hung up, and the phone was switched off."

Tahera gathered together her children and her son's medical records and went to the prison, where she begged the prison chief to release him. "We shook hands, and he said that by order of the Taliban leader, a number of prisoners would be released for the holy month of Ramadan."

On the fifteenth day Tahera's husband was released, and the family almost collapsed with relief when he came home. "The Taliban had beaten him so much that he could not even stand up, and we rushed him to the hospital," Tahera says. It took time for her husband to recover, but as he healed, the family remained determined to leave Afghanistan and go to Pakistan or Iran, even if it meant entering the other country illegally. Susan Glazebrook and the other judges from the IAWJ persuaded her to wait, as crossing the border illegally would make it next to impossible to acquire the papers for the next stage of their journey to a safe country. Susan told Tahera that she could now apply online for a passport and a Pakistani visa. In Pakistan the IAWJ would be able to house Tahera in basic accommodations and provide some food and other bare necessities.

Tahera and her husband used every last penny from their savings to pay for the passport applications and visas, but they still faced a long wait to find out if it would be successful.

"We waited for fourteen days and there was still no sign of the passports or visas," Tahera says. "My husband and I were in a terrible financial situation, and we worried constantly about our security. We took turns going to the houses of friends and relatives. My children had no future, schools were closed, there was no work and no income. We were people who had once served our country with pride, and now we were living in secret, hiding our identity and afraid to be recognized."

As the months passed, Tahera's son's heart condition had become critical. Every day life in Afghanistan worsened, and there was now nowhere in the country where he could receive the operation he desperately needed. As Tahera waited through each agonizing day, all she could cling to was the hope of news of a dangerous and uncertain journey across the border. Without safe passage to Pakistan and medical care, Tahera knew, her son would surely die. She could only pray for escape.

PART TWO

Building Justice

6.

A Sisterhood Formed in Vermont

THE HUMAN EYE CAN SEE MORE SHADES OF GREEN THAN ANY other color. In Vermont during the spring, the number of those shades can seem endless. "In May it's almost like Ireland," Patti Whalen says.

It was 2004, and the women judges of Afghanistan were visiting Vermont for the first time. Two judges, Anisa Rasooli and Hamida Panjshiri, were staying in Patti's home. Overnight it rained, and when Hamida came downstairs in the morning she asked Patti and her husband if she could go outside. Patti's house was deep in the woods, way up on the top of a mountain. Outside the grass was wet with dew and the morning was misty, and the hills of Vermont rolled off into the distance. "Hamida came downstairs with a headscarf on, and she went outside and she took her shoes off, and she started dancing. Then she took her headscarf off, too, and was swirling it around like a banner behind her. And I looked over at my husband and I saw that he was crying. I have only seen my husband cry twice before in our married life—once when his mother died and the second time when he found out he was free of cancer. Then I realized that Hamida was crying, too, and I thought it was because she was free to take her headscarf off, but it turned out it wasn't that at all. It was the color green. She had never seen so much lush nature in Afghanistan. She was crying at the sheer beauty of the color green."

Patti Whalen was a new judge herself in Vermont when the Taliban took over in Afghanistan in the 1990s. "My family are Irish American coal miners from Pennsylvania. My dad was the first in our family to get a college education, and he was a computer engineer in the 1930s with IBM. So I came out of two backgrounds—a very poor coal-mining town in northeastern Pennsylvania, and the middle-class American suburbia of growing up in Chappaqua, New York." She smiles. "And then I became a hippie—and that's how I got to Vermont."

Living in a commune with other families in Vermont in the 1960s brought Patti into contact with women who were victims of domestic violence, and her efforts at assisting them made clear how few resources were available.

"Our neighbor was beaten up by her husband. She was pregnant and I remember taking her to the hospital, where she lost the baby. I was trying to get her help, but there were no women lawyers in Windham County, where I lived. The police were completely dismissive of everything. I went to a women's center which was just being founded in Brattleboro, our nearby town, and the three women that I met at the women's center were the three women who would later help me found the exchange program for Afghan women judges."

At the Brattleboro women's center, they decided that someone needed to go to law school—and that person was Patti.

"I went to law school solely to help with domestic violence issues. All I cared about was getting women access to the courts. I had very little interest in the law, or anything bigger than that. Later I got a fellowship with Howard University in Washington, D.C., a historically Black college, which allowed me to continue domestic violence work in Vermont and work to help poor people get legal services. That's what I did for ten years."

When Vermont elected its first woman governor, Madeleine

Kunin, in 1985, the state had only one woman judge. Kunin decided to appoint more, and increased the number tenfold. "I was one of the ten judges," Patti says, "and that changed my life overnight. I had to get much more serious about the law."

By the time the Taliban took over Afghanistan in the 1990s, Patti had been sitting as a judge for five years. "I read an article in a legal journal that talked about women judges in Afghanistan losing their jobs, and how there was a high suicide rate among women at the time, and I remember thinking about how much I loved my job and I just couldn't imagine losing it."

Back then no one could help, but a few years later, in 2003, Patti found herself standing in line for the bathroom at a meeting of the U.S. National Association of Women Judges in Washington, D.C., with Marzia Basel, then one of the very few women judges in Afghanistan. The Taliban had been overthrown, U.S. troops now occupied the country, and a fledgling interim government under Hamid Karzai was taking shape. As a figurehead for the kind of democracy and human-rights-based rule of law the United States wanted to build, Marzia had been all over Washington, D.C., including a visit to the White House, but when Patti asked her what women judges in Afghanistan really needed, she immediately said training and education.

During her trip Marzia had visited district and federal courts in the District of Columbia, but feared that they were so different from courts in Afghanistan that Afghan women judges would find the courts and the technology intimidating. Vermont was a small state, with fewer resources for judicial training than larger states, and still "did everything the old-fashioned way," Patti says. "We didn't have much technology, and we still had stenographers in trials. And Marzia thought that would be much better."

Traveling home on the long Amtrak journey, Patti imagined what she would like to see if she was visiting another country as a judge, and began to sketch out what an educational program would look like. Back in Vermont she pulled together her three good friends from the women's center and they started to talk about how to make the project work. One woman was the chief of staff to Vermont governor Howard Dean, another was a nurse and a vice president of Planned Parenthood, a nonprofit that provides reproductive and sexual health care in the United States and abroad, and the third worked in international education, mostly in Asian countries.

"We thought about what kind of program we could put together that would give us an opportunity to feel comfortable and get to the real questions that women care about. How could we get us all sitting around the kitchen table just talking as women? We decided the only way to do that was through homestays: they had to live with us and see how we lived and worked. So that's what we did. We designed a two-week homestay program, and the judges got to see us living with our husbands, partners, and same-sex partners. And it was just amazing, because they were exposed to a lot—but we were exposed to even more."

For a year the women planned and immersed themselves in learning about Afghanistan and Afghan culture. They worried that they could never match the legendary standards of Afghan hospitality that they read about—but then realized that such hospitality was already a part of how women in Vermont lived. The program itself would consist of two weeks in Vermont and one week in Washington, D.C., which would be more formal and involve meetings at the State Department and stays in hotels. In later years the women would visit Washington first, but that initial group of four Afghan women judges flew into Boston and would travel from there directly to Vermont.

Patti, her friends who had organized the homestay program, and two interpreters loaded up two vans with welcome gifts and headed out on the four-hour drive to the Boston airport. "We brought flowers, we had food, we had nuts, we had all sorts of stuff, and we were incredibly excited, and we were in the airport and the plane arrived. Everybody got off—no judges, no judges at all!"

At first the women thought the judges had been held up in immigration, then perhaps that they had missed their connecting flight through Pakistan or that there had been a problem because they were traveling without a male chaperone, which was still a cultural norm in Afghanistan. Eventually the arrivals area emptied out "and, finally, we realized we were alone—there was nobody in the airport."

When Patti tracked down a security official, he casually confirmed that a group of Afghan women had indeed arrived, but because they did not have any documentation with them, they were being held in detention. Patti says, "I was horrified. I told him, 'Get them out right now!'" Amid the muddle about paperwork (which the Afghan judges had carefully packed away in their luggage) and State Department–approved translators, Patti threatened to ring Supreme Court justice Sandra Day O'Connor, a loyal member of the IAWJ, who nonetheless probably knew nothing about the homestay program.

"Eventually it got smoothed out and they emerged—and that was my first conversation with Anisa Rasooli. I immediately started apologizing to her for being in detention, and she just pulled her glasses down, looked at me over the top, and said, '*That* was U.S. detention?'" Anisa told her that the women had been treated very well—they had been resting on white leather couches and had been served juice.

"Anisa was a tough cookie when she came," Patti says. "She wasn't in love with the United States—she was fairly cynical about it, and she had very strong feelings about how the U.S. should be involved in Afghanistan. And she was absolutely right on about everything. All of her concerns were completely legitimate. I had so much respect for her."

Anisa asked her if she knew President George W. Bush, and Patti admitted that she did not. "So she said, 'Well, what influence *do* you have?' And I said, 'I only have one vote—that's it.'"

Anisa insisted that it was important for the United States to understand that flooding Afghanistan with money would be disastrous. "She said, 'If you do, it'll ruin everything. Afghanistan has to stand on its own two feet, and we have to get rid of the warlords, and we cannot do that if foreign money is in the country.'" Patti adds, "Of course, no one listened to her, or any of the women. We had briefings at the time at the State Department, but they were token meetings out of politeness and I don't think anybody took the women judges seriously, or thought that they should be consulted on foreign policy issues. That is the arrogance of foreign diplomats, and who they choose to listen to is usually wrong, in my opinion. Later I worked as a judge overseeing war crimes trials in Bosnia, and it was the same there, too."

Eventually the women left the airport, and the Afghan judges crammed together into one of the two vans for the drive back to Vermont.

"We left Boston, which is a big city—freeways, bright lights—and immediately started driving up through the back roads of New Hampshire, where there are no streetlights, there's just little lights in homes, the roads are very dark, and the women started asking the interpreter if we were driving defensively to avoid checkpoints." The Afghan women thought Patti was potentially leading a group of military rebels and urged her to answer the questions very seriously.

Nafisa Kabuli says: "I came from an Afghanistan that had only recently been freed of the Taliban. And the first Taliban government of Afghanistan was very bad. As a woman, I didn't have any freedom, so we had to wear all these veils in front of our face and we had to wear, for example, black pants—and if we didn't they would beat us up, or they would slash us if the colors were not what they were demanding. I had come from a space of all this horror and all these hard experiences, and all of a sudden I arrived in a place of democracy, a place of freedom, and everybody was very kind and very humane."

As Patti had predicted, sharing their homes with the Afghan women would make all of the difference in forging relationships. "When we first landed in the U.S., we were very excited and there were a lot of new things that we were not familiar with," Nafisa says. "In Washington, D.C., we visited the courts, and we learned a lot. We learned about how many rights a person had to defend themselves, and that a defendant had to be represented by a lawyer. This was very interesting because we did not have that in Afghanistan. But we did not meet many ordinary Americans, and it felt so good to be staying with ordinary families in Vermont."

The inaugural group of the program was in some ways the easiest group because everything was new, but in other ways it was also the hardest group because no one knew what to expect. "We had a lot of preconceived ideas that were kind of silly," Patti says. "None of us were wealthy, but we all had dishwashers and an array of modern conveniences, and we felt uptight about it. We were worried it would be intimidating, or that their takeaway would be that America was all about material things. As it turned out, they didn't care about any of that. They had a mild interest in it, but they only really wanted to talk about [serious] issues."

Their first discussions as a group were defensive. "They were questioning me about how much were we getting paid to host them, and I said, 'This is a volunteer project. Nobody's making any money, we don't get paid at all, and in fact we had to raise money to bring you here from people in our community and they donated it.' That was a real surprise to them, but we could see they were beginning to warm to us." Anisa told Patti they were really concerned about all the foreigners who came to Afghanistan as a result of the U.S. and NATO invasion. These people worked for various aid agencies and organizations and seemed to make a lot of money—far more money than local people could ever dream of. Patti agreed that while some people might be motivated by financial gain, others were possibly just trying to cover their expenses back home.

The Afghan and U.S. women discussed their salaries. Nafisa says, "When we came to the U.S., we saw that women were independent, and that a woman judge in the U.S. could have a good income. Back in Afghanistan, the men were very prejudiced against women, and especially against women judges. Women judges made very little money; in those early days we had a very hard life and could hardly make ends meet. Not only were the women judges in the U.S. financially independent, they were powerful, too. That surprised us."

The American and Afghan women would have many conversations like this, driving through town, visiting the local hospital and its maternity ward, or talking about what parking meters were for or how the small town funded road repairs.

"While they were here we had this annual parade called the Strolling of the Heifers, when cows walk down Main Street. It's a Vermont tradition, and it's a huge fundraising event for all the local charities, with a parade and lots of floats, and everybody in the community volunteers. You put wreaths of flowers around the calves' heads, and local children bring their cows down, and the farmers bring the larger cows. [US senator] Bernie Sanders is from Vermont, and he always started off the parade." As a judge, Patti explained, she couldn't fundraise, but she always volunteered in a booth and put on an apron and cooked. The Afghan judges found the event extremely curious, because they had no similar culture of volunteering for events—but were happy to put on aprons and join in.

"I saw how women were free, how women could have their rights, and how they could live their lives as they wished—and this had a great impact on me," Nafisa says. "When I went back home I started an organization for the women judges and I helped another woman to become the head of this organization because she knew English, and I started working a lot in civil society."

Other conversations were more disturbing. "One day when I was driving along with a judge called Marzia we were talking about my law clerk, who was a lesbian and had children with her partner. Marzia asked me, 'How can they have children? How does that work?'" Patti started to explain that it was through artificial insemination, which was sometimes jokingly called "man in a can." As Patti delved into more detail about "man in a can," Marzia shrieked and begged her to stop, putting her hands over her ears: "You have to stop! I don't even know how men and women have children, never mind this!"

Patti was astonished. "'But you rule on rape cases. How can you do that if you don't know how babies are conceived?' Marzia said, 'Well, we don't really ever define it.'"

Marzia was not married, and Patti asked her how Afghan women and girls learned about sex. Marzia told her there were two ways. One was from your mother on the day before you got married. "The other way, she said, was sometimes people had experiences as children, and they learned as children. That opened my eyes to the extent of the sexual abuse going on. So I would think what we were going to tell them was shocking, but often we were the ones who were shocked."

That first year Patti took the women up to Bread Loaf, a prestigious summer writers' workshop at Middlebury College in

Vermont. She was looking forward to showing the women the campus, which was especially charming in the summertime, but when they arrived the Afghan women descended into panic. None of the doors to their rooms had locks, and they told Patti they couldn't possibly stay there. Patti was flummoxed; the police were actually providing strict security for their visit, but it was true that few people in rural Vermont ever locked their doors. Patti herself didn't even know if she still had any keys to her own home. "I don't think anything serious had ever happened to anyone in the Vermont judiciary in about two hundred years." A meeting was quickly convened, but it became clear that the problem would not be easy to solve; the women were terrified to sleep in rooms without locks, and no locks could be fitted at such short notice. In the end the Afghan judges agreed that they would all sleep together in the same room, and with the security of strength in numbers they were able to get through their time on campus—but it was an eye-opener for their American peers.

"I said to them, 'All the men that you see are colleagues. These are the men that we work with all the time. You have nothing to fear from them.' The Afghan women responded with, 'How can you not fear them? They're men!'" Patti recounts. "It was the most amazing conversation I think I've ever had with women. Because we were saying, 'Wait a minute—we don't expect men to engage in criminal behavior. When men rape or abuse or beat, it's abnormal behavior. That's not acceptable.' But for them that was all they knew."

During the legal part of the program, Patti took the judges to watch hearings. "One time we had a man that was arrested for public nudity and he even came into the courtroom and disrobed. It was a very exciting moment! The judges were stunned. They were very amused by all our antics to preserve his right to express himself, but also to try to get the guy dressed."

Every night the women shared potluck dinners—a new concept for the Afghans, who were keen to take the tradition back home, where entertaining was usually a long and expensive process. "We would feed our children first, and in Afghanistan children would have to wait until everyone else was fed," Patti says. "We said, 'There are two reasons to feed children first. One is that we value our children. But it's also just much easier to feed them and not have hungry children running around.' They were just fascinated by that, because their idea is that children should be trained to be patient and wait and respect their elders—and no child in Afghanistan would eat before the elders ate."

Each potluck dinner had a different theme, and the questions flowed back and forth. One night they talked about religion, and the American women spoke about their own disillusionment with the churches they had been brought up in. Anisa says, "I told them I was very angry at the Taliban for destroying Afghans' love of Islam and turning it into a miserable and harsh experience."

When discussing health care another night, one of the Afghan judges revealed that she was terrified her husband's family would murder her because she was unable to get pregnant. Another woman told the group that she had been diagnosed with cancer but had delayed starting chemotherapy to come on the trip. That woman later died of her cancer. Patti says it was humbling to realize how much the trip meant to them.

The women laughed a lot and had fun together, too. They danced, wrote poetry, did yoga, played volleyball, and went bowling. "We had a lot of fun, and sometimes the fun was over our own misunderstandings or communication issues," Patti says. "But it was also true women's humor. Because we were women we saw things the same way."

One night at dinner in Middlebury, the chief justice of Vermont asked the women what would happen to them if the Taliban came back. They became incredibly animated and replied, "We would get out. There would be blood in the streets." The chief justice then asked them how they would get out, and one of the judges said she would jump in a truck and drive off. The chief justice asked, "But can you drive?" The women said that none of them knew how to drive. But later, as Patti started to drive them home, they asked her, "Will *you* teach us to drive?"

Middlebury College, where the dinner had taken place, was near the site of a well-known barn where world-class cross-country skiers signed their names on a ski-waxing table. The barn is at the edge of a flat parking lot with no barriers at all. Patti turned into the parking lot, and all of the judges got out of the van, apart from one. The interpreters declined to take part. "They bailed, so I told them to teach me the words for stop and go," Patti says. Then the Afghan judge climbed into the driver's seat, and things began smoothly. "She was perfect, she turned left and right." Feeling cocky, Patti said, "Now let's go down the hill to the lower parking lot."

"What I didn't realize was the weight of the van, and when it started to go downhill it freaked her out. All of a sudden she could feel the speed picking up. So I said to her, 'Stop, just stop!' And she slammed her foot on the accelerator instead of the brake, and the van just lifted up and smashed into the side of the barn—the precious barn with all of the names written on it—and got hung up there in the wall. The van was off the ground with all four wheels spinning." Both Patti and the judge were uninjured, but in the background Patti could hear her friend Jack, a ski enthusiast, moaning, "Not the barn. Dear God, not the barn!"

The interpreters ran over to help, and Patti told them they would have to call the police—a prospect that struck fear into the Afghan women. When the police came, Patti explained that the women were from Afghanistan, where police questioning often had very dire consequences. The police officer was very nice to them—but he did want to see the Afghan judge's driver license.

One of the interpreters managed to come up with something that resembled a license. The cop looked at it in the dark, and the interpreter offered to make a copy for him. Then the police officer asked the judge if she had had anything to drink. She laughed and said, "No, I've never had any alcohol to drink in my whole life."

As their two weeks together drew to a close, Patti found herself reflecting on what both groups of women would take away from the experience.

A colleague whom Patti worked with in Vermont was responsible for sending out notices for court hearings. "One of the key parts of the justice system is notice and opportunity to be heard. You can't do anything unless you give people notice ahead of time that you are holding a court hearing, but one of our staff people who was in charge of sending out these notices was often complaining about them—and when they weren't delivered properly, she'd have to redo them or reschedule the court hearing with proper notice." Patti and her colleague showed the Afghan judges how they did notices and explained why it was a significant part of the U.S. system, and the Afghan judges shared that it was difficult to give anybody notice in Afghanistan—because of the lack of telephones and no real postal service—and that it was a huge barrier to any court proceeding. "Afterwards, my colleague said, 'I am never going to look at my job again the same way, I just feel incredibly privileged that we have these systems that work.'"

Above all, the Afghan women were interested in what they could learn and take back. Some of those lessons were practical, like how to organize a filing system, or the importance of keeping a clean and well-run courtroom. "When I went to Afghanistan a few years later I could see the courts were actually in poor condition," Patti says. "In juvenile court, people were just piled on top of each other in a room, and babies and kids were crying, and I asked, 'How do you manage all of these people?' It was just chaos." Anisa confirmed that the courts were unorganized, but they were trying to implement better processes.

"When we told the U.S. judges how we wrote our opinions of sometimes twenty or thirty pages by hand, they were amazed. They asked, 'How can you do that?'" Nafisa says. "After the fall of the Taliban in 2001, we didn't even have any law books to refer to in our courts, and when we told the American women that, they helped us to put together a law book to use."

Other conversations among the women delved deeply into what it meant to be a judge. They talked about how to ensure you were aware of your own biases, or how you could tell someone was lying.

Nafisa Kabuli says, "The most positive impact the trip had on me was that it made me look at my own culture. There were so many negative things in my culture, and in the U.S. I learned how open-minded people are, and how they think about other people in general, not just themselves. In our culture we have a lot of harsh ways of thinking, and I learned to stop thinking that way.

"In particular, I started thinking about the rights of women and children, and how, as a judge, I could be more inclusive. For example, part of our culture and law mandated that if a family made a mistake, including killing somebody, then the two families must reconcile through the offending family giving a girl child to the other family to compensate for what they had lost. The term for this means 'to give away a bad deed.'

"It's incredibly harmful to treat girls like that. I thought, why should a woman or girl be forced to make up for another person who has committed a crime? So one of the first things I did when I returned was to dismantle this culture and law.

"I started an organization with three other women to work on this, and we talked with many girls who were the victims of this trade, and the worst part was that if the family didn't have a girl that was ready to be married, they would just give a baby girl away, and this girl was treated like a slave.

"As a result of our work, I wrote a report about this practice, and the recommendations were taken up by the Afghan president, Hamid Karzai, who explicitly addressed this practice and made it illegal. From then on anyone involved in trafficking girls like this was committing a crime. This all came about from the way in which my trip to the U.S. had changed my thinking about our culture."

At the time of their visit to Vermont, Anisa Rasooli was head of the juvenile court in Kabul, and she remembers a crucial case she ruled on, invoking this law.

Two boys, ages fourteen and twelve, had gone out into the fields to get food for their animals. After a few minutes they started throwing stones at a tree to knock down some leaves—but one of the big stones rebounded off the tree and hit one of the boys in the head. He fell to the ground and started screaming that he was paralyzed. The other boy got down beside him and tried to help but ended up with blood all over his hands and clothes. He was trying to wash the blood off his hands when someone else saw them and accused the boys of fighting. The ambulance arrived and took the injured boy away, but he died on the way to the hospital.

Soon after, the family of the dead boy approached the family of his friend and said that they had to pay for the funeral—and also give up one of their daughters in marriage to the family.

The family was prepared to do almost anything to avoid this. The father sold his land and his animals and gave all the money to the family of the dead boy—but they said it wasn't enough. They still wanted the daughter. "She was only seven years old," Anisa says, "and the man they wanted her to marry was forty-five. The family said no again, and moved out of the area to avoid them."

It still wasn't enough, and the other family hunted them down from village to village until they found them again and the case went up before a gathering of village elders. The village elders met and ruled that the family must hand over the girl. But at this point the child's mother said, "No. You will have to kill me. You can take my daughter, but you will have to kill me first."

Although the village wanted to keep the matter a secret, information leaked out and the case came up before Anisa and her two colleagues in juvenile court.

"It was a very important case," Anisa says. "It is against the law in Afghanistan to marry a seven-year-old girl to a forty-five-year-old man, and we sentenced the man who wanted to marry her to jail. Then we sent the girl and her parents to a safe house, where she would not be attacked by the other family, and we punished all the villagers who wanted to give a seven-year-old baby to a middle-aged man."

What struck Anisa was not so much the details of the case but the fact that the girl's mother had assumed that the court would agree with the villagers.

"She didn't know what a courtroom was like, or the basis upon which a court makes decisions. When I decided not to give her girl to the other family, she was so happy and excited. Then I remember looking at the little girl, who was standing there with no idea about what was going on, and I just knew that at some point someday in the future her mother would tell her what had happened in the courtroom that day." Anisa's ruling had changed the course of their lives.

These changes, and effects, were momentous—but there were also things that could not be so easily taken back to Afghanistan from the United States.

When this first group of judges embarked upon the second part of their trip, they visited Washington, D.C., and were invited to the White House to meet First Lady Laura Bush. Prior to the U.S. invasion, both Laura Bush and the British prime minister's wife, Cherie Blair, had spoken out against the Taliban's treatment of women in Afghanistan. Now Mrs. Bush seemed genuinely gracious and eager to help, according to the Afghan women and their translators. When she asked the women what they needed, they said that they didn't have any computers. Mrs. Bush immediately offered to supply the courts with computers—much to the amusement of some of the interpreters, who noted among themselves that first the U.S. forces would have to build a power plant, because in Anisa's court, for example, there was no electricity in the building.

The first years of the exchange were exciting and profound for everyone, but as time passed the needs of the Afghan women judges changed.

"At the beginning there were only a hundred women judges in Afghanistan, but by 2021 the number had almost tripled. We couldn't bring them all to America during the summertime, and they progressed in their legal system quickly," Patti says. The program then shifted to focus on what women could learn within Afghanistan. In 2007, Patti flew to Kabul to take part in the first Afghan women's judicial conference and witness the training in basic women's rights that the Afghan women judges had set up for high school girls, and often their mothers. "A lot of those girls are the women that you saw protesting in the street in 2021," Patti says. "That kind of training was huge—and everybody just ate it up. I think 2007 was one of the last really good years in Afghanistan. After that, corruption just started to overwhelm it."

7.

An American in Kabul

PATTI WHALEN WAS SITTING BACK IN HER ECONOMY-CLASS seat when the plane she was on crossed into Afghan airspace and began its descent into Kabul. It was February 2007. Suddenly the plane lurched to the left, then to the right, then dived steeply. Patti clutched the back of the seat. Her neighbor leaned over to let her know that the pilot was flying defensively to avoid being shot down. While the explanation reassured her that the plane was not crashing, it was also a warning of the dangers on the ground. Below, Patti watched the starkly desolate and beautiful landscape of the Hindu Kush mountains give way to the smoggy gray outlines of the city. Once the plane landed, it taxied past a long line of burned-out warplanes and wreckage from previous conflicts and disasters, until finally pulling to a stop near the terminal. Somewhat shakily, Patti climbed down the rickety stairs to the tarmac and crossed to the airport building, which had no electricity and was in total darkness, with wires hanging from the ceiling.

At the head of the passport line, Patti watched the border officer carefully scan everyone's passport through a reader, which she eventually realized was not plugged in. She couldn't tell whether it was a training program or whether it was designed to provide a false sense of security. In the baggage claim area, suitcases were piled up, unmoving, on the luggage belt.

Patti was traveling with the executive director of the IAWJ, Joan Winship, a paid member of staff from the group's head office in Washington, D.C. After reclaiming their luggage, both women were escorted into a small room for a briefing with private security guards employed by the U.S. embassy. When she emerged outside into the sunlight, Patti immediately saw a group of women judges, including Nafisa Kabuli, who were waiting for them with flowers and gifts. "There was a fence between us, and the security guards, who were from a group like Blackwater, didn't want us to approach the judges. They said, 'No, that's the Afghan section. Don't go there.'" The separation between foreign and Afghan would be one that plagued the entire trip—and for Patti it symbolized so much of what was wrong with the mission in Afghanistan. Her immediate response, however, was just to say, "'No, we're going to go and say hello to them. They're our friends.' I was there for the women judges, not the American embassy." When she reached them, Patti was moved to see that somewhere in the depths of winter the women had found fresh flowers to bring to them. "I've no idea where they got them from, honestly, because I never saw any fresh flowers the whole time I was there; they use plastic flowers and they give those to each other."

After Patti had been reunited with Nafisa and the others, she climbed into the car with the security guards to leave for the guesthouse where they would be staying. The guard, who was armed with an automatic weapon, said, "This is the protocol: If we're stopped, we'll get out of the car. But if anything happens to us and you're left on your own, you just pick up these guns, and don't stop shooting." The guard handed Patti a gun with a large number painted on it in white—like on rental bowling shoes. "I thought, 'Oh my God, this is how war crimes happen.' There was a kind of cowboy attitude about the whole thing."

If they needed to escape, the guard told them, they should smash out the rear window of the car and climb out, guns in hand. Patti looked back and saw her colleague Joan in the backseat, along with the mountains of luggage they had brought, which included medical supplies for an orphanage that Anisa was running. "My colleague and I are not exactly small ladies," Patti says, "and the idea that we were going to clamber over the luggage and then squeeze through the rear window seemed pretty unlikely. I just thought, 'OK, if they catch us, they will have to shoot me. If that happens, we are dead.'"

Patti and Joan had been invited as private citizens to attend a conference organized by the Afghan women judges, but they were staying at a U.S. Department of Justice guesthouse, where Patti was assigned a soldier who stood guard over her bedroom door with a rifle. Each evening she returned from a day out with the judges, experiencing incredible meals and hospitality, and chatted with long-serving U.S. officials, some of whom had never tasted Afghan food in the years they'd been stationed there, instead eating Cheerios and pasta flown in from overseas. This only emphasized to Patti how far removed U.S. officials really were from local culture.

In the United States, Patti had heard about the work the women judges were doing in Afghanistan, but now she could see it firsthand. "We saw Afghanistan from their point of view. We were in their homes. Some of them lived in nice apartments, others lived in very poor circumstances, but nothing was very fancy. That happened later in Afghanistan, as more money poured in.

"I thought I knew a lot about Afghanistan before I went there," Patti says. "I'd hosted the Afghan women in Vermont. I'd read a lot of books. After being there, though, I realized I knew nothing about Afghanistan. It was far more complex than I thought, and people's motivations were something that was very difficult to pin down. I've been cautious about that ever since, because I got the sense that people survive by shifting allegiances all the time, and so it's essentially a country without a lot of trust."

Traveling with the judges in their own cars, rather than in the easily identifiable U.S. vehicles, Patti was struck by a city transforming at a feverish pace. "Kabul had the atmosphere of a post-conflict city, with everything changing all at once. It was not a pretty place, but it had an air of excitement to it. It had also had an air of fear. When I got home, I realized that I was scared of a terrorist attack a lot of the time I was there."

Visiting the judges in their courts and watching them at work made the most profound impression on Patti. "My visit coincided with money coming in to redesign their courtrooms, so some of the judges were in temporary buildings, like containers fitted out with electricity and office equipment. But Anisa Rasooli was in the juvenile court at the time, which had a stone floor and was freezing. She had a potbelly stove in the middle of the courtroom. They were using scribes. There was no electricity. None of the judges had computers. They would make the files themselves out of a type of wax cloth that they could cut up to make a folder to keep their papers in."

The judges that were working for the internationally supported courts, like the antiterrorism courts, were housed in modern, high-tech buildings and got much bigger salaries. Anisa Rasooli could have taken one of those jobs, but she was committed to reforming the juvenile court.

"We'd talked a lot in Vermont about what we called status offenses—for example, punishing young people who had run away from home and had an affair, or wanted to get married. Anisa said, 'That is just really a status offense, and we can change their status if they get married.' So she would have a religious leader, like an imam, there at the court and would tell them . . . , 'If you change your status and you're married, there is no case against you.' Anisa was a very creative person in that way."

Patti was most shocked by a case she saw involving a boy who had stolen a bicycle. "The person that brought him into court had probably robbed him of his coat and shoes, so he was barefoot on the freezing floor. I remember being in a state of total crisis, thinking, 'How can I just sit here and watch this?' I wanted to give him my socks, but I felt paralyzed in a state of total inaction."

One of the things that stopped Patti from acting was Anisa's response to the situation. "She didn't get him socks, but she went after the official who brought him and demanded to know where his shoes were, and told him never to come back to the court with a child in that state again. As it happened, the case couldn't go forward because he was a juvenile and he didn't have an attorney, but I remember the control that Anisa had, and the authority in which she spoke."

In a country where women were often invisible, Patti was impressed by the calm authority the women judges projected. "There was another judge named Rahima Rezai who was working in family court at the time. One of the Supreme Court justices stood up and gave her a lecture about how they shouldn't divorce women and they had to honor Islamic principles. Rahima stood up and challenged him in an unbelievably gracious way and, referring to the Quran, talked about women who are abused, and women who aren't supported, and so have a right to divorce—and it's their obligation to do so."

With Patti and her colleague in attendance, the Afghan women now gathered for their first conference. At the time there were about a hundred women judges in Afghanistan, and ninety-two of them had traveled from all over the country to Kabul—which was not an easy task in winter. Patti had strongly suggested that the women hold their first conference alone to debate things between themselves and decide on their goals, but the Afghan women wanted to augment their legitimacy and so had invited their male colleagues from the Supreme Court.

Invited to give the keynote speech, Patti worried about what she should talk about. "I wanted to expose them to other women that had struggled and had really achieved things when people thought it would be impossible." One of Patti's friends was the Kenyan activist and Nobel Peace Prize–winner Wangari Maathai, who had started the Green Belt Movement, an organization that promotes environmental conservation and women's rights.

Wangari had often visited Patti's town in Vermont and was a big influence in her life. "I decided to talk about Wangari, and in that way it would be inspirational but not overtly political." Over the course of her life, Wangari mobilized Kenyans to plant more than thirty million trees, and inspired a pan-African movement. For Wangari, the tree was a symbol for democratic struggle in Kenya, and in 1992 she confronted President Daniel Arap Moi over giving state land to cronies. "She went and sat in the park under a tree and did not move," Patti says. "Each day a few women would come. Then a few more. And finally they arrested Wangari, and after they arrested her and beat her, a thousand women came and then more. It was a huge show of solidarity. So I told that story because of how much she had personally given up because she had been arrested and was still in jail while this was going on, but also how the support of other women helped her achieve victory."

Patti thought she had successfully avoided controversial topics, including the Taliban and the role of the United States on the world stage. "So I was surprised when afterward someone from the U.S. embassy came over and thanked me for speaking so bravely." Patti was taken aback. She hadn't been trying to be brave. The woman told her that stealing land and giving it to warlords was a huge and incredibly controversial issue in Afghanistan, and that Patti's speech had been televised and watched widely.

After the conference was over, the Afghan women judges looked aghast. They approached Patti and told her, "You have to leave right now. Immediately."

Patti says, "I felt incredibly stupid for not thinking about the implications of what I'd said, and what it meant for them, too. It was awful."

Patti's plane left the following day, but it was not until she arrived back in Vermont that she learned of the most harrowing aspect of her visit. "The most terrible thing that happened was that one of the women judges was killed that night. The cause of her death is still not clear. Her name was Karima and she was a judge on the drug court. She had stayed with me in Vermont, so I knew her well. Karima believed that some of the judges on the drug court were corrupt, and she wrote a letter about it. There was no judicial conduct board or anything like that in Afghanistan at the time, so she decided that she would give the letter to the U.S. embassy and a copy to the British embassy." The U.S. embassy refused to take the letter, saying it was an internal issue, but the British embassy did accept the letter. Two days later Karima was dead.

"They said that the roof on her house had collapsed from snow and it killed her, but we'd had dinner there a couple of nights before, and I didn't remember any snow. It hadn't snowed in Kabul while we were there, so it was hard to believe," Patti says. It was a reminder of the life-and-death consequences of being a woman judge in Afghanistan.

8.

Nafisa: A Pioneer

NAFISA KABULI WAS ONE OF THE WOMEN WHO HAD VISITED Patti Whalen in Vermont, and she had been an instrumental part of Patti's trip to Kabul. By the mid-2000s she was a senior judge and a founder of Afghanistan's own association of women judges. In the course of her life, she too would face many threats and dangers, but her story shows, she insists, that her commitment to justice has been lifelong.

When Nafisa was a little girl in the 1960s, a well-known policewoman patrolled the streets of District 1, in old Kabul. District 1, with its labyrinth of ancient alleyways and sweeping new boulevards, had been home to Nafisa's extended family for generations. "I vividly remember her—her name was Torpekay, and I always wanted to be like her and help people. I wanted to join the police force, too." Even as a little girl, Nafisa sympathized with people whose rights were abused. "If I saw anybody threatening or scolding children, that would really upset me, so without even consciously choosing to, I would defend that child and not allow such things to happen. That is one of the first memories from my childhood."

In those days, families often chose not to send their daughters to school, but Nafisa remembers that one day, when she was five or six years old, her mother walked her to the local primary school and enrolled her.

"My mother wasn't feeling well. She knew that she was ill, and she was afraid that she would die, so she wanted to make sure that I went to school." The school said that Nafisa was too young—they did not accept children under the age of seven—but Nafisa's mother insisted. "She said, 'I understand that she is young, but if I die I am afraid that nobody else will enroll my daughter in school.'"

Her wish was granted and the school offered Nafisa a place, but Nafisa did not want to go. "My mother talked to me and said, 'Look, what can I do for you? What do I have that I can pass on to you?'" Nafisa's mother was a religious woman who wore the burqa and had no education. She explained to Nafisa that she felt that she had little to offer her, but school could offer her many opportunities. "It's a sad memory for me, because it is one of my last memories of my mother, but she said, 'I want you to go to school.' And that's when I started my education."

Soon after beginning her first year at primary school Nafisa was walking home one afternoon when one of her classmates started taunting her: "Your mother is dead! Your mother is dead!" Nafisa was so distraught she shouted back, "No, my mother is alive and it is your mother who is dead!" But when she ran home she discovered that it was true.

"I cannot tell you how devastated I was. How sad. I still get sad every Mother's Day, because I barely remember my mother." At the time traditional women did not appear in photos, so Nafisa now has no way of seeing what her mother looked like. "I don't have an image of my mother in my mind, because I was very young when I lost her. I just know that I loved her."

However painful the last memories of her mother are, Nafisa says, "I'm thankful to her for taking me to that school. That was the beginning of my life." With her mother gone, Nafisa's father stepped into her place and looked after Nafisa and her brothers and sisters. "My father was our hero; he was a mother, a father, a caretaker, and everything to us. He took care of us and did everything in his power to make sure we wouldn't feel the empty place left by my mother."

Nafisa's father was modern, enlightened, and open-minded. He worked as a typesetter for foreign newspapers, so he was exposed to a variety of ideas and read widely. In the evening he would bring different newspapers and books home with him for Nafisa to read. When she protested that she wasn't old enough, he would tell her to try just a little, to just look at the alphabet. "That was how I familiarized myself with the alphabet, and later how I learned how to read and write." With the encouragement of her father, Nafisa went to primary school, then high school, and eventually took the university entrance exam, the Kankor. "So much of what I've achieved I owe to my father. He steered me toward what I wanted to become and what I wanted from life. He steered me toward my dreams."

After finishing her local primary school, Nafisa was accepted at Zarghona High School, a very well-known and respected Kabul school. Zarghona picked only the best students, but if they didn't show sufficient effort or got bad grades, they were kicked out.

Nafisa was hardworking, stubborn, persistent, and mischievous. She played card games and jumped rope with her brothers and sisters—and everything that she learned she wanted to perfect. She preferred the active and exciting games the boys played. Despite receiving the best education, going to university was the furthest thing from her mind; her dream was still to join the police force.

"I used to tell my father that as soon as I was finished with tenth grade I was going to leave school and join the police. He would always say: 'No, wait until you get your diploma, then you can go to the police academy.'" When she eventually finished high school Nafisa told her father that becoming a police officer was still her dream. He asked her to explain her reasons properly. Nafisa recounted the story of someone who had recently been murdered in their neighborhood and explained that she wanted to understand all the factors that had led up to that happening.

Her father said, "OK, kid, if you become a police officer, that is not your job. Your job will be to just go and arrest the murderer, and then deliver them to the attorney general or to the person who is in charge of taking the case to the court. But if you become a judge you will learn about the whole incident and consider all the different aspects of the story." With her father's encouragement, Nafisa decided to apply to university and study to become a judge.

"Kabul University was the place for young people to be. Everybody was dreaming; it was the place everyone wanted to go to. I liked my classmates. We were very free, and we would talk to each other about everything. The university had a wonderful atmosphere; it was academic but there was a sense of excitement. Progress was in the air."

Nafisa took the entrance exam in 1979 and won one of the coveted slots, but by the time she officially began her studies, Afghanistan was already in a state of war.

"A lot of things were happening, and there were obvious changes," Nafisa says. "I was aware of the fighting and the Soviet invasion, but I was immersed in my schooling and my own dreams and life. I was very young, but the biggest change I saw in those days was good. Girls had more opportunities to study and to go to school and to be part of society."

There were other women who had become judges before Nafisa, and others would follow in her footsteps, but Nafisa was unusual in that her family was neither well connected nor well educated. She was a scrappy self-made city girl, a pioneer not only in her family but also in Afghanistan. "Our country was very traditional and a lot of people didn't like the fact that there were women judges, because they thought that women were not allowed to judge men under Islam. But that way of thinking was changing. By the end of the 1960s many women could go to school to become judges—and I was one of them."

Nafisa was accepted at the *shari'a* law school rather than the civil law school, but at university the young men and women still took most classes together, apart from the specific *shari'a* law classes, where the sexes were separated. Competition was fierce. "There were many girls who were interested in becoming judges, but the university would only take students who were first, second, or third in the rankings, so you had to have very high grades in the entrance exam in order to be accepted for the judicial school."

After graduating, Nafisa was sent to train for two more years at the Supreme Court, where she studied under the country's highest-ranking judges. Eventually she qualified as a judge in her own right and could take part in hearings and cases on a panel with her peers.

"Even in those days life was not peaceful in Afghanistan. There was little security in the country. There were not suicide bombers, but rebel fighters fired rockets into the capital all the time. We lived in constant fear for our lives." One day Nafisa was at the Supreme Court sitting for an exam on the constitution when a rocket hit the building. "I was terrified. We escaped from the building, and we were all just running around looking for somewhere to hide. After about half an hour we went back to the exam hall again and sat down and took the test."

A life of insecurity and mortal danger would stalk Nafisa for her entire career in Afghanistan—but she had committed herself to serving justice.

"When I graduated and I received my permit to be a judge, I kissed my father's hand and I took my oath—and I always remembered my oath. I always thought about people and their side of the story. I knew that their only hope often rested with me as a judge, and they wanted a judge to bring justice based on the facts of the case. I promised myself that I would not be influenced by power or authority, or whatever anybody else told me. I would bring justice."

One of the conditions of starting work as a woman judge in Afghanistan in the late 1980s was a Supreme Court mandate to work in a remote area outside Kabul. Only Nafisa and one other woman decided to accept the offer of a judge's permit based on that criterion, and Nafisa chose to move to Balkh province, where her uncle lived, to begin work in the public security court.

Balkh is a large, ethnically diverse Afghan province that sits on the border with Uzbekistan, Turkmenistan, and Tajikistan. It includes the city of Mazar-i-Sharif, from where many of the Afghan women judges would later flee the country. During Nafisa's stay, the province was ruled by a regional strongman named General Rashid Dostum who was on bad terms with the central government in Kabul. From the beginning of her tenure there, local corruption made her work perilous.

One of Nafisa's first cases involved a local Taliban commander who had kidnapped a prosecutor. As soon as Nafisa received the case, the prosecutor in charge told Nafisa: "This person kidnapped a prosecutor. He's been arrested, and we know that he should be found guilty." When Nafisa discussed it with the chief judge, he backed up his colleague, telling Nafisa: "You are in charge of this case, and you should find him guilty. That's it."

The conversation was literally chilling. "I felt cold all over my body," Nafisa says. She replied, "A judge can't just take the order from the chief judge and come up with a verdict before hearing the case. If you are afraid of the commander because he has all these rockets aimed at you, and you are afraid that he is going to fire them, then that is on you. I'm not going to sign a guilty verdict unless I hear the case first." The chief justice ignored Nafisa's protest and signed the guilty verdict, but the case marked the start of Nafisa's struggle with an inherently corrupt regime.

"I went through a lot of pain because I believed in justice and I wanted to follow the rule of law. I wanted to give my orders based on law, and because of this I was always under a lot of pressure. Yet I always felt like my conscience was greater than my fear. I thought, if people kill me because I have passed a judgment, that's fine, but if I stay alive and pass a judgment that goes against my conscience, I will never forgive myself."

Nafisa continued to work in Balkh for four years before accepting a new role as a judge in the traffic court in Kabul. Her return to the capital was dramatic. Nafisa's family had moved into a new apartment in the upscale Macroyan district and she was eager to get back to help them financially, but according to Nafisa, Afghan roads at the time were unsafe, and many people were stopped, even kidnapped or murdered. Nafisa decided to travel by plane, but because a woman could not travel without a male chaperone, she booked two tickets and asked her nephew Massoud Kabuli to accompany her. At the time there were no direct flights from Balkh to Kabul because the relationship between Rashid Dostum and the national government was so bad. Nafisa decided to take a military plane to a newly built airport in the Saqawiya plain area instead, but the aircraft that served that route had already been damaged in a rocket attack and had been badly patched back together, so Nafisa's family begged her not to use it—and especially not to risk the life of her nephew Massoud, who was then still studying to become a doctor. Nafisa told them that Massoud had made his own decision, and they boarded the plane together.

In those days Kabul had no electricity, and so Nafisa was carrying a large bag with her belongings, an oil lamp with a glass chimney, and a flask of tea. As they approached the capital, an announcement was made that rockets were being fired at the airport and there was gunfire on the ground. By now seven rival groups were fighting for control of Kabul, and the atmosphere was febrile and extremely dangerous. The plane eventually hit the tarmac in a hard landing, and everyone disembarked and started to run toward the terminal in panic.

Nafisa says, "As I was running, I lost my shoes and fell on the ground, and everything fell out of my hands. The lamp was rolling everywhere, the rockets were flying overhead. Someone picked my shoes up and thrust them at me, so now I had to continue but also holding my shoes, too. People were stepping on me on the ground, and then some Taliban men ran up to me and started shouting, 'You must cover your hair!' In the midst of this craziness and terror, my headscarf had slipped and my hair was showing. That's when I started shouting and screaming and said, 'How the hell should I care about this stupid hijab when I am dealing with all of this and everybody is just trying to save their lives? And you are worrying about my hijab?'"

By the time the Taliban took over Afghanistan in September 1996, establishing the Islamic Emirate of Afghanistan, Nafisa had been working in the traffic court for several years. "When the Taliban came the first time, I was sent home from work, and I immediately became a homemaker," she says simply. She had been shut out of her job and prevented from taking on any other professional public role, but Nafisa was determined to ensure that her life wouldn't stop.

In those days Nafisa was living with her family in Macroyan, the suburb on the east side of the city where the Soviets had built new, modern apartment blocks. A local woman named Homa Jan started a class under the pretext of teaching girls sewing and the Quran—both activities that the Taliban deemed suitable for girls. Home schooling for girls was strictly forbidden under the Taliban regime, but Nafisa agreed to help, secretly teaching girls social science subjects, including geography and history, in Homa Jan's classes.

"We asked the students to carry the Quran and a needle and thread, so that if the Taliban stopped them they would see those items in their bags. The Taliban followed us a lot. Each teacher was in charge of one subject, and we would carry one book on that subject so that there were not a lot of books lying around if the Taliban came. All the girls were passionate about going to school and learning, and their parents were so glad to send their daughters to Homa's home that they would sometimes rent a car to travel from different parts of Kabul."

Despite their best efforts to hide the secret school for girls, someone reported their suspicions to the Taliban, and the knock on the door came one day.

"They threatened us and told us that if we continued to have classes they would arrest us and throw us in jail." It was winter, the end of the school year in Afghanistan, when students traditionally were getting ready to take their final exams. The women decided that they would not stop teaching the girls, but instead of meeting at Homa Jan's house, they would ask their students to visit their homes to take the tests.

The students visited Nafisa's apartment, but a member of the Taliban was living on the top floor of the apartment building and became suspicious of the number of girls coming and going. Nafisa's brother protected them by claiming that the girls were carrying out religious good works, like cooking for the poor, but privately he begged Nafisa to finish the classes as soon as possible. Nafisa refused. "I told him, 'I cannot let go of any of these girls unless they pass their exam, because this is the final exam and it's important. Otherwise they won't be able to go up to the next grade.' Everybody was very serious about teaching those girls, and we were prepared to risk our lives to make sure that the girls could take their exams."

Nafisa says the girls were intelligent and serious. "After the ousting of the Taliban, all those girls went and took a comprehensive exam and, depending on what grade they got, they restarted formal education and a lot of them went to university. One of my students became a judge."

In those dark years, Nafisa had no idea how long the Taliban regime would last, but she knew that it would not be forever. In the past, all the best and worst regimes in Afghanistan had been swept into power on strong currents and then swept out again. Nafisa's students often cried, asking her, "You're teaching me about altitude or geography—but what am I going to do with all of this?" Nafisa told them, "Don't cry, just take this teaching and learn. You're going to use this, because there will be a day when you will take the entrance exam to the university." It was obvious, Nafisa says, that the Taliban regime would not last. "And we knew that, because no Afghans liked them. People were really devastated, and were sick and tired of all the laws and regulations that they imposed."

When life seemed impossible, the women of Afghanistan went underground—to meet, to teach, and to wait. Across the country, in another province, Nafisa's colleague and close friend Anisa Rasooli was also secretly helping girls learn.

9.

Anisa: The Advocate

ANISA RASOOLI GREW UP IN A VILLAGE IN PARWAN PROVINCE, north of Kabul, in a notably scenic part of Afghanistan where an annual weeklong festival, called the Mela-e-Gul Arghawan, commemorates the beauty of the purple flowers of the *Cercis siliquastrum*, the Judas trees, that carpet the hillsides and valleys.

"Parwan has seven or eight big towns, and I grew up in a small village where people were friendly. We have very nice weather there—a beautiful and sunny summer where most of the time you could grow all kinds of fruits, vegetables."

By the 1970s more people were educated, including her own father and, to a lesser extent, her mother. "Starting with my generation, everyone was very passionate about education. The country needed higher education in any field, and we educated lots of doctors, engineers, and teachers that not only taught in Parwan but spread out over the country to do good things.

"My mom was actually the main driver behind our success, and she encouraged all of us to study, to work hard, and to do something for ourselves and for our community and society." As with Nafisa, it was Anisa's mother who first encouraged Anisa and her brothers and sisters to go to school.

Anisa went to primary school and high school in Kabul. Based on her success in the Kankor, Anisa won a slot to study law at

Kabul University and, after completing her degree, decided to study for the judiciary.

"It wasn't easy for me, or my family, to let me go to law school and then become a judge. At that time society wasn't open to accepting a woman judge, or lawyer, or prosecutor. Even some of my relatives, including my uncles and aunts, didn't want me to take that path. My mom stood up to them and told them that she would allow me to follow my dreams and become a judge in Afghanistan, no matter what. My siblings also supported me and stood by me."

Four of Anisa's brothers qualified as doctors, one became an engineer, and another achieved a master's degree in law—but Anisa was the only daughter in the family who wanted to continue her education. "I was passionate about it. Without that passion I would not have made it, even with my family's support. It was my passion to graduate from law school and become a judge and help others. We were living in a country full of injustice, and I was hoping somehow to do something positive for the whole community, especially for women. I felt like it was my responsibility to encourage women to advocate for their rights, so that all women could speak up for themselves, like me."

Anisa's initial inspiration was her eldest brother, who was a judge and her role model. "I wanted to be just like him, an honest and responsible judge. As time passed my ambition grew—we were living in the most male-dominated society, and Afghanistan was engulfed in war. I wanted to help my Afghan sisters have basic rights. You can't imagine how it feels if you are a girl and you can't go to school."

When Anisa completed her education she began work as a judge alongside only twenty other women, including Nafisa. "In a country of thirty million people, twenty women judges was quite unique." Their role, as Anisa saw it, was to help all Afghan women progress, not only in law but also in medicine, education, and all other fields. "We live in a world which is dominated by gender, and women need help from other women to solve their problems. Men can't solve women's problems."

After years of study, Anisa could finally start work—and it was as sweet as a breath of fresh air. As happened to Nafisa, too, however, Anisa's time as a judge, sitting on the Kabul public security court, was abruptly cut short when the Taliban took over the country and she was immediately fired.

"I felt terrible when the Taliban took over. You can't imagine how it felt to finally achieve my dream, and then be told to go back home and sit inside—and all the studies and all the things that I had experienced and achieved were all gone. It was for nothing."

Anisa joined the more than six million Afghans who crossed the border into Pakistan and Iran during the Taliban regime of the 1990s, but she found no solace in a life in exile. After a year teaching math and religion in a girls' school in Pakistan, Anisa decided to go home and to contribute to her country in whatever way she could. "I couldn't live abroad. I needed to go back home, and I decided to go back to my homeland, Parwan, where I was born."

Back in her village, Anisa despaired over the fact that girls were forbidden from getting an education—although boys were free to go to the local government school. Anisa asked her father for money to buy supplies and books, and he readily agreed. She opened her own school for girls, attracting an initial group of sixty students. "I really owe it all to my dad, because he was the only one who could imagine an Afghanistan of literate men and women, living in peace in a well-governed society."

At first the school existed in name only, due to a chronic shortage of teachers and supplies. In the early days, Anisa, her sister, and others in the village would teach the students about a subject they knew. They donated supplies and notebooks when they could. For

Anisa it was a strange turn of events—because she had been one of the top students at university, people had often encouraged her to become a teacher, but instead she had been determined to become a judge. Now here she was, a teacher after all. It was God's will, she decided, and a way for her to serve. "Destiny brought me to a place where I could be a teacher and I could teach five- or six-year-old girls and somehow make their future brighter."

Slowly the school attracted more and more students, and expanded to include classes for older girls, too. Eventually more than two thousand girls were learning at Anisa's school.

"It was scary. It seemed crazy to do something like that in the time of the Taliban, but there were two reasons why it was successful. Firstly, I was brave enough to do it. The second reason is that we were living in a place far from the Taliban-controlled areas. War in Afghanistan is tribal, and it is also a war between the city and the countryside. The Taliban are Pashtuns, but in Parwan we are Tajiks. The Taliban were based in the cities of our province, but we were in the countryside—and they were afraid of our people. The Taliban couldn't come near us, so we could establish a school."

Anisa says that she asked people not to gossip because the teachers' lives depended on keeping the school a secret, but many parents were still afraid to send their daughters. Often they would tell her that it was not the time to do such things. Why couldn't she just stay at home and keep quiet?

"I said, 'No, I can't do that.' And in order to encourage them to send their daughters to school, I would go to their houses to teach the girls myself. After I'd been doing that for some time, they trusted me and allowed their daughters to come to the school."

Anisa's school thrived and grew, and when the Taliban were overthrown it stayed open, operating as a primary and secondary school for both girls and boys in the area.

"Each one of those parents came and said, 'Thank you so much.

We all pray for you, because thanks to you our children are educated now.' With the help of my father, we paved the way for the children of my village to be educated," Anisa says. But freedom brought new choices, and for Anisa it brought the opportunity to fulfill her true destiny, as a judge.

10.

Anisa: A Supreme Court Nomination

IN THE TOWNHOUSE WHERE SHE NOW LIVES IN NEW ENGLAND, Anisa Rasooli keeps a mug on her desk decorated with a cartoon image of Ruth Bader Ginsburg. The mug is a reminder from her many admirers that Anisa was considered the "RBG of Afghanistan." She was nominated to the Supreme Court in 2015, but her confirmation failed in an antagonistic and corrupt parliament by only a few votes, with many believing that it was a foregone conclusion that the parliament was going to thwart the confirmation of the first-ever woman nominee. Her nomination by Afghan president Ashraf Ghani drew howls of protests from Kabul clerics, and mockery and derision from male parliamentarians, but Anisa says, "I am happy with the outcome. I believe it was a good step forward. I knocked on the door."

With the Taliban swept from power in 2001 and the installation of a new regime, Afghanistan found itself with a shortfall of educated people, many of whom had fled overseas during the previous years of war and oppression. There was an almost total absence of educated women who could step into the void and set about rebuilding their country with democratic and human-rights-based laws and institutions.

In rural Parwan, Anisa had spent the Taliban years educating the young Afghan women of the future, but now she could fulfill her potential as a judge and legal scholar. Her first appointment was as head of the primary juvenile court in Kabul.

The juvenile court was special, Anisa says. "I was so happy to have become the president of that court. It was the very first place I worked when I graduated from my judicial course, and back then I dreamed that someday I could be the head of that court. Now I'd achieved my dream. I was the head of a court in Kabul and I would help children and their parents."

Juvenile cases, however, were every bit as complicated and dangerous as those in adult courts—and the results could be just as frustrating and futile. One case in particular involved a seventeen-year-old boy who was charged with being a Taliban terrorist. The boy had two brothers, one who was working with the U.S. Army and another who had been killed fighting with the Afghan National Army.

Anisa asked the boy to speak in court and explain his side of the matter. She told him: "What you say has a huge impact on what I decide in your case, so be wise and don't say stupid things. If I give you a second chance, tell me what you would do with your life." The boy replied, "You know what? I don't want anything from you. I just want one thing from God—to give me a second chance at life so I could carry out a bomb attack on you, and then a second bomb attack on my brother who is working for the U.S. Army."

The boy was laughing as he made his threats, and Anisa said, "You're insane. You're brainwashed, and you have no idea what you are doing." She wondered how a boy could make a plan to kill his own brother, his own blood. "The brother with the U.S. Army was the breadwinner of the family, and the seventeen-year-old in front of me was no one; he was a liability to the family, and they'd still had to raise money to hire a lawyer to come to court to try and get him released."

The boy was an active member of the Taliban, and he had been taken hostage fighting against the Afghan National Army. Anisa says, "When the previous Taliban government took hostages they killed them, but when our new government arrested people it was according to the law, and we needed to treat them properly, feed them, send them to court, and put them in prison. Justice had to be served."

The juvenile court had more leeway than adult courts and could help young people return to society and be productive. According to the law, Anisa had to send the boy back to prison, but she had been hoping to find another solution for him and his parents, one in which he would take responsibility for his actions and be allowed out of prison on day release to work in the community. "The law gave me many ways to deal with this situation, but when I heard his threats I was afraid, and I told his parents that I couldn't do anything to help. It would have been hard for him to find and attack me, but easy for him to kill his brother and his family. I had to send him back to prison."

Anisa was head of the primary juvenile court for five years, and in that time she worked closely with the Ministry of Justice and the Supreme Court to shape new laws that expanded children's rights. Initially Kabul had one small juvenile court, but under Anisa's leadership the juvenile court system expanded to other provinces, and in 2007 Anisa became head of the appellate court for juveniles. At the same time she worked hard to get the Afghan president and parliament to recognize that, according to the United Nations Convention on the Rights of the Child, a child should appear in juvenile court until age eighteen, rather than being sent to an adult court at as young as sixteen.[6]

"We had signed the Convention on the Rights of the Child, but in reality we did not obey it. We were trying so hard to convince the government to obey that convention, and also to find a way to protect children's rights."

Anisa was carrying out her day job as a judge, teaching as the first woman tutor for the Afghan judiciary course, and leading the Afghan Women Judges Association when the Afghan president put her name forward to be one of the nine members of the Supreme Court in 2015.

Anisa had to appear before the Afghan parliament twice for her confirmation. The first time was an introduction, but during the second appearance she had to make a presentation about what she would aim to do with the role, and then wait for the vote.

"I found that place completely bizarre. It was a place that you couldn't imagine actually functioning as a national parliament," she recalls. The day of her second appearance, Anisa stepped up on the dais at the front and saw before her a sea of men. She says they were "sitting and hanging out with each other, while others were laughing, asking how it was possible that a woman could present herself as a candidate for the Supreme Court."

Anisa was used to having authority in a courtroom, so she refused to be unnerved, instead she raised her hand and knocked on the table. "I said, 'I'm here to present myself to you and I'm here to introduce my plan for what I could do in the Supreme Court. But I am also a teacher, and a teacher can't give lectures in a situation like this where everyone is talking and no one is listening. I kindly ask you all to listen to my presentation.'"

Some parliamentarians started shouting, "Who do you think you are to stand here and tell us how to react and how to talk?" Then the head of the parliament took the microphone and said, "You can continue with your presentation, but we don't care about what you're saying." As she began to speak someone slipped Anisa a piece of paper from the floor that said she should apologize to the representatives for telling them to listen to her.

Anisa thought, "Why should I apologize to these people? They have no right to that. I am a judge and I am here to present myself for an important position. They need to listen to me. Our people voted for them to take these seats in parliament, to receive a high salary and all the benefits that a representative deserves. They are here to listen to debates, consider people's applications, and pass the law—and they haven't done the things that they are supposed to do." She also thought that if she apologized it meant that she would be begging them to vote for her, and she didn't believe judges were supposed to do that.

Anisa could see, looking at some of the laughing, mocking faces, that the parliament was not even going to consider her presentation or her candidacy. When she finished speaking she silently folded up the piece of paper demanding an apology from her and sat down.

When she stood up to leave the room so that the vote could take place, one of the representatives approached her and showed her another piece of paper. He said, "Do you know what this is?" Anisa replied that she had no idea. Then he told her, "It is the voting paper. This is the paper that we are going to put in the voting boxes for you. We are so powerful that we can take these papers out of the room and vote for you or against you. So if I'm a businessman and you are going to be a member of the Supreme Court for my area I need something from you when I come to court. Will you do that for me?" Anisa replied that if he came to court and asked for something that was legal, of course she would hear his case. He replied that this would not be "legal" work in front of the court, but issues that they could discuss together elsewhere. Anisa said, "No, you know we can't do illegal work. My response is always no." The man replied, "OK, then we will see what happens in the vote."

As if she could be left in any doubt how high the odds were stacked against her, when Anisa left the chamber a parliamentarian who was himself a former judge stood up and announced: "If you vote for a woman to become a member of the Afghan Supreme

Court, you all will sin an unforgivable sin—and God will make sure that you face the consequences of what you do."

When the vote was announced, Anisa did not get the votes she needed to join the Supreme Court, but she remains proud of what she stood up to and achieved. "I was five votes short. But I will always be the first woman candidate for the Afghan Supreme Court, and I have paved the way for others to follow me one day."

Anisa's place on the Afghan Supreme Court went to another man who shamefacedly admitted to her that he did not have her judicial experience. Instead, he was confirmed by the parliament and then chosen by Ashraf Ghani to become the president of the Afghan Supreme Court. Only a short time later he asked Anisa to come in and have a special meeting with him. Much to Anisa's surprise, he offered her the role of head of the appellate court for serious crimes and corruption. This was not the normal way to be offered such a job, but as the role would involve the dangerous duty of sentencing the richest and most powerful people in Afghan life, the judge wanted to give Anisa time to think it over. "I knew that this position was the most important, dangerous position in all of the Supreme Court, but I thought that if a man could hold this position, then a woman could, too. I accepted." Anisa would go on to hold the job for the next four years.

"When I got the job I knew that it wouldn't be easy," Anisa says. "It was completely fraught and problematic for everyone connected to the court—for the prosecutors, for the lawyers, even for me as the head of that court. Ministers, generals, vice presidents, and mayors would pull up to the entrance in their government cars and go out the other side to prison. It is extremely hard in Afghanistan to send people at that level of authority to jail."

Anisa was working in a country where it was almost impossible to progress if you weren't a member of a political party, but her refusal to be associated with any one group meant that she was also deemed likely to be trustworthy and honest. "That is why they chose me to head up that court. I wasn't corrupt and I was loyal not only to the court but also the community and the people."

During her time as head of the court Anisa sometimes ruled in cases in which numerous members of the Afghan government, apart from the president, would call her and ask her to help whoever was the subject of the case. "In the four years of my duties there, we worked according to the law. I never caved to pressure or felt overwhelmed about sentencing people. In spite of all the calls and messages, I was never too terrified to do the right thing."

As president of the court, Anisa had seven judges working underneath her. All of them were men, and she had to fully trust each of them. "You can imagine that if one of them was corrupt, the whole team wouldn't work. I was lucky to have an honest team that was true to the Afghan constitution and law."

As an honest judge at the head of a corrupt system, Anisa was living on borrowed time. Two events hastened her departure.

One day the chief of the Supreme Court called Anisa to his office and asked for a favor. He mentioned a case that was currently before the court and told her that the Afghan president himself had requested a certain outcome. Anisa said, "The moment that you chose me to become the head of this court, I told you that I'm going to do everything according to Afghanistan's constitutional law and the criminal code. If you don't feel satisfied with what I am doing here, then move me to any other court in the country. It doesn't matter to me. I can't do anything for you." Then she left the office.

The second event was a case where a former government minister was about to go to jail, "but he was innocent," Anisa says. "One of the members of the Afghan Supreme Court called me and said, 'You know the other court sentenced him to prison, and if you don't do the same thing, you could lose this job.'" Anisa knew that even if she was no longer head of the corruption court she would still be a judge with her state salary. Since she didn't accept any corrupt payments, she had nothing to lose by moving to another role. "This man was actually innocent, and I couldn't do it—I couldn't send an innocent person to prison to serve someone's political interests. I freed him." But that act meant that Anisa's career as head of the corruption court was over.

"They wanted to smooth things over. They told me I'd served the country well. They gave me a certificate to hang on the wall. And they offered me a new position inside the Supreme Court as the senior consultant at the Court for the Elimination of Violence Against Women."

Anisa's boss told her that if she accepted the job it would position her well to eventually become the president of the high court judging cases of violence against women, but in truth, Anisa had long worked for the rights of women and was more than happy to accept the role as consultant, and to be free of the headaches of the anti-corruption court.

"We'd tried so hard to set up the violence-against-women court. I'd tried my entire life to have that court, because in a male-dominated country like Afghanistan judges did not rule fairly in cases where something happened between a couple, or even inside a village. The male judge would rule in favor of the men in the case, based on their gender."

The Court for the Elimination of Violence Against Women had been established in 2009 as a means of implementing a new law aimed at reducing violence against women. It was bitterly contested by traditional groups within Afghan society who saw it as an American imposition. Even though Anisa only worked with the court for a short time, she saw cases flooding in from all over Afghanistan. "I could see how beneficial establishing those courts were, because we were supporting and protecting women all over the country—and letting them know that they were not alone. They were seen, they were heard, and they were living in a society where there were some people who were willing to protect them and let them live freely."

The court was crucial, Anisa says, for letting men know that they couldn't kill their wives and get away unpunished anymore; for letting parents know they could no longer marry off their daughters while they were still children; and for letting people know they couldn't discriminate against women more broadly. Anisa says that all the women judges worked to establish those courts for their "sisters," and were ultimately successful.

While she was consulting on the Court for the Elimination of Violence Against Women, Anisa was teaching criminal law and reporting as the head of the Special Investigation Commission for Afghan Women's Prisons and Prisoners. In that role she led six other commissioners in conducting interviews with the prisoners, examining the conditions they lived in, and investigating the social and economic problems they faced—culminating in a two-hundred-page report to the Afghan president. She had almost reached the pinnacle of her profession, and the mood in the country had changed sufficiently so that by 2019 it seemed like she could finally claim a seat on the Supreme Court. When President Ghani told her that he was prepared to nominate her to the Supreme Court again, it was with the confidence that on this occasion parliament would vote in her favor.

"The whole of parliament was willing to vote for me, because ideas about women were changing," Anisa says. "Unfortunately, the Taliban came and took over again, and we suddenly lost everything." Anisa's career was bookended by two terrible Taliban regimes, and the role she so justly deserved on the Afghan Supreme Court remained a dream unfulfilled.

11.

Nafisa: Tackling the Narcotics Trade

NAFISA KABULI'S CAREER ALSO BLOOMED, AND THEN DIED, during the twenty years of the U.S.-backed Afghan Republic. She vividly remembers September 11, 2001—the day her life as a judge could truly begin. The Taliban were still in power, but on the streets of Kabul there was a feeling that change was coming. "The next day we could see that the Taliban were frightened. They were really losing it. They felt the danger." By October 7 the U.S. and allied bombing campaign was underway, and just over a month later the Taliban lost control of Kabul. "They were so afraid that, as they were leaving, they would just let go of their guns. They would leave them in the street and escape." Men who had been forced to wear long beards suddenly shaved them off. "Everyone was so happy. I remember one person walking through the streets carrying a radio playing music, because until then music was banned."

Nafisa could not contain herself for one more minute: "The first thing I did was run straight to the Supreme Court." No one had told women that they could go back to work, and some of Nafisa's former colleagues were shocked to see her, especially as she was not wearing the Taliban-mandated burqa and just had a scarf draped over her hair. Nafisa remembers that they said, "What are you doing? Why are you here? Don't you know the Taliban are still here, and you just cover your hair with a scarf?" Nafisa replied,

"No, I know they are gone, and I am not afraid of anything. It's time for me to come back here."

After the Taliban were ousted, Nafisa would walk the streets of Kabul without wearing the burqa; small children would stare, and start speaking to her in English. "I would say, 'No, I'm Afghan, I'm like you, I'm just not covering my face.'" Young men on bicycles would wave and shout "Viva freedom, viva freedom!" But other women fretted that the change was not permanent or safe. When Nafisa visited the newly opened UN Office of Women's Rights, friends and family urged her to tell the United Nations to provide security for them so that they too could give up the burqa. "I said, 'No, they are not providing any security for me. I am doing it on my own. And you can do it on your own as well.' It took some time for women to unveil."

After years of waiting, women returned to work with astonishing speed, and by the fall of 2001 Nafisa was established in a new role in the civil court northeast of Kabul in an area called Deh Sabz. In civil court she dealt with issues including disputes over house deeds and warranties, but was soon moved to a court for criminal misdemeanors.

"It took about a year until we felt a sense of normalcy. At the beginning we had to work from memory, because a lot of laws and regulations had been dismantled. Most of us hadn't been working for years, so even using our memory was hard. Writing cases and judgments was difficult, because we hadn't used those skills for such a long time." Eventually organizations like the IAWJ helped the judges with new law books and equipment. "In those twenty years there was a lot of development, and we really felt like we were building a new nation."

Just as her friend and colleague Anisa Rasooli had taken a difficult and controversial appointment to the anti-corruption court, after five years in criminal court Nafisa agreed to take up a senior role with the narcotics court—a notoriously complicated and dangerous area.

Despite the efforts of allied forces and the new government, Afghanistan retained its total dominance in global opiate production, producing 83 percent of the world's heroin in 2011. Although they were no longer in government, the Afghan Taliban were still very much in operation and were collecting more than $170 million in "taxes" each year from the illegal trade. The problem was so acute that the United Nations Office on Drugs and Crime reported that "the Afghan opiate trade continues to represent a severe global threat to public health, governance and security."

Narcotics were cultivated primarily in five provinces, Nafisa says, including Helmand, Farah, Balkh, Nangarhar, and Badakhshan, and were a deeply embedded problem in Afghan society. "Talking about narcotics is not a new issue in Afghanistan. It's been going on through the ages—and of course it's not just about narcotics, it's about cultivating narcotics, about the use and abuse of narcotics, and also about the trafficking and smuggling of narcotics. The history of narcotics and Afghanistan goes back long before the history of the court system."

Nafisa outlines one drug smuggling route from Afghanistan through Helmand province, across the border into Iran, and down through Balochistan to the Gulf of Oman, where the drugs are put onto ships to Europe and around the world. Other routes channeled the drugs down through Pakistan, or north through Tajikistan and Central Asia. "That's the way the narcotics mafia works, and a very small amount of it is ever caught. Sometimes if the smugglers have their own internal fights, someone gets caught and a case goes to court, but there are thousands of kilograms and only a tiny amount is ever recovered."

The narcotics court dealt with crimes relating to smuggling drugs in quantities above fifty kilograms (over 120 pounds), so most of those Nafisa encountered were people in authority, including the police and those who were supposed to be involved in fighting the narcotics trade. "In one case, the police chief was very much involved in the narcotics trade and he would use police cars, with police markings on them, to smuggle the drugs."

Another case involved a high-ranking government official who was using his state car to transport narcotics. A family member had been traveling in the car on the day when it was stopped and searched. Shocked, he had initially confessed, but then immediately retracted his words and forced the driver to take the blame. When the case came before Nafisa's court she knew instantly that the driver had only been moving the drugs on the official's orders.

"Like any other mafia-type group, the official must have told the driver either 'I will kill you or harm your family' or 'If you take the responsibility, we will make it up to you.'"

While the powerful official never appeared before the court, Nafisa had some leeway in determining sentencing for the driver and the family member. She was under pressure to send the driver to prison for a long time and to let the family member go with only a slap on the wrist. "I awarded a ten-year sentence to the driver, but also an equal sentence to the family member. I wanted both the driver and the official to understand that there is some justice, and some equality, too." Nafisa adds that later that official became a member of parliament.

Even as she awarded harsh sentences in some cases, Nafisa found people innocent in others. In one case a man came before the court who had been driving between two villages in a small truck during Ramadan. As he drove along with his mother they saw two men walking down the road with large sacks on their backs. The men wanted a lift, and his mother said: "Give them a ride—they're carrying something heavy and it's Ramadan, everyone's fasting and hungry." The men jumped in the back with their bags, and they drove off down the dirt road until they reached a checkpoint. Of course, as soon they saw the checkpoint the two passengers jumped out of the back of the truck and ran away, leaving behind their bags, which the police soon discovered were full of drugs. When Nafisa met the defendant he had already been found guilty and was appealing the verdict. The man came from a poor family, with no means to pay for an expensive lawyer. Nafisa says, "I could see he was not a smuggler. I'd never met a smuggler who carried drugs around in the back of their truck in large sacks. They were always hidden—in doors, in parts of the car, or equipment." Nafisa upheld his appeal and found him innocent, at which point the man collapsed. "He fell back, hit his head on the wall and fainted."

After he was released the man called Nafisa every night for a year asking what he could do to help her in return. "I was tired of him calling me every night," Nafisa says. "He was a poor man, so I said to him, 'If you really want to make me happy, please just send your children to school.'"

Unfortunately, not everyone who called had such good intentions. Nafisa was working in the appeals court on a case relating to an amount of drugs so enormous that even the president of Tajikistan had written a letter explaining the devastating effect this amount of narcotics would have had on his country should it have reached its destination. "It was huge, absolutely huge," Nafisa says, but the man responsible had originally been found innocent and was walking around as a free man. Not only was he responsible for smuggling the drugs, but he also owned all of the necessary equipment to manufacture heroin, morphine, and cocaine. Nafisa wrote a judgment outlining twelve reasons he was guilty of the crime, and the order was sent out to rearrest him and send him to prison. That night she received an unknown call from someone purporting to be the man's lawyer. He insisted that he wanted to see her. Nafisa replied that until she knew who he was she wouldn't meet him. People were always pretending to be lawyers and trying to set up secret backdoor meetings. Nafisa said, "You know what—if you are a lawyer, come to court. The only place where I need to see you is in court, and the court is always open to you." Immediately he hung up and, Nafisa says, "I never heard from him again."

If Nafisa felt threatened, it was with good reason. In 2008 Alim Hanif, the director and chief judge of the Central Narcotics Tribunal appeals court, was shot and killed on his way to work. Later that evening, Nafisa received a warning that said, "Your boss was 'released' from this life, now it's your turn."

A few months later, criminals came for Nafisa, too. As she walked down a quiet street in Kabul near her apartment and stepped off the curb, a car accelerated toward her and hit her hard, throwing her up into the air. Before she landed on the pavement, Nafisa thought, "They are trying to kill me. This is my assassination." Once she rolled over on the ground Nafisa knew that her only hope was to try to crawl the short distance to her home. Clutching a few bits and pieces from her handbag, she made it, and her family then rushed her to the local hospital. The doctors ran a series of tests and X-rays but seemed to treat the matter lightly, and breezily told Nafisa that she had a fracture. "They said, 'Oh, nothing has happened, you are fine.' I said, 'No, I'm in a lot of pain. I was thrown up in the air like a rag doll and my foot is in agony.'" The doctors agreed to put Nafisa's foot in a cast, but when she told them she also had terrible chest pain, they said, "Don't worry about it, just go home and rest." Nafisa realized that whoever the terrorists behind her assassination attempt were, they had also warned the hospital not to treat her—so her family took her home for the night and then the following day traveled to another hospital, where she was diagnosed with broken ribs and a broken big toe and immobilized in bed in a full body cast for more than a month.

Nafisa was shaken to realize that the government cared so little for the safety and security of their judges. "They placed so little value on, and paid so little attention to, my life." Until then Nafisa had felt confident that she was building a new democracy in Afghanistan, but now she saw the mood darkening. "Things changed. Soon after that they told the judges that they could have their own drivers, and hire people that they trusted as their security guards. A lot of judges hired their brothers or family members, because those were the only people they could trust. Our drivers took us from our homes to court every day—even to different cities where we were sitting. Later they gave us the option to carry a gun."

Nafisa hired her cousin to be her driver and security guard, and returned to work. "I had to. I still had a passion for my job, but I also had no other choice. I was a judge, and I had to work to make a living. I continued working for myself, and for all the judges. All the judges were going through the same hardship. We were under extreme psychological pressure. Every day that we left home to go to the court, we were not sure if we would get back home in one piece. Every single day."

Even the presence of a driver and a security guard offered little real protection. As she left court one afternoon and walked the short distance to her car, somebody called to Nafisa and said, "Judge, I am the man that you sentenced to ten years in prison, and I have just been released." Nafisa recognized him as a prisoner who had just been pardoned by the president.

"I was worried, I was scared, but I didn't want to show my feelings because I was surprised to see him standing there right in front of me," Nafisa says. "So I pulled myself together, and I stayed strong, and I said, 'I'm glad you are out of prison. Congratulations.'" Then, before he could respond, she quickly turned and left.

Despite all the passion she had for her work and justice, Nafisa admits that she felt hopeless. "If I had any way to stop what I was doing, I would, but I had no other choice. We were defenseless."

Nafisa's career was long and colorful, and like Anisa Rasooli's, it wove like a strong thread through the history of a nation during twenty years of struggle to provide fair and democratic rule for all of its citizens, regardless of their ethnicity or gender. Nafisa kept reports of all of her cases, a history of her time on the bench, but on the night the Taliban came, she was forced to throw them all away. "I had to get rid of all the pictures and all the documents that I had. I threw them in the river." The once spectacular waters of the Kabul River were now little more than a trickle in places, dried by droughts, and running over with sewage—but that was where Nafisa had to dispose of the remnants of her career. Nafisa's translator interrupts and says that there should be a poem about what the river carries on the night of a coup d'état, because everybody throws everything that they have in the river—and the river takes all the documents, and the water wipes away the ink. Nafisa agrees. "You have to let it go, and I don't know if this is letting go of history or if the river is separating from you from what you had and giving it to eternity. Is our history wiped out when the ink is gone?"

12.

Raihana: The Next Generation

ANISA RASOOLI AND NAFISA KABULI WERE THE PIONEERS OF Afghan women judges, but now there was a new generation; the ambitious young women who had sat in Anisa's classroom and learned from Nafisa in meetings. They were ready to push forward toward an Afghanistan based upon the rule of law and human rights. Sometimes they got the worst jobs or were sent to the most remote places—but despite how much they were pushed to the periphery, their very existence meant that they were at the heart of the new Afghanistan. They sat in judgment of the old way of doing things, and they opposed the corruption that, their stories show, was still systemic.

Raihana Attaee says, "When I was growing up in the 1990s, the Taliban was governing Afghanistan. Boys could go to school and were free to do whatever they pleased. Girls had to stay home with many restrictions. My dream was to go to school. I loved riding a bike like my brother, but I was not allowed. I hated people saying, 'You cannot do this and that because you are a girl.' I did not want to live like other women in my village. I wanted to be a boy and be respected as a man in my community. There was only one way that I could become a boy. The solution was to cross over a rainbow, but I had to pay the price. The price was losing one of my legs. When a rainbow appeared in the sky each spring, I wanted my dad to help me cross over it." Crossing the rainbow was a famous folk story among Raihana's people, and her father told it to her many times.

"There was a beautiful girl named Mah Gul. She lived with her dad and had no brothers. Her father went to the mountains daily and collected grass and thorns to sell in the village's small bazaar. The girl was not allowed to go and work with her father. She cooked, cleaned the house, and waited for her dad to return home all day. Years passed, and her dad became old and could no longer go to the mountains to collect grass. Mah Gul wanted to help her family by going to the mountain, but in her village, it was a great shame for a girl to leave home and be seen in public. So she had no way to realize her dream. Soon her dad became sick and could no longer get out of bed. Mah Gul was helpless. Her dad was about to die from sickness and hunger, and she could do nothing to save him.

One night, when Mah Gul lay down to sleep, she wished to become a boy upon waking so she could go to the mountain. That night, in her dream, she met an angel. The angel reached out to Mah Gul, wiped away her tears, and took her outside. In the sky there was a colorful painting that Mah Gul had never seen before. The angel said to her, "This is magic. You can call it rainbow. I can help you to cross over it, and you will change into a boy. After becoming a boy, you can go out and support your dad."

Mah Gul was excited, but the angel was hesitant to help her. The angel told Mah Gul that when she crossed the rainbow, transforming into a boy, she would lose one of her legs forever. Mah Gul did not know what to choose. She thought if she stayed a girl, she would not be able to save her dad's life. What is the point of being alive when you are not free or able to do what you want to do? She told the angel that she would pay the price to become a boy. The angel spoke to the rainbow, which then reached down and touched Mah Gul's feet.

When Mah Gul opened her eyes in the morning, she wished her dream had been real, but she knew it wasn't. When she tried to get up from bed to check on her dad, she couldn't move one of her legs. Mah Gul thought she was still dreaming until she reached for her mirror. In the mirror, she saw a boy—the angel really had turned Mah Gul into a boy. Mah Gul went to his dad and told him everything. His father was happy because Mah Gul could go out and work. Mah Gul learned how to walk on one leg and go to the mountains. After some time, he could collect grasses from the hills and sell them in the bazaar. He was able to buy food and medicine for his dad.

Even so, Mah Gul looked at himself in the mirror every morning and felt sad because he no longer saw a girl in the mirror. He had lost his natural identity. Although Mah Gul looked like a boy, he remained a girl inside. He was happy to be able to save his dad's life, but always wished he could still have a woman's face.

"After that, the rainbow always appeared in the sky to give people a choice," Raihana says. "It is always girls who choose to change their gender, not boys—and everyone knows the reason for this sad story. The story of Mah Gul reached other parts of the world, and many girls choose to change their gender, to be free. But in some parts of the world, people couldn't understand Mah Gul and her feelings. This is because they were free since birth, so they couldn't understand how hard it is to be a girl and have no freedom. "

Raihana understood the story very well. "After a long and snowy winter, our village welcomed the spring's sunshine. It was midday when the rain stopped, and a rainbow appeared in the corner of the sky. Children rushed to the top of the hill close to our house to see the rainbow. As I approached the mountain, the rainbow was coming down and down. Dad was chatting with some other men on the hill. I thought Dad could reach the rainbow if he tried. I shouted to Dad, 'Please catch the rainbow. I want to cross over it.

Please hurry. It is very close to you.' Dad did not try to catch the rainbow, which disappeared when I was at the top of the hill.

"'Dad! Why did you not catch the rainbow? Now I can never become a boy.'

"Dad laughed as always and said, 'I don't think crossing over the rainbow is a good idea. As I told you, if you cross over it, you will be a boy, but you will be disabled for the rest of your life. Do you want to be a disabled boy or a healthy girl?'

"'I want to be a boy even if I become disabled.'"

"'Don't worry, my daughter. I will catch the rainbow for you another time, and help you to cross over it. It is spring, and the rain and sun will create many rainbows.'"

Raihana says, "The next night, I sat beside Dad and said that if he saw a rainbow again, he must try to catch it for me and help me cross over it. I wanted to be a boy and go to school. Dad looked at me and said, 'It is only a story, darling. You cannot cross the rainbow. It is only colors. People made up the story to show how hard it is to be a girl without freedom. Now you are old enough to understand what is real and what is fiction.'"

After hearing her dad's words, Raihana felt hopeless. "It was my only chance to go to school and be educated. It was the only way that I could ride a bike." After that day, she went back to the hill many times and watched boys attending school below. "I wished for the same opportunities. It seemed an impossible dream."

Raihana is from the Hazara ethnic group and was born in a small village called Mahajireen in the Jaghori district of Ghazni province in central Afghanistan, southeast of Kabul. Hazaras are the third-largest ethnic group in Afghanistan, after the dominant Pashtuns and then the Tajiks. While Pashtuns speak Pashto and identify as Sunni Muslims, Hazaras usually speak Farsi and the majority are Shi'a Muslims, with a minority of Sunni Muslims.

Raihana explains, "The Hazara people have endured various

forms of oppression from Pashtun rulers and governments, including slavery, systematic expulsion from ancestral homes and lands, and massacres."

It is estimated that in the late nineteenth century the Hazaras lost approximately 60 percent of their population to ethnic cleansing by the Pashtun ruler Abdur Rahman Khan, and in the following decades Hazaras continued to face repression. They were often forced to conceal their identities and faced discrimination at work. "Until the 1970s, a large percentage of the Hazara population were discriminated against by the government, and could not access higher education, enroll in the army, or secure higher-level government jobs," Raihana says.

During the Taliban rule in the 1990s Raihana says that a popular Talib mantra was "Tajiks to Tajikistan, Uzbeks to Uzbekistan, and Hazaras to Goristan [graveyard]." In 1998, the Taliban laid siege to the Hazara homeland, Hazarajat, starving civilians, and in August of that year Taliban fighters captured Mazar-i-Sharif, killing at least two thousand people of different ethnic groups. Hazaras estimate that the death toll was actually as high as fifteen thousand.

The fall of the Taliban brought new hope for the Hazaras. Although they continued to face discrimination, they could now participate in public life and attain a formal education. Raihana says, "Hazara women pushed for women's emancipation."

Raihana describes her village, Mahajireen, as being surrounded by vast mountains, deep valleys, and clear and cold springs. Ghazni province in total had a population of just over a million people, compared to the four and a half million people who live in Kabul. When Raihana was growing up, there was little government infrastructure and people were poor, she says. "My people had no access to government schools or to government jobs."

Raihana says that if you travel by plane and fly over her village you might think it was only mountains and that no human being could live in such a place, "but life is going on there, and people work hard to survive. There are children waving and saying hello to you. When I was a child and heard the voice of a plane flying overhead, we shook hands and wished for the people on the planes to have a safe trip. We thought those inside the plane would see us and wave to us, too."

Women did not go to mosque. Instead they cooked and looked after the children, which kept them busy all day. People ate what they could grow. Wheat was the most important crop, and most people grew potatoes, tomatoes, and vegetables for their animals. There were cows, sheep, and goats for milk, meat, and oil. Fruits were rare in the village, and Raihana ate little fruit until she moved to Kabul.

"Most of the village was illiterate," Raihana says. "Some men had primary education and could read and write in Farsi and Arabic. The men learned from some Muslim clergy, the mullahs, who went to Iran and became religious scholars."

For men, the essential work in the village was agriculture; for women it was housekeeping, although women often worked on the land, too. "People never talked about working in the government, or traveling to big cities and working there. The only thing we knew about the government was fear of police and government agents. It was as if there was a government just to punish people. If there were any disputes between people, they tried to solve them without taking the case to the government. People believed that if they involved the government, both parties would suffer. Instead the older men in the village solved all types of disputes."

Raihana explains that another important means of survival for her people was to leave Afghanistan and work as laborers in Iran. "Most of the Hazara men in my dad's generation, along with my older siblings, went to Iran. They would try to save money to live on when they came home. Usually two or more young men left the village together at a time, traveling to Iran with no legal documents. The trip to Iran was dangerous. Some of the men returned home after being arrested and imprisoned by Iranian soldiers at the border, but some of them went on to cross the border successfully. Back home their families would wait for someone to come from Iran and tell them their men were safe."

When Raihana's brother and his friends left Iran to make the journey back home to Afghanistan, they were captured in Kabul by mujahideen fighters under the leadership of an infamous warlord named Abdul Rasul Sayyaf. The mujahideen stole Raihana's brother's belongings and beat him, knocking his teeth out. After months of torture he escaped from prison and made his way back to the village, but he no longer had any of the money the other men in Iran had given him to bring home to their families. To compensate, Raihana's father had to sell his business in a bazaar to pay the other families.

People in Mahajireen were highly religious. Men went to the mosque every day to pray and listen to the mullah. When there was a problem, people went to the mullah for advice. According to Raihana, no one questioned his words or ideas.

The mullah talked about women most of the time, Raihana says. "'Hey, ladies! Allah obligates you to obey your husbands and respect them. These are not my words; they are the words of Allah, the Prophet Mohammad, and imams. If your husband is unhappy with you, the angels will curse you until tomorrow, and God is disappointed with you. Hey, ladies! The Prophet Mohammad said, "If prayers are allowed to anyone other than Allah, I would want women to pray to their husbands." Husbands must be nice to women, as the Prophet guided us. However, if a woman does not obey what her husband says, the husband can separate his bed, and if it does not work, he can physically discipline his wife. Girls can marry after they have their first period. Women's obligation to their husbands is to give them food and a place to live and obey their husbands. Men's obligation to their wives is to give them food and a place to live.'"

According to the mullah, every disaster came down to a woman's behavior. "When there was an earthquake, the mullah said it was because women did not cover themselves and made Allah angry. If people experienced a dry year, it was because women had illicit relationships with men." What the mullah said was law, and people obeyed it. Although men in the village could hear news on the radio, the women never listened. "Dad listened to BBC Farsi news, but Mom never did," Raihana says.

Raihana's mother could read the Quran but, like other women in the village, was illiterate in Farsi. A woman with sons was respected by her husband and family; a woman with daughters could be divorced, or faced the prospect of her husband taking a second wife. Raihana remembers many sayings about the woes of having daughters: "A girl is for others, and a boy is for the family." "A girl brings sadness to her family three times. Once, when she is born, second, when she gets married and leaves the house; and third, when she dies."

Girls and boys played together when they were small, but once girls turned seven they were told never to play with boys. "Our brothers could punish us if they saw us playing with boys. Girls learned housekeeping, and boys learned to have no responsibility at home. Girls cleaned the house, washed the dishes, and brought water from the spring even when they were still children. Boys kept playing. When we argued with our brothers at home, our parents reminded us to stay silent because we were girls." When mothers had pregnancies close together, the older girls would have to look after their younger siblings. "Daily life teaches girls and boys how to grow and understand their roles. Girls learn to be silent and respectful and be responsible for the home; boys learn to order people around and accept no responsibility at home. There was a lot of encouragement for boys to study, be educated, and be brave, but not for girls."

Underage marriage was common in the village. "The culture and religion tell girls that they are born to get married and have children. When a girl was fourteen everyone asked her family when she would get married. If a girl behaved in a way that other family members did not like, they would tell her, 'You are not a good girl, no one wants to marry you.' Or 'You are not beautiful enough for a good marriage.'"

Men paid all the expenses for their sons' marriages and received money for their daughter's marriages. "Every girl has a price," according to Raihana. Beautiful or wealthy girls had higher prices. Men who were not rich could not get married for a long time and had to work in Iran for years to make enough money to marry.

In addition to paying money to the girl's family, the groom had to arrange a wedding party and provide food for hundreds of people. The man had to buy clothes and jewelry for the girl. "This tradition is still compelling in Afghanistan. Men must spend a lot of money to marry, which is not a good custom. It makes the families see their daughters as property and causes a lot of problems. Some men borrow money for their marriage. Some treat their wives as their slaves and say, 'I paid for you, so you have to obey what I want.'"

Girls take nothing from their family home. Parents use the money from the groom's family to buy their daughter's clothes, jewelry, dishes, and other things for her new home. On the wedding day, the girl leaves her father's house with a box of her belongings. "After leaving the place where she grew up and spent her childhood, everything changes." Her family may still love her and miss her, "but when she returns from her husband's house, everyone treats her differently, and she feels like a stranger."

When a father passes away, his daughter is not entitled to an inheritance—everything belongs to the men. "According to Islamic thought, each girl shall inherit half of a boy's share," Raihana says. "Receiving half of a share in inheritance is discriminatory but is better than nothing. Most girls did not know about their share in the inheritance, and those who knew their rights could not ask for their share. Even today in Afghanistan, it is considered shameful for a girl to ask for her inheritance. When some women asked for their claim, the brothers refused to give her the share. There were many cases before the Court for the Elimination of Violence Against Women about this. According to the law on the elimination of violence against women, brought in after 2001, not giving a woman her inheritance was a crime punishable by imprisonment."

After becoming a wife, life becomes more challenging, Raihana says. A woman often moved far away and couldn't see her family for a long time. Now she would have to share a house with her husband's family—cook, clean, and look after all of the other family members. "She has to become pregnant as soon as possible and bear many children. She has to obey what her husband wants." If a woman can't have children, or only has girls, her husband can take another wife, and either choose to remain married to his first wife or divorce her. "For most Afghan girls, marriage seems horrible," Raihana says, "but they prefer to get married because they have no place in their father's house. Girls who stay single for a long time experience a lot of humiliation in their daily life."

If a woman was divorced, she had to leave her house with the items she had brought with her on her wedding day. She could not take her children with her and had no ownership of the house no matter how long she had lived there. After divorce, a woman had no place to go, no skill or ability to look after herself, and no hope for a better future. If her parents were still alive, a divorced woman would return to her father's house. If her parents were dead, she would turn to her brothers, who likely would not want to take her in. "That is why Afghanistan women accept violence and do not want divorce. If they are divorced, they lose everything, including their children. The patriarchy leaves women with nothing."

Raihana vividly remembers the story of Gul BiBi, a woman from her village. "I will never forget the day Gul BiBi left our village and went away forever. Gul BiBi was married to Dawood. Dawood was a poor young man who did not have a house of his own and lived with his mother in a house owned by his uncle. Soon after their marriage, Gul BiBi became pregnant and gave birth to a beautiful girl named Halima." Halima and Raihana grew up together.

"Gul BiBi was a strong woman. She encouraged Dawood to go to Iran and work there. When Dawood went to Iran, Gul Bibi was pregnant again. Her second baby was also a girl. When Dawood was in Iran, his mother became sick. Gul BiBi took care of Dawood's bedridden mother for three years as well as caring for her children and working in other people's houses for food, clothes, and anything people gave her. After four years Dawood returned from Iran and brought some money with him so they could build their own house. Gul BiBi worked as much as Dawood did to build the house, and by the time the cold winter had arrived the house was finished and they could move in. Gul BiBi was happy in her home and proud of all her hard work. She became pregnant for the third time. This time, though, she was worried—Dawood had told her that if she gave birth to a third girl he would take another wife."

After Gul BiBi gave birth to her third daughter, Dawood married again. Gul BiBi had begged him to wait—she was young and could have many more children—but Dawood did not listen. "After Dawood's second marriage, Gul BiBi and her daughters changed enormously," Raihana says. "They laughed less and seemed sad most of the time." Gul BiBi didn't talk with the other women in the village anymore. She looked defeated. One morning

Gul BiBi left the village with a small box, the one she had brought with her when she got married to Dawood. "Mom said that Gul BiBi had fought with his new wife and Dawood had divorced her. He told her to leave the house forever."

After a week, Gul BiBi returned to see her daughters, but Dawood would not allow her to speak to them. She cried and asked Dawood to let her stay with her children. Gul BiBi said that she had no place in her brother's home. "Dawood closed the door in her face and told her not to come back. No one saw Gul BiBi in the village ever again.

"Every woman in Afghanistan knows someone like Gul BiBi," Raihana says. "It reminds them to live the way that others decree, to accept violence, to accept her husband's second marriage and not to become like Gul BiBi. The situation changes only when laws and customs vary, and it is only possible when women become educated and gain the skills to direct their lives."

Raihana longed to "burn discriminatory laws and create new laws to support everyone." As a judge in the Court for the Elimination of Violence Against Women, Raihana saw how women suffered. "The rules were designed to support men and oppress women, and women had to choose between a life made up entirely of tension and violation, or lose their children. If they chose to get a divorce, they had to leave their children forever. Some women stopped their claim for divorce after they understood they would lose their children if they got divorced."

All of that lay in the future, however. Before she could become a lawyer, Raihana had to go to school.

Under the Taliban regime in the 1990s girls could not go to school, but in Raihana's area they could go to the mosque. "My dad kept telling me that the situation would change and I would be able to go to school one day. He encouraged us to keep going to the mosque and learn what I could from the mullah."

In spring, summer, and autumn the boys went to the government school and the girls helped their families in the house, but during the winter, when the land and roads were covered by snow, most of the children over the age of seven went to the mosque. The mosque had a young mullah and an old mullah, and the young mullah taught the students every day.

"The class was divided into two parts; half was for boys and half for girls. The mullah sat in the middle of the class like a borderline. The first book that every student had to learn was the Qaida Baghdadi, a basic guide to the Arabic alphabet, which we all called the Pangsara. After completing the Pangsara, students learned the Quran. After learning the Quran, students could learn to read in their own language, Farsi. We had to learn two books of Farsi poetry; one was called Pang Ketab, and the other was called 'Hafiz' by the poet Hafiz Shirazi. If students could read Hafiz, they could read any other Farsi writing."

In addition to learning religious books, students also had to learn how to pray, which was the most difficult part of studying in the mosque. "The prayers were in Arabic, and the children did not know the meaning of the prayers. We had to memorize them, and they were long and complicated." Although they could read Arabic, none of the children learned how to write in that language.

"Each Wednesday, the mullah asked each student about their previous week's lessons. Those who could not answer the mullah's questions were punished, and the punishment was physical and harsh." Early in the morning the mullah would ask some students to bring some tree stems to the mosque to be used as lashes. "The stems were long and robust. The mullah lashed students on their hands and feet, and often left marks on their bodies. Wednesdays were the worst day of the week for students," Raihana says.

Raihana was attending the mosque and learning the Quran when the villagers fired the mullahs and hired two new mullahs.

"The new mullah was very serious and angry," Raihana says. "He used long lashes every day and he punished many students for not staying silent. On Wednesday, everyone was afraid. I was terrified when he called on me to go up to him and read the previous lessons. He asked me many times to read, but I could not speak. On that day, he lashed a lot of students, and everyone was crying. My hands were red and swollen. When I got home, my parents told me not to go to the mosque anymore. After that my dad taught me and my siblings at home, and I learned writing and reading in Farsi."

Eventually the angry mullah was replaced by another new mullah, and Raihana returned to the mosque. This young mullah moved from the middle of the class to the girls' part. "He divided the girls by the age. The older girls had to sit close to the mullah, and he spent the day talking and laughing with the teenage girls while the rest of the class played among themselves."

One day Raihana's father visited the mosque and saw the mullah chatting with the older girls. After that he told Raihana and her siblings not to go to the mosque anymore, and taught them at home again.

"My dad had to work on the land, though, and he did not have much time to teach us at home. I was getting older and I tried to accept my destiny. I did not search for rainbows anymore. My life was simple, and my thoughts went no farther than my small village's boundaries. I thought it was a girl's destiny to live like other women in the village. One day, like other women, I would have to get married and have children, and I should not dream for more. Maybe that was the life that Allah wanted for girls."

Like other girls in the village, Raihana stayed at home and learned embroidery—a skill the Hazaras were famous for. "Girls in the village came together and shared their stories while doing embroidery," she says, and she was happy with her mother and her siblings. "I grew up in a big and happy family. My parents had nine babies in total, but two—a boy and a girl—died when they were babies. I grew up with six siblings—three brothers and three sisters. I am the fifth child of the family, and like other families in my village, my family wanted to have more boys than girls. Before I was born, Mom wished for a boy. She always told me, "You are a good girl because you brought luck to the family. After your birth Allah's gift was another boy." That was my brother, Jawad. Then finally came my youngest sister, Najiba."

Raihana says her mother is the kindest woman she has ever met, loving everyone in the family unconditionally. As a village woman, Raihana's mother was always in a hurry. "Mom had to feed cows and sheep. She had to collect grass and prepare it for the animals. She had to help Dad on the farm. She had to do the cleaning and washing." It was only many years later, after the family had moved to Kabul, that Raihana's mother could spend some time on herself.

"Dad was a well-known community leader. Most of the time he left home early in the morning and returned late at night. He solved disputes, organized community affairs, and brought peace between people." Raihana says her father was the oldest in his family and had no formal education, but he had a deep knowledge of life and was a good leader and a lovely father. She says she owes her success to his support.

When the Taliban took power in Afghanistan in 1994, people were afraid and did not know what would happen to their lives when the Taliban reached their village, Raihana says. There was horrible news about the Hazara genocide in cities such as Mazar-i-Sharif, Bamiyan, Herat, Ghor, and in other parts of Afghanistan.

"When the Taliban reached our village, they announced that all men must gather at the mosque urgently. No one knew what the Taliban would do. When the men arrived the Taliban announced their rules and said they wanted people to obey their government and their restrictions on women. They wanted the village to choose a representative who would be responsible to the Taliban government by the following morning. Men returned home and did not know who was going to represent them. No one knew what would happen. During the evening, the men gathered again in the mosque to make their choice. No one volunteered for the role, and everyone remained silent. All the men were afraid of dealing with the Taliban. When Dad spoke up and volunteered for the role, everyone in the mosque was incredibly relieved, but my mom and older siblings were not happy. Mom said, 'The Taliban might kill you. Think about your children.' Dad replied that the village needed a representative, and all the men would be punished if they did not choose someone."

Raihana's father represented the village until the Taliban regime collapsed in 2001. "He was proud of his decision. That period was a remarkable time in his life—but it was also the most challenging part of his life, as he had to work with the Taliban to protect people. During that time, he built a good relationship with the Taliban, as the Taliban respected him and promised him not to arrest his people without letting him know. Sometimes he left home in the middle of the night to save people from the Taliban."

The Taliban did not obey the law in terms of arresting or punishing people—and they had spies in the village. Often people were arrested because someone in the village had a grudge against them, and Raihana's father had to mediate to try to save them.

When the United States and its NATO allies invaded, ousting the Taliban from power, most of the representatives left their homes and fled to other parts of the country, Raihana says. Her father did not. "When my uncles asked Dad if he wanted to leave the village, he said, 'I always put my people first, and supported them during a hard time. There is no reason for me to leave my home.'" Raihana and her family stayed in the village, and the new government took power. "A new phase of life started in Afghanistan, a new life for the Hazara people and the women of Afghanistan. It was a step toward hope and progress, and signified our desire for a better life."

When her father heard on the BBC radio news that the Taliban had fallen, he told his family that things were going to change. "No one knows what the future holds," he told them, "but people will have more freedom and I am sure now that my girls can go to school." This was the best news that Raihana had ever heard—and it was true.

Mahajireen had a small primary school for boys, but the nearest high school was in another village called Zeerak, two hours away. Raihana's older brother, who is now a pediatrician, went to the high school there, first on foot, then by bike, and finally on a motorcycle.

Soon after the new government was established, most of the girls in Mahajireen started going to school. Some girls from the village went to the Zeerak high school, but for others it was too far. Raihana's father volunteered to go to Kabul to raise funds for a new school in the village, and returned triumphant. People volunteered to start preparing lessons, and anyone who had enough knowledge, including two or three women, was accepted as a teacher.

"Before our new school started, winter arrived. My brother was preparing for the Kankor [the national university entrance exam] in Kabul and returned home that winter. Dad asked him to teach mathematics to my older sister, my younger brother, and me. My very oldest sister was illiterate, but she had already married and left home by then, so my brother could not help her. Unlike her, my sister and brother and I could already read and write in Farsi but knew nothing about math. That winter we worked hard, and after a few months our math was good enough to pass the entrance exam."

When spring came everyone in the village was excited. "Girls were counting the days to start the school. Anyone who wanted to start school had to pass the entrance exam. According to our grades, the examiners would decide what class would be appropriate for each student. After the exam my younger brother, Jawad, was put in grade five. My older sister, Gul Jan, was put in grade four.

Najiba, Raihana's youngest sister, was not old enough to attend school. She had to wait another year to be eligible—but she was desperate to start school alongside her brothers and sisters. "Most people in the village had no ID card and teachers guessed the age of the child by checking their teeth. Those children who had lost one of their teeth were considered to be seven years old and were eligible to start school. After Dad told Najiba she could not go to school because none of her teeth had come out, she tried to pull a tooth out herself by shaking it. On registration day, Najiba went down to the school and showed the registrar her loose tooth. Her plan worked, and she started the school that year."

At first the children began studying under tents donated by the United Nations. There were no chairs, and sometimes nothing to cover the bare ground. Children sat on a piece of stone or wood while teachers stood on their feet all day, and books and paper were sparse. Despite the hardship, however, everyone was delighted to be there, and worked hard. "Classes were arranged based on students' understanding, not their age, so girls from different generations were in each class," Raihana explains. "Due to the lack of teachers and resources, grade five was the highest class in our school in the first year. Those who were above fifth grade went to the Zeerak high school." As the students improved, however, so did the school, and by the time Raihana finished grade five, another year was added.

"There were fourteen students in our class. Some of my classmates were twelve years old, but some were older than twenty-five and were married with children. What brought us together was our desire to learn. Those who were married always told the rest of the class not to get married until finishing their studies. Looking after children, doing all their housework, and studying was very challenging. Our married classmates left school quite soon. Their difficulties were greater than their desire to continue learning. They had no support from their family to keep going."

Raihana saw her father at school every day—he was one of the trustees and traveled to Ghazni every month to collect the teachers' salaries. After he'd lobbied officials in Kabul for a long time, the government agreed to fund a new school in the village, and three years later Raihana moved into her new classroom.

"Walking into the clean and beautiful classroom with tables and chairs seemed like a dream. The building was modern and the outside was covered by stone and cement, which looked different from all of the other buildings in the village. It looked like a city building."

Despite so much progress, the village girls still had to work at home in the morning and could only attend school in the afternoon. Younger girls carried water from the spring, washed the dishes, and took the sheep to the mountains. Older girls helped their mothers with cooking, cleaning, washing, and working on the land. Sometimes there was so much to do the girls had to rush to school without eating any lunch.

"We grew up alongside our school. As we reached the end of every year, another year was added to the school—until we reached ninth grade. When we finished ninth grade, most of us stayed in school, but the rest of the girls got married and left. Most of them did not want to get married, but they accepted what their family wanted. In my village, girls could not stand up for their own desires, and they did not learn to fight for their dreams. Our religion and culture taught us to keep silent and listen to older people because they knew better. Marriage was seen as the goal for life, and those girls who got married earlier were seen as more prestigious than the others. My older sister got married in grade eight. There was no pressure from my parents, and when her husband's family came to our house and asked for her, my dad asked her if she wanted to get married or continue her studies. She said she wanted to get married as long as her husband's family allowed her to continue her studies."

Raihana's sister was really too young to get married, but she had seen other girls in her class doing so and didn't want to be left behind. Her husband's family promised to support her studies, but after she was married she was never allowed to go to school again. Soon after her wedding her husband went to work in Iran and left her with his parents. When she said she wanted to go to school, her in-laws said no other married women were attending school in the village and it would bring shame on them.

"My sister went to live in Iran, too, but she became sick and lived a hard life. She got pregnant many times, but only one of her daughters lived; her name is Tamanna. My sister always wished she had stayed in school and not got married. After living in Iran for a few years, she passed away from kidney disease. She always wished to live longer to take care of her only daughter. Tamanna was only nine when her mother died, but she is a beautiful and bright girl living in Iran with her dad and stepmother."

After completing ninth grade, Raihana had to move up to the high school in Zeerak, which meant getting up at the crack of dawn and leaving home in the dark. Raihana felt daunted: "Zeerak high school was big, with a vast building and many students. Six of my classmates went to Zeerak high school with me, but there were more than thirty girls in our class and I was unsure if I could keep my position as head of the class. After the exams, though, I achieved the highest score and became the top student."

That year the Mahajireen school needed teachers for the lower classes, and the villagers asked the high school students to teach part-time. Raihana and her classmates agreed, so she went to high school in the morning and then taught third grade in the village school in the afternoon. "Mom was the one who took on most of my responsibilities at home and gave me time to study and teach. Dad always encouraged me to dream bigger and not stop in my efforts for a better future."

One day Raihana's father asked her what she wanted to become in the future. Raihan thought about it and said that maybe she should be a teacher. "Being a teacher is good," he replied, "but you must consider being a leader."

Raihana said, "There are no woman leaders. Maybe women cannot be leaders?" Her father told her women could be leaders if they worked hard, dreamed big, and had support.

Raihana's father allowed her to decide her own future. He never told his children how or when to marry, saying: "Everything has a time. Now is the time to learn and be educated." Whenever anyone asked for Raihana's hand in marriage her father would tell them that Raihana was wise enough to decide for herself.

"In our village, most of the families supported their girls in studying. Parents worked harder to give their daughters more time to learn. Despite many financial challenges, families paid for their children's studies. For girls, school was not only a place to study. It was a place to be happy and have our own time. It was a place to share our stories and be ourselves. It was a place to meet our friends. From our old books, we learned about the world and understood that the world is not only our village. We learned to dream of a better future and try to achieve it."

The Taliban does not allow women to go to school because they are afraid of educated women, Raihana says. "An educated woman does not want to be the second wife of a man. Educated women fight for their freedom and challenge barriers. Such women teach their children and community to be wise and free. Educated women want to be respected as human beings. Through education we have learned to stand up for our dreams and open our eyes."

In tenth grade, everyone was talking about preparing for the Kankor, and Raihana's brother wanted to go to Sang-e-Masha, the center of Jaghori district, to share a room with other students and take extra winter courses. At that time, girls did not leave home and live separately from their family, so Raihana was sure she would be left behind. She was sure that if she did not take the extra winter courses she could not pass the math exam. One night at dinner, when her brother was talking about going to Sang-e-Masha, Raihana burst out: "Dad, what should I do? I can't take the winter courses and in the spring the boys will be ahead of me."

Raihana's father sat and looked at her. He could see how sad she was. Finally he said, "Do not lose hope. I will find a way."

Eventually he told her, "You can participate in winter courses. I will not let my daughter be left behind. We will go to Kabul. In Kabul, all of you can go to better schools and classes. There you can prepare for the Kankor and learn English."

Before he uttered those words, Raihana had never thought about leaving her village. "It was where my ancestors lived, where my dad was born and lived his life, and the home where we spent our childhood."

The news of her dad's plan spread like wildfire. People could not believe that the family would leave the village forever. Raihana's father had a good life and reputation, but he decided to leave everything behind and start from nothing in a big city to give his children a better future. "Especially his daughter's future. If Dad had not decided to move to Kabul, I could never have achieved my goals," Raihana says.

"My parents seemed very sad and worried the day we left our village. I asked why, and Mom smiled and said she already missed her home and her brothers. Dad looked into my eyes and said, 'I have mixed feelings. I am unhappy because I am leaving behind what I love the most: my people, the school, and the village. But I am happy because my children will have a better future.'" At that time, Raihana could not understand her dad's feelings, because she was over the moon and dreaming of a better life in Kabul. But now, after being forced to flee from her homeland, she understands exactly what he meant. "I had the same feeling. I felt sad because I had to leave behind whatever I had achieved, including my job and my lovely family and friends. But I was happy because I was moving toward safety, and a better future for my son."

13.

Raihana: The Right to See the Sky

BEFORE RAIHANA AND HER FAMILY MOVED TO KABUL, HER father asked her older brother Arif to rent a house for them. Arif was living in Kabul and was a student at the Kabul Medical University. He rented a one-story home with three bedrooms in Dashti Barchi, the western part of Kabul, where most Hazaras live. "The house was almost new, and it was in a good location. We used one room as our bedroom. Another room was for us to do our studies in, and the biggest room was dedicated to our guests. Mom designed the guest room like our guest room in the village. She put mattresses and pillows all around the room which were covered with colorful handmade covers."

In Afghan culture, visitors are welcomed, and Raihana says people dedicate the best room in the house to guests and prepare the best food. People rarely stay in hotels, preferring to stay with friends and relatives, and in Kabul Raihana's family had guests most of the time.

Life was much easier in Kabul, and everything was more accessible than in the village. "We did not need to fetch water from a long way away. We did not need to burn wood fires. Cooking on gas was much easier than on a wood fire. We could buy bread from the market. We could get up later on the weekends. However, it took time to get familiar with life in a city. We arrived in Kabul at the beginning of the cold winter. Sometimes during the morning the taps were frozen with ice, and we did not know how to open them."

Other things about city life also took time to get used to. Washing dishes in the kitchen seemed strange if you were used to spring water, and Raihana's mother was suspicious that clothes washed under the tap would not be clean enough. Moreover, neighbors were standoffish and unfriendly. "Mom was unhappy about that. She said, 'We are human beings; we need to talk to each other. These people living around us behave as if they are deaf and blind. They look at us but do not say a single word.'"

Nor was the family wealthy. Raihana's family had been comparatively rich in the village, but her father had followed the local custom of lending money to poorer villagers and few had repaid him before it was time for him to leave. Now, in Kabul, he could cover only rent and necessities, but he still insisted that Raihana and her siblings should attend the best schools—even if they were private schools. Raihana enrolled in Marefat High School, the best school in that area of the city, and began studying.

"At that time, Afghanistan's economy was growing, and people were hopeful. The security situation was good, and there were no bombs in Kabul or other parts of the country. Thousands of refugees were returning home from Iran and Pakistan, and the property market was booming."

Soon Raihana's father was able to buy a piece of land to build their own house on. Raihana was blossoming at Marefat High School, and as the top students in their classes, neither she nor her brother Jawad paid fees. As part of the new curriculum, Raihana studied anthropology and learned about human rights, the purpose of human beings, freedom, equality, gender issues, and more. Anthropology was full of discussions and questions—and Raihana thrived. At Marefat Raihana could also study music, drawing, and English. "In the morning, before students went to class, classical music was played from the school loudspeakers. Some conservatives criticized the school for playing that music, as under a strict interpretation of Islam music is not allowed."

Now that Raihana was close to graduating from high school, she was studying for the Kankor, and her university place, in earnest. Each year the Kankor was held in the central part of each province, and all school graduates could take the exam. Most high school students took private Kankor preparation courses to get better results in the exam.

Kankor day was a big day for students and their families. The most prestigious universities in Afghanistan were government universities—and they were free for those who successfully passed the Kankor. Those who did not get a place at a government university could apply to a private university, but they were expensive and most low- and middle-income families could not afford the fees.

Raihana and her brother Jawad prepared for the Kankor examination together. "We worked hard all year to get better results and we took part in each practice exam. Jawad's marks were three or four points higher than mine in most practice tests. I tried hard to overtake him, but couldn't. His marks were higher than mine in the real Kankor exam by three points."

On the day of the Kankor, Raihana's father took them to the exam. "It was a stressful day, but also one that was full of hope." After twelve years of school, the exam would determine their future—but they wouldn't know their results for months.

"Jawad and I both did well and we were admitted to Kabul University Law School. We were classmates for two years, and then I chose to continue my studies in judicial law and prosecution. Jawad continued his studies in political science."

In Afghanistan men and women are separated most of the time—at home they often sit and eat separately, and parents warn their children of different sexes not to play together. At university boys and girls met and mixed, sometimes for the first time. "We shared the same classroom, but boys and girls sat in separate rows." Most of the girls in class were very shy, Raihana discovered, some so much so they were reluctant to even walk into the room. "They said they thought all the boys looked at them when they entered the class. They found it difficult to answer a question from the lecturer or share their thoughts."

Classmates from traditional families found it hard to continue their studies, in part because they got no support from their families. "At any time, their brothers or fathers might order them not to go to the university anymore. They had to do everything to convince their family not to stop them from being educated." In contrast, some of Raihana's friends came from very low-income families whose parents were dedicated to helping them move forward and have a better future.

"Traditionally, girls had to get married as soon as possible. Most of my classmates married during school, but I refused to do so. Fortunately, I had the support of my family, especially my dad, to continue my studies; otherwise, it would have been difficult. It is hard to fight for your dreams when you are still very young. During my university years, some of my relatives told me that it was the proper time to marry someone. They said, 'If you wait until you graduate from university, no desirable man will want to marry you because you will be too old.'"

Raihana didn't care about the social or financial background of her future husband; she just wanted to marry an educated man, someone who believed women were equal and would respect her as a human being. In her last year at university a young man from her village, Maqsood Rezayee, asked her to marry him. "It took me seven months to decide." Maqsood and Raihana had gone to school together and he was in his final year studying engineering at Kabul Polytechnic, a public university. "He kept messaging me and asking about my decision, and we shared our thoughts and ideas. I was worried about my decision and did not know if he was the right person for me because it is impossible to know someone just by talking to them on the phone. Even so, I could see that we had a lot in common and could have a happy life together."

Even today, many traditional Afghans would think it is terrible for a girl to chat with a boy on the phone. "They believe the family should decide about the marriage of their children, not the children. I felt I should decide whom to marry. Knowing someone's ideas and thoughts is essential before you marry them. Most Afghan men do not want freedom for women. They do not like independent women who argue for their rights. They like women who accept what the men want. I need to live with a man who believes in equality and respects women."

Raihana decided that Maqsood was the man she wanted to marry, and told her family, who were happy about her choice. The couple got engaged in 2013 and married four years later. "Maqsood is a supportive and lovely man. We have a precious little boy, Arsam, who is four now. Just like everyone else, our life has happy and challenging moments, but the good thing is that we both try to create a happy life for our family, and love each other."

All the students from Raihana's class at university had different dreams for the future. Some wanted to be prosecutors, or defense lawyers, or work in the Ministry of Foreign Affairs. Others wanted to apply for postgraduate degrees overseas. None imagined, however, that one day they might have to leave their country permanently. Raihana's brother Jawad decided to accept a place studying in Germany, and their paths diverged for a long time. For Raihana, however, the decision was simple: she wanted to become a judge.

"In law school, I noticed that it is not only our culture that discriminates against women. The discrimination in my country is systemic. It is inside our laws and our legal system. Afghanistan has a written constitution and written laws. Our family laws are old and the source of discrimination against women. For example, a man can divorce his wife for no reason. He does not even need to go to court. However, if a woman wants a divorce, she must have a legal reason for the divorce and prove it in front of a court. Similarly, a father can even marry his daughter to someone when she is under fourteen years old.

"Like family law, our criminal law had discriminatory articles. Fortunately, some of those articles were amended in recent years. According to Afghanistan's previous criminal law, if a man sees his wife with another man and kills his wife, the husband shall not be punished as a murderer. His punishment was much lower than that of a murderer. The case was not the same for women. If a woman saw her husband with another woman and killed him, then she was punished as a murderer."

Raihana wanted to challenge this discrimination. "I believed our laws were bad, but if we had judges who understood women, and who believe in equality and human rights, they can try to apply the law in a way that does not create so much harm to the parties."

Every two years the Afghanistan Supreme Court holds a national exam for the highest-performing students to train as future judges, and Raihana applied. The exam was delayed for a long time because of contested election results, but when Raihana was told she could sit for the test, her friends and family couldn't believe it. "Some said that under Islamic rules a woman should not be a judge, that only men can be judges. They did not know that we already had female judges in our courts."

Thousands of students from all over the country came to take the 2015 judicial exam. "When the results came out, I saw my name on the first page with a good grade. It was one of the most exciting days of my life," Raihana says. "More than sixty women passed the exam, which was a higher amount than any other year."

Classes started almost immediately, and Raihana plunged into two years of full-time judicial training. "Men and women were separated. There were two classes for women and five for men. Some of our lecturers were Supreme Court judges, and they were highly discriminatory against women. They said humiliating things to us; one of them said, 'You are here for nothing. Women cannot be judges. You are misusing your time. If I were a woman, I would prefer to sit at home, eat what my husband provides, and look after my children.'"

Women who had babies during the training were not allowed to take any time off, and one woman had to sit for an exam the day after giving birth. "It was clear that such pressures were put on women to stop us from continuing our studies and becoming judges."

When female students wrote a letter to the Supreme Court Judicial Training Department asking for childcare services, the head of the department brought the letter into the classroom and said, "Today, you ask us to build childcare for you! Tomorrow, you will ask for child delivery services! If you want to go home and care for your children, do so. We are not here to deliver your baby services."

Security was also becoming a greater challenge. In the two years that Raihana studied to become a judge, the number of bomb explosions in Kabul increased. The training was in Shirpoor, the area of Kabul where most foreign guesthouses and high officials' homes were located. One day Raihana had an exam, but as her car approached the building, she saw that the road was blocked and there were a lot of soldiers. They told her that a Taliban suicide bomber had attacked a guesthouse and killed a lot of people. Raihana had to walk past the scene of the attack to get to her building.

"I saw many dead and burned bodies. We had to walk in the blood of the innocent people that was running down the street. I don't know what I wrote on my exam that day, as I was totally distracted by thoughts about the people who had been killed."

Despite all the challenges, Raihana passed her course and was appointed as a judge by the Afghanistan Supreme Court and the Afghan president. But her happiness did not last long: The Supreme Court decided that all the new graduate judges had to begin work in the province they were born in. It was a decision that affected women judges in particular, as many had families in Kabul, and a woman couldn't travel or live alone in most parts of Afghanistan.

"The only way to continue our career was to ask the Supreme Court to change their decision. We all gathered in the Supreme Court for many days and stayed there from morning to night to talk with the chief justice, Mr. Halim. Unfortunately, the chief justice did not want to see or speak with us. We all sat on the floor in front of his office all day, and he never showed up. It felt awful that your organization does not want to hear your voice." The women met with members of parliament (MPs) to ask for their help, and Raihana and a colleague accompanied an MP to speak to the chief justice. "Again, the chief justice told us to stay out of his office. He talked with the member of parliament alone. Sitting outside his office door made me feel useless."

Finally, the women took the issue to the U.S. embassy in Kabul, which gave financial support to the Afghan Supreme Court, especially for judicial training. A few days later the Supreme Court changed its policy and said that female judges should work in provinces outside Kabul—but not necessarily those they were born in. Although not ideal, this meant that women could choose provinces that had better security or were closer to the city so that they could return home at night.

"It was the time to make a decision," Raihana says. The Supreme Court appointed her to work as a judge in the Court on the Elimination of Violence Against Women in her home province, Ghazni—but Ghazni was dangerous. In June 2016, the Taliban attacked the court building there and killed at least six people, including a judge. After discussing the situation with her family, Raihana decided to go to Herat province, which had better security and where she could live with her aunt. "It was hard to leave my family and go on my own. In Afghanistan, girls live with their parents until they get married, then with their husbands and family. So girls do not live on their own, but I had to leave my family because I did not want to give up my dream of being a judge."

Before going to Herat, Raihana had to go to Ghazni to arrange to transfer her job to Herat. "I could not go by car because the Taliban stopped vehicles on the road daily and searched for government officials. The new judges decided to go to Ghazni on a military helicopter, which could offer extra protection. That day I wore my long black clothes, covered my face, and left home. Dad and Mom prayed for me. Soon we all found ourselves in a military helicopter flying from Kabul to Ghazni. The helicopter flew with the doors open, and two soldiers sat behind massive guns pointing out the door, ready to fight. My colleagues and I were sitting opposite each other. The helicopter flew so close to the mountains I thought it would crash into the hill and we would die. When we arrived I went to my friend's house and stayed in town for three days to finalize transferring my job. Each day I went to work and I saw women who had covered their faces with the chadari coming to the court. I wished security was good enough in Ghazni so that I could work in that court and hear from those women."

One week later Raihana flew to Herat. "I dressed as I did in Kabul: a small headscarf with a top that reached my knees and ordinary pants. I had to wait for a taxi by the road, and while I stood there people were staring at me. Some cars stopped and asked me if I wanted to go with them. I couldn't understand their behavior. When I asked my taxi driver he said, 'If you want people to stop staring at you, you must wear the same clothes as the women here.' Women in Herat wear chadar namaz, which is a long hijab that covers the entire body from head to foot. If you wear different clothes, people stare in a way that makes you feel like you are wearing nothing."

The next day Raihana went to the court wearing official judge's clothes, but she noticed that all the women judges were wearing the same long hijab as the women in the city. "I don't like wearing a long black hijab. I wanted to wear my official clothes, but my female colleagues asked me to wear chadar namaz. They told me that if I did not wear it, I would be recognized very quickly by the Taliban, and it was unsafe."

Bowing to pressure, Raihana bought a black chadar namaz but found wearing it difficult. "I had to dedicate one of my hands to keeping it on. The women of Herat have effectively had one hand cut off. You have only one hand to do the rest of your work. During the three years I was in Herat, I never got used to wearing that hijab."

Raihana asked to be appointed to the Court for the Elimination of Violence Against Women, where there were six judges, including the head of the court, who was a man. All the other judges were recent graduates, "fresh, energetic, and ready to bring changes for the people."

"The procedure of the cases started with the police report of the violation and then went to the prosecutor's office for investigation. Following the prosecutor's investigation, the case was sent to the primary Court for the Elimination of Violence Against Women. After the administrative part of the court received the case, the head appointed two judges to work on it. One of the judges was responsible for reading, investigating if necessary, deciding, and writing the case. The other judge read the case once. On the day of the court hearing, the three judges decided on the case. To make a judicial decision, a majority must agree on the decision."

Each province had one primary court and one appeals court that dealt with cases of violence against women. If one of the parties disagreed with the decision of the appeals court, they could appeal the case in the Supreme Court in Kabul.

"The types of violence against women and their punishment were determined by law. The crimes of violence were murder, rape, forced suicide, underage marriage, the sale of women, preventing marriage, forced marriage, stopping women from the right to education and work, assault, harassment, and financial violence, including stopping a woman from ownership or [receiving an] inheritance, and some other crimes. There was a specific punishment for each crime; most punishments were imprisonment. The minimum imprisonment for a violent crime was three months, and the maximum was twenty years. Considering the aggravating and mitigating features, the judge could decide between the maximum and minimum punishment."

Both men and women can be victims of violence, but the Court for the Elimination of Violence Against Women only had jurisdiction over women victims.

"Before working at the court, I thought educated men would treat their wives better but many of the perpetrators I saw were educated men. Some were university professors. Also, not all of the perpetrators were male. There were many women, including mothers-in-law, sisters-in-law, and daughters-in-law, who were the perpetrators of violence. These cases did not only happen to poor people; many were from wealthy families."

Although some of the cases were minor, Raihana found most of the cases she dealt with overwhelming.

"Some of those cases, and the victims, remain with me forever. Fatima was a girl from a remote part of Herat. She lost her mom when she was young and she lived with her brothers before being married to a man in Herat city. After her marriage, she was violated harshly by her husband and her mother-in-law. They inflicted different punishments upon her, including biting her and not giving her food. They imprisoned her at home with no access to food for a long time until she died. The reason for their cruelty was that the husband thought she was not a virgin when he married her. When her brother understood his sister had died, he took the case to the court. Fatima was killed for nothing; her husband's belief about her virginity was wrong. Her beautiful, sad eyes stay in my mind."

Reported suicide was much higher among women in Herat than in any other part of Afghanistan, although Raihana says it's unclear whether this meant that more women died by suicide or whether it was just that more families in Herat, which was a liberal province, reported cases, as the stigma and shame were not so great as in other parts of the country. "Some women burned themselves; some ate chemicals or took overdoses of medicine. Some threw themselves off buildings. Those cases came before my court. According to the law, if a person violates a woman and, as a result of the violation, she kills herself, that person is responsible for her death. In some of those cases, both parties were the victims of poverty and social injustice. Poverty, illiteracy, having many children, having no access to social welfare, and having no income put the families under extreme mental pressure in ways that resulted in violence and then suicide."

The judges had to discuss the case together and reach a shared decision. The cases they disagreed about most often were those involving men who wanted to take second wives.

"According to family law, if a man wants to marry more than one woman, he has to have some specific issues, such as if the first wife cannot get pregnant. Also, the man has to be wealthy enough to support both women. According to the law on the elimination of violence against women, if a man marries for the second time without legal reason, it is considered violence against his first wife and is punishable by imprisonment."

This new law was highly controversial in Afghanistan, and religious people often railed against it as being un-Islamic. "I liked this article of law," Raihana says. "I wanted to punish those men who married for the second time, or more, against the law. Some of my colleagues disagreed with me and did not want to punish those men. They believed Islam allows men to marry four women at the same time, and why should laws or courts stop them? I, as a woman judge, believe that it is not justice to allow a man to marry more than one woman at the same time. It causes distress to women and their children. Unfortunately, in Herat, many men have more than one wife. Even some of the male judges wanted to marry for the second time."

During the time she lived in Herat, Raihana saw the security situation worsen in Afghanistan. She lived alone and told her neighbors that she was a nurse at the hospital while her husband, Maqsood, studied for a master's degree in Malaysia. Then in 2020 her son, Arsam, was born: "My life changed forever. My silent home was filled with the sound of a noisy baby. Being a mom is challenging, but it is a challenge that I love. Arsam brought me a depth of love that I had never felt, and I became more cautious and sensitive."

Now Raihana felt the pain of the women who separated from their husbands and had to give up their babies. Most women accepted violent partners, she realized, just because they did not want to lose their children. "I will never forget the women who came to the court to keep their children, but the law did not support them in that. Sometimes a judge has to follow the law against their own wishes."

In the year that Arsam was born the Supreme Court announced

that there were some provinces that had never had a female judge and asked women to consider taking up appointments there. Raihana knew that she was secure and relatively safe in Herat, but she wanted to help women in areas where there was even greater inequality. She asked to be transferred from Herat to Nangarhar.

Raihana says that Herat and Nangarhar are both considered major cities in Afghanistan, but they are culturally very different. Nangarhar, in the east of Afghanistan, is closer to Kabul and shares a border with Pakistan. "It was a stronghold for ISIS and the Taliban for many years before the Taliban took control in August 2021, making it unsafe for government officials, women, and minorities. It is a monocultural province, predominantly Pashtun, with Pashto as the main language." By contrast, Herat shares a border with Iran and is a multicultural city where most people speak Farsi and there are different ethnicities, including Tajiks, Pashtuns, Hazaras, and Arabs.

"I grew up in a remote village, lived in Kabul, Herat, and Nangarhar, and spent some time in Mazar-i-Sharif, but I never witnessed such strict restrictions against women as I did in Nangarhar," Raihana says. "People in Herat seemed more open compared to Nangarhar. Many women worked with the government and NGOs, and people were proud and willing for their women to work and girls to study. Many women worked in the Herat court for years, including judges, clerks, and administrators. In Nangarhar I was the only woman working in the court. In Herat women followed a dress code that covered their bodies but left their faces visible. Many young women did not follow this dress code and wore shorter clothes, similar to those in Kabul. People were open to changes. Women went to gyms, and driving for women was more common in Herat even than in Kabul. Restaurants were full of families, including men, women, and children, who could sit there openly. When people got married, they could choose to live separately from the boy's family, which was not common even in Kabul. In other parts of Afghanistan, they had to live with the boy's parents after getting married.

"In Nangarhar, few women worked with the government and NGOs. Most women wore chadari, covering their entire bodies, including their faces. Some women, especially students and those who worked, wore long black clothes and covered their mouths with a black mask, leaving only their eyes visible. People trusted religious schools more than governmental schools. These schools, run by religious leaders, had many students, including girls and boys, who learned fundamentalism and radicalism."

Crucially, "Herat was much more secure than Nangarhar, especially for a woman. There were targeted killings of government officials, especially in the last few years, but as a woman, I could live there by myself, something that would have been impossible in Nangarhar."

When Raihana submitted her request, the head of human resources at the Supreme Court told her: "I am a man from Nangarhar, but even I am afraid to go and work there. If you knew what it was like, you would not want to go. In addition to the Taliban, ISIS is very active, and they are the enemy of the Shi'as and Hazaras. A few months ago, ISIS killed many Hazara workers in a coal mine in Nangarhar. As a Hazara woman, going there is a big risk."

Raihana thought over his comments but did not change her mind. The Supreme Court agreed to the appointment and asked the Nangarhar court to give her a house inside the court grounds for greater security.

"On the first day when Maqsood and I went to the Nangarhar court, the chief justice of the Nangarhar appeals court welcomed us warmly and said he was happy to have a female judge in the Nangarhar court. He believed they needed more female judges to come and work in Nangarhar, especially in the Court for the Elimination of Violence Against Women."

One of the court staff, Wahidullah, showed Raihana the house she would live in. A small door opened into a driveway at the end of the court building, with six homes. The house Raihana was assigned had a huge yard and was surrounded by old trees, but it was clear that no one had lived in the building for years. "The house seemed very old and had wooden doors and windows. When Wahidullah opened the door and asked us to go in, I suddenly saw a snake escape and slither into a hole in the building next door. Maqsood and I were scared! Wahidullah said, 'Oh, you will get used to seeing snakes after a few months. Children here play with snakes all the time!'"

At work Raihana shared an office with two other judges, both men. On her first day one of them said, "I don't know why you chose to come here. I respect you as my sister, and want to advise you about some things. You speak Farsi, not Pashto, which is the language here. You are a Shi'a Muslim, but people in this province are Sunni. You are a Hazara and a woman. These things make you very vulnerable. I'm not sure people in this province will accept a female judge and, as a Hazara, you have a lot of enemies here. I don't think that you can continue to work in Nangarhar." Raihana says, "I knew he was right." Working in Nangarhar would not be easy, but she was at peace with her decision.

"From that day on, I breastfed my baby every morning, wore my long black hijab, covered my face, and left home for the court. For the few first days, everyone was silent when I entered my office, like they had turned to stone. The social segregation between men and women in the province caused both genders to be afraid and feel ashamed of each other. I could feel that my colleagues were praying not to have me in the office. When people came to the courtroom, they only greeted the men, as if I was not there. Women wearing burqas followed their men to the courtroom but never spoke, and no one asked them anything. Most of them entered the courtroom and left without saying a word. Women in Nangarhar had no voice."

On the day of her first sentencing Raihana saw two women enter the courtroom wearing burqas. When they saw Raihana they greeted her enthusiastically and introduced themselves. One was a defense lawyer and the other was a prosecutor, and they had arrived for the sentencing. "I was so grateful to meet women working in the justice sector in Nangarhar. We talked a lot, and I asked questions about the Nangarhar women's situation and their culture. They were pleased to have a woman in their court, and invited me to meet women from other sectors who were working for the Human Rights Department and women's support organizations."

The women came to a meeting organized by the chief justice. "They brought me beautiful flowers and many other gifts. They gave me makeup, headscarves, and perfume, and I still have a mirror that they gave me. We drank tea and ate dry fruit, and some of those ladies became my friends after that."

Later other families in the court cooked Raihana and her family a traditional Afghan dinner, qabuli, which is a rice dish with slow-cooked lamb, golden onions, glazed carrots, raisins, and toasted pistachios. The wife of the chief justice asked to be invited to Raihana's home, which she redecorated at her own expense. Raihana asked her husband, Maqsood, to leave and welcomed the ladies and their young children. "They all wore the burqa and removed them inside the house. We talked for more than two hours and drank tea. I asked them why they wore the burqa even when leaving home and coming the short distance from their house to mine. They said it was their culture. They never went out without wearing a burqa."

Raihana told them how hard she found it to wear the burqa. She explains, "The burqa is long and covers the entire body, including the face. It has very tiny holes in front of the eyes. Most of them are blue. When I came to Nangarhar, I wore this type of burqa for the first time. I could not breathe normally and could not see where I was walking. Before wearing a burqa, I could not imagine how hard it was to wear it because I saw women wearing it in the city all day. I would like to ask those men who make women wear a burqa to wear it once themselves and try to walk with it. Then they would understand women."

Every time Raihana traveled from Nangarhar to Kabul she had to wear the burqa to disguise her identity, but she longed for the day when she could travel freely and take it off. "You can't even see colors properly under a burqa. Women in Afghanistan do not even have the right to see the blue color of the sky or the green leaves on the trees."

After their first meeting, Raihana and the women at the court often visited each other's houses. "They were young and beautiful women with many children. They wished they were educated and were free to do whatever they wanted. They expected their daughters to continue their studies and be free. However, they had very restrictive ideas about life and women. They accepted most of the restrictions as natural and had no complaints. According to their ideas, it is unsuitable for women, especially young girls, to have mobile phones because they might speak to men." Among the six families living in the court compound, Raihana and the chief justice's wife were the only women with a husband who had only one wife. The other women all had husbands with two wives. "I could not understand how they could share their house and their husband."

Despite the restrictions, "Nangarhar welcomed me warmly, and I got used to living there quickly." Soon Raihana's male colleagues started to talk to her in the office, and Raihana felt free to argue with them about judicial decisions. Not long after that, the chief justice asked Raihana to visit his office, and said he had read her judgments and was pleased with her work. He asked the Supreme Court to appoint Raihana as the head of the primary Court for the Elimination of Violence Against Women, and they were happy to have a woman leader in Nangarhar.

In her new role, Raihana started to introduce some reforms. "Women whose cases came to the court did not show their faces during court meetings, and most did not speak. According to law, the judges must ensure the parties are who they claim to be. It was possible that the woman behind the burqa was not the real party in the case. I asked my colleagues why they did not ask women to show their faces in court. They said they were afraid of their men's reactions in case they thought they were just trying to see their wife's faces. After that, I told the parties that I am a woman, too, but I am not hiding my face in the courtroom. According to Islamic rules, a woman can show her face. Women who are the victims of violence or involved in the case must talk and show their faces. The parties accepted."

Sometimes a woman asked to speak to Raihana alone and would reveal some facts that had not been part of the initial investigation. "It proved how vital it is for a court to have judges from both genders. In traditional societies like Afghanistan, talking about sexual matters or sexual harassment is forbidden. Women would never share these things with a man, but they feel more comfortable sharing it with a woman."

In the office, Raihana's male colleagues often discussed issues relating to women with her. "Some did not like women working outside of the home. One man wanted to marry for the second time because he had many daughters but no son. Another colleague did not even take his wife out to let her buy what she needed. He preferred to go out and buy it for her. I challenged their beliefs, and some days our discussions lasted for hours. My point was, 'Why should women not work outside the home? I am a woman working with you in this office. Is it bad?' They said, 'Our relatives and families believe it is not proper. If our women worked, everyone would laugh at us and say we cannot pay for her needs.'"

The man who wanted to marry for the second time said that he loved his wife but that his friends and family asked him to marry another woman to produce sons. "In the office, other colleagues laughed at him too and said he was afraid of his wife, which is why he could not marry for the second time. In Afghanistan, people interfere in other's lives most of the time. They joke about each other, and pressure other people to do what they want."

One day the man who did not want his wife to leave home to go shopping decided to buy her a gold ring. He told Raihana that he had traveled miles to the shop and then when he got back home his wife said she did not like the ring. He took it back, but when he returned with another ring she said it did not fit. After traveling back and forth to the shop five more times his wife eventually chose a ring. "I asked him why he didn't take his wife to the shop to choose her own ring. He said, 'In our family women do not go shopping. My people see it as improper for a woman to go shopping.'" In Afghanistan, especially in provinces like Nangarhar, people lived collectively, and communal opinion was very important. "Individuals live according to what their community thinks, rather than their own wishes."

In Nangarhar, nothing seemed to have changed in twenty years, and women had little freedom despite all the international funding and projects that were started to improve women's rights. In other parts of Afghanistan, however, like Kabul, Bamiyan, Mazar-i-Sharif, Herat, and even the village of Mahajireen, where Raihana grew up, there were traces of social and cultural progress.

"My family left Mahajireen in 2007. I visited my village nine years later, and I could see the difference. When I left my village, women's lives were very restricted. They did not ride a bike or drive a car. Young girls did not talk to boys. The family decided about their children's marriages. But by 2016, driving was normal, and even necessary, for women in the village. Girls rode bikes. People could decide to marry for themselves. Girls had mobile phones and wore short clothes. No one wore a burqa or chadar namaz in my village. All the girls went to school and had dreams for their future."

Raihana says she is not sure why some parts of Afghanistan moved forward and embraced democracy, but the Pashtun areas, like Nangarhar, Kandahar, Paktiya, Paktika, and elsewhere, did not.

"Women in Herat, where I worked previously, were more outspoken and keen to defend their rights. For example, the Court for the Elimination of Violence Against Women in Herat ruled on many cases related to assault, financial abuse, beating, harassment, cases against men who married with second wives against civil law restrictions, and many other minor cases of violence against women before the court. There were terrible cases, from murder to rape to suicide killings, but the majority of the cases were related to minor crimes. In most of those minor cases, women themselves brought their cases to the court and followed the process. However, in Nangarhar, most of the cases during the time that I worked there were murder. After the victim was murdered, their family brought the case to the court. There were cases about harsh beatings or rape, but men pursued those cases, and women covered in the chadari followed the men into the court. In my year in Nangarhar court I did not see a single case regarding the second marriage of a man, financial abuse, or many other minor acts of violence against women which were common cases in Herat. This does not mean that these crimes never existed; it means women did not know that they were a crime."

Yet, despite all the challenges, Raihana says she loved working and living in Nangarhar. "I could see how effective my work was in the Nangarhar court compared to Herat. Every time I noticed women coming to the court, they were happy to see a woman judge there. They could freely share their concerns with me as a woman."

After a while, the chief justice asked Raihana and her husband, Maqsood, to teach English to the judges' children in their free time. "We welcomed the idea. We dedicated one of our spare rooms for the English classes. Almost eleven children registered for the course. Maqsood taught them most of the time, and I taught them one day a week. The children loved those classes."

Her neighbors were good, kind people. "I enjoyed sitting and talking with them whenever I could. In one conversation I asked them to promise me that they would support their daughter's education. I asked them not to allow their men to stop their daughters from going to school. One woman said, 'I want my daughter to be a judge in the future and work in the court. Before you came here, we thought women could not be judges. You are a good example for our daughters to continue their education for a better future.'"

Raihana's happy moments in Nangarhar did not last long, however. By 2021 the U.S.-Taliban peace negotiations, the Doha Accords, seemed to be going in the Taliban's favor, and security was deteriorating day to day. "In August 2021, our cities collapsed to the Taliban one after another. Even then, however, we could not imagine that we would lose everything, and the Taliban would take power." When that day came Raihana and her family were left afraid and alone. "The Taliban destroyed everything, including the judicial system that we worked for. They wiped out the Courts for the Elimination of Violence Against Women. As I left my country all I had was the hope that one day my colleagues and I could come back and start again."

14.

Tayeba: The Promise of Return

TAYEBA PARSA ALREADY UNDERSTOOD WHAT IT MEANT TO return. She was also from the Hazara people but, unlike Raihana, grew up in Iran and returned to Afghanistan only after the fall of the Taliban. "Iran and Afghanistan are very different. Iran seems very modern compared to Afghanistan." Afghanistan seemed to have far fewer facilities and far older ideas—and returning exiles were mocked for their "foreign accents" and the different way they spoke Farsi or Dari. "Leaving Iran for Afghanistan was a huge adjustment," Tayeba says, "but I was young, and I was happy because I had the opportunity to go to university." Life in Afghanistan under the Taliban had been virtually impossible, but life for Afghan immigrants in Iran was difficult as well. As Raihana explained, even the most educated Afghan men were forced to take manual jobs.

"In Iran my father worked doing embroidery on sewing machines. When he could not pay his workshop expenses he brought his machine home and worked there. My eldest sister also learned to do embroidery, and they worked together at home. After she got married at the age of nineteen, my other elder sisters learned to do that. Gradually our home turned into an embroidery workshop. My mother, my younger sister, and even my seven-year-old little brother and I would help them by drawing patterns on fabrics, ironing, removing extra threads, and scissoring. It was like a factory. Everybody had their job. We would go to school and come back to our duties. Life as an Afghan in Iran was so difficult because they all are laborers. We would all work and pay all of our income to the owner of the apartment. But we were proud that we could work and support our family—and we learned that women can work as well as men."

When Tayeba was in eleventh grade her sister returned home from school one day crying. Tayeba's sister was in twelfth grade, and she said that the principal had announced that there was a new order stating Afghans were not allowed to study above eleventh grade anymore.

In light of such devastating news, Tayeba's family believed the best solution for their family was to return to their homeland.

The Parsa family crossed the border together and reached Herat. The family was supposed to stay for three days while they waited for a flight to Kabul, but the only accommodation available was in a dirty, run-down hotel, and Tayeba and her sister felt the fear and insecurity on the streets whenever they ventured out. The city was crowded and jostling, and the eyes of strangers seemed to follow them everywhere. "I was seventeen years old and my sister was fourteen but tall. Every time we went out it seemed like every man stared at us because we didn't cover our faces," Tayeba says.

Tayeba's parents quickly came to the conclusion that it was too dangerous to stay in Herat, and decided to hire a taxi to take them to Kabul by road instead. If staying in Herat was dangerous, however, crossing the country on Afghanistan's poorly maintained highways was also extremely risky. Everyone they encountered was a threat.

"We got in the taxi and the driver was a Pashtun. He stared at us in the mirror, *really* stared. Maybe it was habit, or perhaps we looked a little bit liberal because we didn't cover our faces. But in the end we realized that he was a good man."

One night, outside Kandahar, the driver pulled up by the roadside and said that it was too dark and dangerous to drive any farther. He led the family into a huge hall where men slept in one room and women in another. As there was no electricity, the driver handed Tayeba's mother a flashlight. Then he said, "Lock the door, and do not open it during the night for any reason."

The drive was dusty and long, but after three days of fearing every roadblock and stranger, Tayeba's family reached Kabul and drove to the Hazara part of the city, where they had left their home twenty-five years earlier. Everything in the city was dirty and covered in soot from the coal fires used for cooking and heating. Street children sat, disconsolate, at crossroads, begging for change and crowding around car windows. When they found their old house Tayeba could see that the traditional red mud, plaster, and straw building was almost falling down due to the years of decay and fighting that had torn the city apart. The family had an old-fashioned Afghan toilet that was a hole in the ground, and cooked in a large kitchen with kerosene burners because there was no electricity. Like all houses in Kabul, they had a well for water, but as the well dried up they had to dig deeper and deeper, until the family eventually paid a private company for water deliveries. Tayeba's mother cried when she saw how dirty and decrepit their old home had become, with one of the rooms almost totally destroyed by a rocket attack. The only small saving grace was that half of the building was still occupied by Tayeba's uncle and aunt, who rushed out to warmly welcome them home.

"One benefit was that we had a huge yard," Tayeba says. In keeping with Islamic tradition, Afghan houses usually presented blank walls to the street so that outsiders could not see the women within, but often had beautiful enclosed courtyards. Tayeba's yard was large, with mature trees offering shade. Later, when Tayeba became a judge, the family gave their half of the original house to their uncle and built a new, more modern house in the yard, filling it with rugs and furniture that Tayeba bought in Iran.

Tayeba's mother was unhappy and unsettled in their new life in Kabul. She had left three married daughters behind in Iran and worried for them, as well as for the future of Tayeba and her sister in Afghanistan. But Tayeba's father forged ahead, taking Tayeba first to the Ministry of Education to certify her Iranian education certificates and then to the Ministry of Higher Education so she could apply to take the university entrance exam, the Kankor.

Tayeba studied the new Afghan textbooks, which she had not had access to in Iran, and took the exam. She was admitted to study *shari'a* education at Al-Beroni University, a prestigious public university, outside Kabul. She had wanted to study civil law, so at first couldn't decide whether to accept the place—but her father urged her to accept. In the era before the Taliban, Hazara people were often not allowed to go to university, and during the Taliban regime girls were not allowed to study at all. Tayeba's father told her to take all the opportunities she could while they were available to her, and although it was highly unusual for a girl to live away from her family, Tayeba was happy to go to a university in a dominantly Tajik area: "The teachers encouraged me, especially when they realized that I was a good student and good at Arabic."

Women were not allowed to study Islamic jurisprudence at the time, but Tayeba's teachers at Al-Beroni University allowed her to take classes in *shari'a* law. Later, however, traveling back and forth by road became too unsafe and she had to transfer to Kabul University. Despite its prestigious reputation, at Kabul

University the teachers told Tayeba she was only allowed to study Islamic education.

"There are many similarities between Sunni and Shi'a Islam, but sometimes I did not believe in what I was studying. As a Hazara, I am a Shi'a Muslim, and Islamic *shari'a* law and education in Afghanistan are based upon Sunni teachings. In *shari'a* law schools we study four divisions of Sunni: Hanafi, Shafi'i, Hanbali, Maliki, although Sunni Afghans are all Hanafi. So there is no Maliki, Hanbali, and Shafi'i in Afghanistan. But there are no Shi'a teachings even though we have a large Shi'a population in Afghanistan. When they teach different ideas of different divisions of Islam they do not mention Shi'a's ideas at all. It makes you feel as if they do not accept you, and that even as a Muslim they consider you a pagan. Professors always were surprised at seeing me in the class because Hazaras can be recognized by their faces. So they knew I was a Shi'a and wondered, 'What is this pagan doing here?'"

In time, however, Tayeba was admitted into some civil law classes at Kabul University and applied to the civil law school. Judges in Afghanistan could study either civil law or *shari'a* law, but they were expected to work with both when they graduated. Despite her hopes, however, Tayeba was not admitted to the civil law school, and had to continue to study civil law in her own time.

"I did not like the classes that were about teaching *shari'a* principles in primary schools, but I liked the law classes better. I started to read the civil laws of Afghanistan, which were based upon the Napoleonic Code." Tayeba bought her own law books and used all the information and resources available in Kabul from the influx of international organizations. In *shari'a* classes, however, she struggled.

"The *shari'a* law curriculum was old and out of date, and the professors were imams who didn't take girls seriously. They'd been pressured by international organizations into accepting women into their courses, but they only wanted us to learn basic edicts about our personal lives and dissuaded us from joining the judiciary."

Men and women studied separately, but the women who did get admitted to law school were usually successful, Tayeba says, because they studied harder and were twice as motivated as the men. As both a woman and a Hazara, Tayeba faced double discrimination. In the university, just as in all areas of Afghan life, the old ethnic divisions played out, with infighting between Pashtun and Tajik professors.

"In Iran my teachers liked me, one even hugged me when I came first as the top student among twenty schools. But in Afghanistan I soon realized that some of the professors did not like me. The professors were all men, and they thought it was ridiculous that they had to teach a Shi'a student. One professor often insulted me and gave me lower grades. The dean of the law school told me that I could ask for a formal review of my grades, but I was afraid of that professor. "

Tayeba was now an Afghan living in her own country, but in many ways she felt more discriminated against than when she was growing up in Iran. "Sometimes I felt incredibly sad when I was studying at university. The dean of the Law Department really believed in me, and encouraged me, though. He was a Pashtun man, but I won his respect in my third class at law school when he asked a question relating to Arabic that only I knew the answer to. After that he spoke up for me and supported me."

Later in her career, taking the *shari'a* route into law would seem like a disadvantage, but at the time *shari'a* law graduates were more commonly accepted into the judiciary, while civil law graduates often chose to work in higher-paid jobs with international organizations. "Now secular law school graduates find it easier to get scholarships and retrain overseas, but at the time there were only four secular law graduates in my judicial training class of twenty-five. It was difficult for secular law graduates to find work in civil courts, family courts, or commercial courts. They could only work in criminal courts."

In her judicial training Tayeba learned about both secular and *shari'a* law—although in practice *shari'a* law was not often implemented. "Secular law dominated, but we were allowed to use Islamic jurisprudence if we could not find a rule or order in our codes that were translated from the European codes."

Islamic jurisprudence studies the verses of the Quran that discuss the fundamental principles of a contract, like hiring an attorney, renting, or selling, as well as what are considered crimes in Islam, including adultery, same-sex relationships, robbery, drinking alcohol, and falsely accusing a person of adultery.

Although Afghan law appeased the imams by stating that crimes specifically mentioned in the Quran would be punished according to Islam, it also stated that other crimes would be tried and punished according to secular law. "It was a way of deceiving clerics and allowing the judiciary to apply the Napoleonic Code," Tayeba says, and adds that she did not mete out any of the Islamic punishments applicable to a criminal court, like cutting off hands or lashing.

After two years of judicial training, Tayeba got the highest grade in the entrance exam for the judiciary and was one of the top ten students, who were permitted to work in the Supreme Court assisting more senior judges. She chose to work in the civil division of the Supreme Court.

"I wanted to avoid working in criminal law. I didn't trust the criminal justice system; all areas of law in Afghanistan are corrupt, but in criminal law that meant putting innocent people in prison."

Tayeba joined the civil division and worked there for a year writing up reports of cases and summarizing court decisions made in the primary courts, the appeals courts, and the Supreme Court. After a year, newly qualified judges moved up to a role in a primary court, and Tayeba chose commercial court.

Each morning she got up before dawn to pray and read the Quran. Then she ate a small breakfast of cheese with raisins and drank some sweet tea. Most people in Afghanistan do not sweeten their tea, but Tayeba liked to add sugar to hers.

After breakfast Tayeba's driver, who was also a typist in the office, would arrive and take her to work. Once she got there she would eat a second breakfast and take her seat in the room she shared with two other women judges. Each woman had a large wooden desk and a leather chair, and usually a flask of tea. During the day the judges would often conduct hearings in the office, under the direction of the chief judge, rather than using the large courtroom.

Slowly life was opening up for the women of Afghanistan. When work finished at 4:00 p.m. Tayeba sometimes went to the gym to exercise—although at the time this was still unusual, so she didn't talk about it very much. She also tried to learn to swim at the swimming pool, but learning as an adult was daunting and difficult, and eventually she gave up. Although life still revolved mainly around the family, women got together with their friends more often to talk, and once a month Tayeba met up with other women judges and former classmates to go to a good restaurant where they could eat and chat. In 2007 the United States decided to provide more economic support to Afghanistan, creating a commercial banking sector, improving infrastructure, building business parks, and giving grants to private enterprises. International money began flooding into the country and, over the course of the next seven years, the average income in Afghanistan would rise fivefold.[7]

Kabul was turning into a boomtown. Shiny new malls were popping up everywhere, but Tayeba noticed they were full of cheap Chinese goods and preferred to buy better-quality things from Iran. More often than not she finished work and went straight home to eat, and then wrote up her cases until late into the night. When she decided to study for a master's degree, she often stayed up reading until 2:00 a.m. before turning off the light.

By Afghan standards, Tayeba married late, which was frowned upon and considered both subversive and extremely risky. "I waited until I met the right person. I didn't care about pressures from society. My father didn't put pressure on me." When another family suggested a marriage with a man who was considered a good match, Tayeba's mother and sisters encouraged her to accept, but her father allowed Tayeba to choose—and she decided to turn down the proposal. "It was regarded as a very good proposal, but I thought, 'I don't want to marry him,' because so much of my character was formed by being a judge and working in the law and I believed that someone who had no experience with that could not be a good match." Tayeba's father told her, "In your work you make decisions about other people's lives, so I don't want to make a decision about your life. You are free to do anything, but be careful because in Afghanistan we have strong traditions."

The man Tayeba chose, Wahid, is a distant relative, and they met for the first time when he came to her house with some family. "I had a strong feeling in my heart the first time I saw her," he says. He had studied law, and a year later he arranged to come back to ask her about becoming a judge. Tayeba laughs when she remembers this. "Was that for real?" she asks him, and he admits that he just wanted to see her again. After their second meeting Wahid sent his aunt to ask Tayeba to marry him. She refused. For two years Wahid continued to send messages through his family, asking Tayeba to marry him—and Tayeba continued to refuse.

Eventually he told her, "I will wait for you for five years, or however long, until you agree." His persistence won her over, and eventually Tayeba accepted.

"I resisted until I met the right person. Wahid was a law graduate and I still think my character is about 90 percent lawyer. All of my achievements are legal, so I can't share my enjoyment of them with someone who doesn't know anything about the law."

Wahid says he wants people to know that as well as her considerable achievements as a judge, Tayeba is a good wife, a good mother, and a good friend (and also an excellent cook).

Tayeba says, "I dedicated my life to my job. My relatives, and other people, used to gossip and say, 'Tayeba didn't get married, Tayeba is still single.' My relatives regarded me as an unsuccessful woman who could not get married. That is why getting married and having children was so important to me. I had to prove that I was not a failure as a woman."

At work, Tayeba was now a judge in the Kabul commercial court, which was extremely busy because all commercial and political activity was in Kabul. "Some of the judges in the provinces had hardly any cases. In some provinces the government would send a judge to an area controlled by the Taliban to try and show they were in control—but there would be no cases because people would know not to take any cases to those courts, and the judge would only attend court to sign in once a week and then leave. They were scared."

Even in her first few days on the job Tayeba noticed huge corruption in the courts. "Senior judges believed they could deceive me because I was only twenty-four. In some cases there was obvious evidence that they were ignoring, and it was clear that the judge was taking money to favor one party over the other."

Tayeba considered whether to stay or leave. But she decided that she could ensure that there was some justice in at least the cases that she was involved in by staying and doing her job honestly. During her first month in the court Tayeba worked under an honest chief judge, but he was soon replaced by someone corrupt who would make life very difficult for Tayeba for more than two and a half years. That chief judge often tried to force the panel of three judges sitting on a case to rule dishonestly in favor of one of the parties. "He realized that he could not force me," Tayeba says. "He abused his authority. Then he would try to deceive me—but again he realized that I am determined and would not change my mind."

Tayeba gives an example of a case where she wrote up her opinion and gave it to the chief judge. He fobbed her off, saying, "I know you are a very talented judge and I don't need to read your opinions." Tayeba reminded him that, as chief judge, he still had to either agree or dissent from the opinion and then sign off on it, but the report sat untouched on his desk for five months. Eventually, Tayeba believes, he received the bribe he was looking for, and he signed off on the case—but in doing so he besmirched the name of the honest judges involved in the case by arguing to the parties involved that he needed a bigger bribe to pay off the others (payments they did not know about and never received). "He would bargain for more money and, of course, he would lie that he had to pay his colleagues' share. I heard all those rumors."

In another instance Tayeba was working on a case involving subcontractors who were renting stores in a market. Tayeba reviewed the case and disagreed with the conclusion the other subordinate judge on the case had come to. "He came to my office, told everyone else to leave, closed the door, and shouted, 'How dare you review my opinion! Who are you, you Hazara girl!" He told me that Hazaras never had any power in Afghanistan—we were the lowest of the low, we were poverty-stricken.

"When I saw that he was trying to frighten me, I went to the door and opened it. He came after me, grabbed the handle of the door, and said, 'What are you going to do about it?' Then he came very close to me and hissed, 'What are you going to do if I do something to you?' And then he left. I burst into tears. It was such a shock. But I didn't cry in front of my colleagues. I insisted on my opinion, and the chief judge assigned another judge to the case. When he realized that my opinion was still different from the new judge's, he reassigned me and took me off the case."

In each case Tayeba felt increasing pressure to give in to her boss and agree to judgments she knew were wrong. Sometimes when she disagreed with the chief judge's wishes he tried to get her recused from a case, breaking regulations stating that a judge could only be recused from a case within forty-eight hours of being assigned to it. In another case he intervened on behalf of a defendant who had to pay back a loan to a government bank. The law stated that the defendant could pay back the loan in a maximum of nine installments, but the chief judge concocted a decision with another judge to say that the defendant could pay the loan back over a period of forty years. "Forty years!" Tayeba exclaims. Feeling more and more coerced to agree to the verdict, Tayeba booked a sudden visit to her family in Iran. "I told him that I would review the case and give him my decision on Thursday, but that morning I flew to Iran instead. I escaped from signing that verdict." But Tayeba could not evade the chief judge forever. While she was gone the colleague who had handed in Tayeba's request for time off was pressured into accepting a reassignment to another court, but when Tayeba decided to ask for a reassignment for herself, her request was denied.

Events seemed to have reached a crisis point. Would Tayeba cave under the pressure and turn a blind eye to corruption? How could she go on and forge an honest career? "The chief justice didn't allow me to go to another court, so I decided to leave the judiciary. It was a huge decision, but the only one I could make. But before I could enact it, the president of Afghanistan changed—and our new president, Ashraf Ghani, asked the judiciary to change the three judges of the primary commercial court, including the head of our court."

Tayeba's nemesis was gone, but while the new chief judge made decisions that were more in line with the law, she could see that the problems were endemic. "The system was still corrupt. The new chief judge came and appointed other judges who were his friends. They tried to issue more justified court decisions, but they would still sell them. They would ask for bribes from a party in the case, and the chief judge would ask his own judges to sign [off on] those cases, but he also asked for my opinion in every case because all of his judges were new to commercial court."

Despite her experience, Tayeba could see that she was often passed over for promotions to permanent senior roles in the judiciary. More broadly, women judges were usually assigned to ad hoc or temporary roles, and often ended up helping more inexperienced men who were appointed as their bosses. "The appointing authority could sell permanent positions to corrupt judges, and corrupt judges were mostly men. Women were rarely corrupt—although I have no explanation for that."

The work was not only frustrating but also dangerous. The dramatic rise in investment in Afghanistan had led to an equally dramatic rise in organized crime. Many of the defendants who appeared in commercial court had connections to the mafia, Tayeba says. Those connections stretched deep into the judiciary itself, as well as parliament and the Taliban. Such men often followed her home and either threatened her or tried to bribe her. "One man followed me home when I was building our new house, and he said, 'I see you are doing construction. I can help you with that.'"

After five and a half long years, Tayeba finally heard that she would be offered the job of chief judge of the primary commercial court. Her colleagues crowded around to congratulate her, and even her boss was keen to share the good news. "I was cautious," Tayeba says. "I wanted to wait for the official letter." Sure enough, the next day someone came along and introduced Tayeba to the new chief judge—a man from another province who was the same age as her and who had no experience in commercial court. Tayeba asked her boss what had happened and why she had missed out. He confirmed that it had been decided to give her the role, but at the last moment the appointing authority got cold feet. "They said I was too young, and commercial court was a place that had cases involving senior figures, even parliamentarians. They said only a man, or an older chief justice, could handle it. But when the new chief judge came he was young, too, and he had no experience. I spent all of my time helping him to understand his job."

After that disappointment, Tayeba was reassigned to a public rights division court, which saw very few cases—though, Tayeba says, "I was happy because I had enough time to study." Tayeba was paying privately to study for a master's degree after two older colleagues had persuaded the chief judge to remove her name from the list for a scholarship and add themselves instead. Now, at least her work in public rights court gave her time to write her thesis.

Tayeba worked in the public rights division for two years and was then reassigned to civil court, where she worked for a further two years. "That was a very good experience because it was a court that was not corrupt. Finally I was assigned to the commercial division of the appellate court for Kabul province, and that was the last court that I worked in before the Taliban took back control of Afghanistan."

Tayeba often looks back on her work in the Afghan judiciary and wonders if her efforts were futile. In her time as judge, Tayeba was a trailblazer for young women, lobbying successfully for more women to be appointed to courts such as commercial court, writing her own judgments on a computer rather than relying on a typist or a scribe and encouraging other judges to do the same, and becoming fluent in English, which often was important in complicated commercial disputes. Even so, she reflects, "My work was not important to people higher up. Higher authorities were not aware of the situation in primary courts. In the primary courts, judges did whatever they wanted, and there was no system. One court could see fifty cases every month. That's a lot, but the chief judge did not complain because he needed more cases—which really meant that he needed more money that he raised corruptly from the parties involved. He did not care if we assessed the cases properly or not."

Even when Tayeba did deliver an honest ruling, her efforts were often immediately overturned on appeal. "It was so disappointing. One case I ruled on involved a butcher against a parliamentarian. The butcher had supplied meat to a wedding hall owned by the parliamentarian for a year," and the parliamentarian had not paid. "But the parliamentarian was a powerful person. He would not take part in the case and never came to the hearings, but when I was assigned to that case, I made him come and, finally, I ruled against him. I was so happy because there was clear evidence, but when it went to the next court, it was reversed easily. It meant that my work was useless. It was so disappointing and tiring—but I was working until the end to try and bring reforms."

In truth, Tayeba was working even beyond the end. "When I arrived in Warsaw [after being evacuated from Afghanistan in 2021] I received a call from one of the parties in my last case asking me why I hadn't issued my judgment in the case. I told him that I had written up my opinion but the Taliban had taken over before it could be submitted. He said, 'I gave $10,000 to one of the clerks. The clerk told me he would give it to you, and you would decide in my favor!'" Ten thousand dollars is a life-changing amount of money in Afghanistan, Tayeba says—it's one year's salary for a judge. The clerk knew that Tayeba had found in favor of the man who paid the bribe because he had printed out her judgment and read it. Then he took the bribe and bought a house. Tayeba notes wryly that Afghanistan's corruption had even followed her to Poland.

PART THREE

Judges in Exile

15.

Somebody's Else's Shoes

THE WOMEN JUDGES ARRIVED IN POLAND VIA UZBEKISTAN and Georgia, and upon landing in Poland each was quarantined for COVID-19 for fifteen days before being taken to another hotel and then transferred to Warsaw. Tayeba's flight was the first to arrive, and when she landed at the airport Anisa Dhanji and Vanessa Ruiz called her to say that neither of them had slept the night before while they waited to hear that she was safe. Tayeba also read a text from her husband saying that he was with her father and that neither of them had yet been able to board a plane: "We are still waiting, we didn't fly, there is no place to sleep, there is nothing to eat." As Tayeba's father was diabetic, her husband had asked a soldier to give them some chocolate. Tayeba texted back and said, "Don't worry. You will come here, and it is safe. I arrived this morning, and we are in a very beautiful area. Everything is green."

Tayeba's father and husband finally got on a plane and arrived later, with some of the other judges. Tayeba's husband didn't have a passport, and she feared that he would be sent back to Afghanistan, but he was only delayed while the airport police took his fingerprints and then sent him on to the refugee facility. When Tayeba saw the bus arriving, she rushed to the window and saw her father. "I started to cry, and then my father started crying too. Later on everyone told me, 'Your father was crying in the bus. We were so happy because we were free and safe.'"

When Nafisa Kabuli landed in Poland in late August, her shoes were falling apart. After days of traipsing around the dusty streets of Kabul the sides were coming away, and she had to grip the shoes with her toes to keep them from falling off when she walked.

Seeing how little Nafisa and the other eight women judges had upon their arrival in Poland—each had been able to carry only a small bag—one of the first things lawyer Anna Kruszewska organized was a collection of secondhand shoes and clothing. Having played a huge role in the evacuation of the women to Poland, Anna was now completely committed to helping them settle into their new lives. Nafisa says, "Anna brought a few different boxes of shoes. But I was so upset, I threw the boxes to one side and said: 'I have bad shoes, torn apart and unwearable, but I cannot wear other people's secondhand shoes. I *cannot* go through these boxes and find a pair of secondhand shoes to wear.'"

To her credit, Nafisa says, Anna completely understood the meaning behind her words. She gathered up the boxes of shoes and arranged to give the women judges gift cards to take to a store to buy a new wardrobe. "I can only thank Anna for understanding in that moment and respecting my dignity."

"They arrived with only the clothes they were standing up in," Anna Kruszewska says. "I was concerned with meeting their very basic needs—and I was not aware of the cultural differences and how much they really matter." Customs widely accepted in Europe and the United States, like passing on previously used baby clothes, were often greeted with dismay by the Afghan women judges.

Money was scarce, and a group consisting of Anna, her Polish friends, Polish NGOs, the women judges of the IAWJ, and Jewish Humanitarian Response were often paying for accommodations, food, and clothing themselves. "For us the most important thing was to address their needs. But they didn't understand what was realistic and unrealistic—and we didn't understand that as well as addressing their physical needs we needed to help them uphold their dignity."

As autumn turned into winter, the judges needed to buy new coats, for example, but when Anisa Rasooli returned from the store with an expensive little jacket that used up her entire clothing allowance, Anna realized she had not explained the clothing budget very well. "A lot of moments like that were challenging," Anna says. "The women had gone from being the most senior figures in Afghanistan to penniless refugees overnight—and it was a huge mental transition. It was very difficult."

As the months passed it became obvious that few countries in the world were prepared to help the Afghan women judges. The women of the IAWJ were struck by the willingness of Poland to take them in, and the personal sacrifices Polish people were prepared to make to house and look after them.

"For us it is like helping our grandparents," Anna says. "We were torn apart by both the Nazis and the Soviets, mistreated and killed. Terrible, terrible things happened in Poland. It's not something that is deep in the mists of history for us—it's only a few years ago. During the evacuation of the judges someone sent me a photo of one of the women's houses, which had a mark on it made by the Taliban to signify that a person they wanted to persecute lived there—and it clicked immediately in my head that is what the Nazis did in Poland to Jewish people. I thought, 'Oh, no, I know these pictures. I remember these stories. No way am I going to see this and not help.'"

In a country that had little experience with mass immigration or refugees, Anna was impressed by the uncomplaining way an official at the Ministry for Foreign Affairs would stay up to 3:00 a.m. to issue documents, or a lawyer would offer to give up his apartment for an entire year so that one of the judges and their family could live there. Most people, including the judges themselves, believed that Poland was only a short-term destination, but while they waited for visas to other countries, the months turned into years, bogged down in a grindingly slow immigration process. Anna says that the strain of holding together the loosely assembled voluntary coalition started to show. "We thought that they'd be taken in by the U.S., the U.K., or one of the big Western countries with a number of ties with Afghanistan. But in time it became quite apparent that those countries didn't feel responsible for them, to be honest. So they spent way more time in Poland than they thought they would."

For Anisa Rasooli that wait lasted almost two years. "When our plane landed in Poland we thought we might be staying for a few days or weeks, like people had done in other places such as Greece or the UAE. It was during COVID, so we were moved to a camp first, but then after two weeks officers from the Polish border force arrived and told us we need to apply for asylum." Anisa explained that it had never been their plan to seek asylum in Poland—their final destination was to be with their friends in the United States. The border force officer shrugged and said, "Well, you caught the wrong plane, and it didn't work out very well for you. But wherever you go you need a legal status, so you have to apply for asylum."

Anisa and the other eight Afghan women judges and their families applied for asylum, the start of a long process. "For the first few months we were guarded by police, because they were worried the Taliban would find us and kill us even in Europe," Anisa says. The women received some funding from the Polish government but were moved from hotel room to hotel room. "We couldn't settle into a regular life, or even cook our own food." Eventually Anisa and her family found an apartment.

The judges from the IAWJ helped the women find a Polish lawyer, Agata Kalemba, and start their U.S. immigration claim, but again the process was long and complicated—especially as the women were now technically living in a safe country. Anisa could see other Afghan refugees settling into life in Poland, learning the language, finding a proper place to live, and even starting new jobs—but she had been told by her lawyer to do none of those things, as evidence that they were living a settled life in Poland would jeopardize their U.S. claim.

After eighteen months the situation reached a crisis point. The Polish government had been providing temporary funding for Afghan refugees but now said that funding would end, and for the Afghan women judges there was still no U.S. visa in sight. Anisa says, "Our landlord told us the lease for our apartment had ended and we would have to move out, but it was very difficult to find another place to live, as most landlords wanted to see proof that one of us was employed—which of course we weren't."

Anisa says those days were the most difficult in her life. "We were stuck in Poland, we couldn't travel anywhere, but we also couldn't stay in the same apartment." With the help of some funding from her friends in the United States, Anisa and her family of ten moved into a hotel, where they rented four tiny efficiency units for three months.

"They were so small we could we could barely cook there. We couldn't fit everyone in one [unit], but we could all fit in two [units] when we wanted to get together to eat."

The hotel owner told them that they had to pay their rent in advance. If it was not paid on the day it was due, he would turn off the electricity. If it was not paid the day after it was due he would lock the door. If it was not paid three days after the due date, he would throw all their belongings out of the window. Anisa sighs, "Somehow we managed to tolerate the situation, trying to stay calm as our friends in the U.S. told us to be patient, that it took time to get visas because there were so many people to process, but one day—one day—it would be resolved."

Anisa's struggles with the hotel owner seemed symbolic of the complicated reality the judges were experiencing in Poland. All of the women understood the crucial, indeed lifesaving support Anna Kruszewska, her many and varied friends, and indeed the Polish government had given them. Out on the street, though, they felt less welcomed by ordinary people and were subject to hostility, racism, and xenophobia, particularly from older people. "They were like, 'We are Polish, we just want Polish people,'" Anisa says.

Nafisa Kabuli agrees that although her family appreciated all the help they received from the Polish government, "the people of Poland were very prejudiced against us. They were so unkind. I have very bad memories. For example, when we'd go to the store to buy something, hordes of other women would go in and out, but the shopkeeper wouldn't pay attention to us; they wouldn't even want to sell us things. When we got on the bus, they wouldn't let us sit down, and if we did find a seat, they wouldn't sit next to us—or they would put their bag between us like a barrier and glare."

Once Nafisa needed to see a doctor and went to the local clinic with her niece Samira. They waited and waited while dozens of other patients came and went, many of whom had arrived after them. Finally, Samira snapped. "She screamed and shouted. Eventually somebody came out and said, 'What is all this commotion, why are you shouting?' Then Samira said, 'You should be ashamed! Where is your humanity? We have been sitting here, waiting and waiting, and you keep sending people in before us. We are sick and we are here like everybody else, and you should send us in when it is our turn!'"

War in Ukraine and the influx of a massive number of Ukrainian refugees only made life harder for the Afghan women judges. Three and a half million Ukrainian refugees crossed the border into Poland in the months after the Russian invasion in February 2022, most of them moving to Warsaw, where the Afghan women judges had finally settled. The attention of the Polish government and the sympathies of the Polish people lay with their neighbors, and support for Afghan refugees shrank even further.

"When we were searching for an apartment we discovered that Ukrainian people didn't need to show any documents to rent a place, but we needed to show lots of documents, which we didn't have," Nafisa says. "When we were walking around our local area people were looking at us the wrong way, as if we had committed some sort of crime in their country." Anisa says she often had heated conversations with Nafisa Kabuli about why the Ukrainians should be given such preferential treatment. Nafisa argued that they had suffered just as much, if not more, in Afghanistan. "They might be a hundred miles away from their home, but we are a thousand miles away from our home," Nafisa said. "They should show more sympathy to us than the Ukrainians because at least when they were in their country, they had a better life than us. Even when we were in our country, we didn't have a good life. Before the Taliban took over, we were struggling against them, and we faced daily bomb attacks and terrorism." Anisa countered that perhaps it was only to be expected that Poles would favor their closest neighbor, just as Afghans perhaps felt closer to people in Pakistan and Iran. One thing was clear, however; there were now fewer resources and less goodwill to go around. Anisa says, "At that point we really felt that we didn't belong there—that we are not the same as them, we're from another country, from another part of the world."

Nafisa's U.S. visa came through first. Soon afterward, Nafisa's sister also received her visa—but the family still had to wait a little while so that Nafisa's niece Samira could get her paperwork done and apply for scholarships to U.S. universities. Even so, life in Poland seemed more bearable in the knowledge that there was a way out.

For Anisa, the anxious wait went on. She felt trapped, far from home but also far from her friends in America and a place where she could set down roots again.

The process of obtaining a U.S. visa seemed long and torturous. "The first interview was a police interview, then there was a second interview. After the second interview, we had a medical examination. We had actually completed an initial medical examination six months earlier, but the medical examination had an expiration date. Of course, the results expired, so then we had to do the medical examination again. Then we got a letter from U.S. Homeland Security telling us we had to go for another interview. It was unusual to have a third interview for a U.S. visa, and we were worried about it."

When Anisa asked why they had to go through another immigration interview, the official told them that he had been ordered to do the interview to try to speed up the process, and also that the U.S. government had some further questions.

"The questions were along the lines of 'Why do you want to leave Poland? Why don't you want to stay in Poland? What's the problem with the Polish government? What's the problem with the Polish people and the Polish community?'" After the third interview Anisa and her family took a third medical exam and then waited again. No one knew how long the process would take. Eventually, though, Anisa got the news that the family was being issued U.S. visas.

Anisa and her family were overjoyed and relieved. But before they even had time to celebrate they heard that they would have to wait at least another three months to arrange everything before their move. Three months more in the cramped hotel! Anisa asked Patti Whalen to find out why there had been yet another delay. Patti made inquiries, and then Anisa and her family heard that if they were ready, they could fly out of Poland immediately.

For Tayeba, the process was even more difficult. While living in Warsaw, she became pregnant with her first child and was applying for scholarships and visas so that she could continue her education and find a way to work in the law again. Other members of Tayeba's family were settled elsewhere in Europe, and her mother was moving unhappily between countries, finding it hard to adjust to her new life; her father remained in Poland, dependent upon Tayeba and her husband. "My father found life in Poland very hard. The Polish language is very difficult, and he couldn't even read the street signs. My husband would take him to his apartment every night . . . [he] might have lost his way if he had not accompanied him."

Soon Tayeba would face a heartbreakingly difficult decision: whether to accept an offer of asylum in the United Kingdom, close to her family in Europe, or accept an opportunity to take up a judicial fellowship at Duke University in North Carolina, which offered a route back to the career she loved but would take her thousands of miles away from everyone she cared about. Most difficult of all, if she went to Duke, her father would not be able to come with her.

When the last of the Afghan women judges left Poland, Anna Kruszewska felt both exhilarated and exhausted. Although the events of the previous two years had pushed her to her limits, they were the most memorable and meaningful of her life. Anna had organized lawyers, psychologists, and housing experts. She had corralled politicians, NGOs, and bureaucrats across the world. She had kept her day job and done another entire job on the side. Now she wondered if this was a life-changing moment. "We are capable of doing things that we would never think are possible. And for me that was the biggest takeaway from this story. There was a moment, to be honest, when I thought about changing my profession. I wondered if I should do humanitarian work, or work with refugees full-time. But I decided that I don't want to stop being a lawyer, because I like being a lawyer. And also, I was tired after those two years. I was really, really tired."

Like many in Poland, Anna found herself drawn into helping refuges from Ukraine, and after her two years with the Afghans she had excellent knowledge and experience. Furthermore, her work with the Afghan women judges was far from over, as many asked for her help in getting visas for other members of their families.

"It wasn't all rosy," Anna says, "It wasn't easy. The Afghan women found it hard to adjust, and there wasn't a huge refugee apparatus in Poland. Sometimes I felt overwhelmed. What do you say to someone who asks you to help them get another thirty visas for members of their family? Or to a family that is living in a Polish person's apartment for a year, but then the person eventually wants to move back?"

The two years the Afghan women judges lived in Poland were complex and challenging, but Anna says: "This is really the story of good prevailing against evil. I'm sorry if that sounds too corny, but it's true. And it is also a story of solidarity—and sisterhood."

16.

Year Zero

RAIHANA ATTAEE FELT LIKE SHE WAS FLOATING ON WATER AS her plane descended into Auckland, New Zealand, in December 2021. So much water—the plane flew over the Hauraki Gulf and its islands, then over the city itself and the two big harbors at Waitematā and Manukau. The trip from Greece had been long and exhausting—and Raihana's son, Arsam, had cried all the way. "I was so tired and, as I looked out of the window, I felt like we were landing on the water. In Afghanistan I'd never seen so much water."

Unlike Anisa, Nafisa, and Tayeba, Raihana was one of seventy women judges and their families who had been evacuated to Greece. In Athens everyone felt tense and under pressure, wondering where they would go and what they would do next. Some judges were getting pregnant and having babies. Others seemed vacant and depressed. The best of intentions could go wrong. The teenage sons of assassinated judge Qadria Yasini, Abdullwahab and Wali, were moved into a beautiful, expensive apartment on their own, but they felt isolated, and eventually they became malnourished because they didn't know how to buy their own food from the Greek stores and cook it; for months they existed on a small bowl of white rice a day.

Having arrived in Aukland, Raihana was free to start her new life with her husband and her son. After two weeks of COVID quarantine in a hotel, the family was transferred to another hotel in central Auckland which they would share for the next two months with almost a thousand other Afghan refugees from Bamyan province, where units from the New Zealand army had been stationed. Everything seemed strange: the water; the new food, which seemed difficult to eat; the canopy of trees in full bloom for summer, which in the Southern Hemisphere was in the months that in the Northern Hemisphere were winter.

On the first day that they could leave the hotel, Raihana and her husband, Maqsood, took Arsam for a walk in the park. "We'd never seen such greenery," Raihana says. In Greece they had gone to the park, too, but had been put off by the signs telling them to keep off the grass. Here in Auckland they could walk barefoot on the grass and stretch out beneath the trees.

Almost as soon as they arrived in New Zealand, Susan Glazebrook from the IAWJ came to see them, and they drove out into the country and spent some time together. Raihana could hardly express how happy she was to be with the woman who had helped her so much, and whose words, messages, and guidance had led her all the way across the world—but in person she felt tongue-tied. Susan's Kiwi accent seemed unfamiliar to someone who had learned English from a textbook, which made it difficult to understand her spoken words, Raihana says.

"New Zealand women and lawyers supported Afghan women judges from the time we arrived in New Zealand. Susan Glazebrook always keeps in touch and makes sure to connect us with lawyers and judges where we live. She mostly emails me and introduces me to new friends. Claudia Elliott, the barrister, helped me with my application to apply to the New Zealand Council of Legal Education to assess my degrees and start my studies in law school. She helps us when we need legal aids.

"A few days after we moved into the hotel, some other women

judges and lawyers, including Judge Nicola Mathers and Judge Mary-Beth Sharp, came to visit us. They brought flowers, toys, and clothes for our children and even managed to provide computers and mobiles for us.

"Philippa Cunningham, a retired judge, is like a mother to me in New Zealand. She always comes and visits us in our home, or I go to her home. She advises and helps us with anything we need.

"One day I tried to ride a bicycle to fulfill one of my childhood dreams—but I fell off and hurt my knee. When I talked to Philippa on the phone, I told her about it, and within a few minutes she knocked on my front door with a Band-Aid. She sat beside me and gently applied pressure on my knee and put on the Band-Aid. At that moment I felt like my mother was beside me taking care of me. She also helps me with my studies, and went with me to the law school to meet with the university staff for the first time. Whenever I feel sad or need to talk to someone, I go to her.

"Pauline Hoyle is a kind volunteer who came often with her car full of toys and kitchen equipment even after we moved [to a new] home. Rachael Reed, KC, bought me a new computer when I was in the hotel, and I still use it for my studies. [The lawyer] Lynda Kearns often invites us to her house, where all of the Afghan judges' families living in Auckland come together. A barrister called Mai Chen offered to let me use her chamber and equipment for my studies. Jo Rice, a retired lawyer, and her husband, Peter, a district court judge, are also kind friends who often visit us. And there are so many other Kiwi friends that I cannot name here. These are the people who have filled our hearts with love after we left our own loved ones behind in Afghanistan.

"We still have the support of the New Zealand Association of Women Judges. They invite us to their yearly meetings and conferences, which gives us a sense of belonging to the judicial field. The New Zealand Association of Women Judges also generously funded my participation in the Women Judges Conference in Morocco in 2023. Going to that conference is one of my loveliest memories because I met those individuals, including the women judges from the IAWJ, who helped me and my colleagues in the hardest days of our life. They saved our lives by helping us to flee the country."

Maqsood was already enrolled to study at the university, so as he began classes Raihana started learning English, Māori, and the history of New Zealand culture. She took Arsam to kindergarten, but he cried and didn't want to be left alone, so Raihana stayed with him and connected with the other Afghan women in the hotel and with the larger, more settled, Afghan community that had been in Auckland for twenty years or more.

Arsam's birthday fell during the time that they were staying at the hotel, and Raihana was incredibly moved when one of her mentor judges in New Zealand, Philippa, organized a birthday party and cake for him. "It was hard for us to know how to restart our lives. We don't know how to celebrate—I wasn't even sure if we should celebrate. But Philippa made him a birthday cake and we held a small party and it was like the beginning of the fusion of the old and new parts of our lives. It was a small thing that we could feel good about."

After two months it was time to move out of the hotel and into their own home but, compared to Kabul, the process of finding and renting a house was extremely difficult. Eventually, with Phillipa's help, Raihana found a house that would accommodate her small family, as well as her mother-in-law and sister-in-law, who had been able to join them directly from Afghanistan.

"We thought about how we wanted to live here," Raihana says, noting that, unlike in Afghanistan, in New Zealand it is not always customary for families to live together. "Here everyone lives their own life. In most of the houses there is only one man or one woman. When you are in Afghanistan you can't imagine that kind of life. Every family lives together, with maybe as many as ten people. Maybe that is bad for young people who want to live their own lives, but it's good for the elderly generation. In Auckland my neighbor is very sick and very old, and they have support from the government carers who come every day and check on them—but there is no family to come or look after them. When I get old I don't want to be alone like that. I want my children to come and see me."

Philippa Cunningham marveled to Raihana at how such large families live together—and also told Raihana that she was happy to live alone and be independent. "In the end we decided to live together as one family," Raihana says. "It's good to be in one place to help each other, and it felt good for all of us to have a home again after such a long time without one."

With help from the New Zealand government and the Red Cross, Raihana bought things she needed for the house, like a fridge and washing machine, and when another Afghan woman judge moved onto the same street, the families could socialize and the children could play together. "Afghan culture is very social. We can't stay alone; we need to go and see friends and talk to each other. That sense of belonging makes us feel good, and I needed that feeling of connection again."

Raihana was also able to start studying again at the university much more quickly than she'd thought—and she got a scholarship and financial support to help her retrain in New Zealand law.

"On my first day I walked into a huge class, with more than three hundred students sitting in a lecture theater, and there were no pens or pencils. I got out my pen and pencil, but everyone else had their own computer that they were taking notes on. I was shocked and I thought, 'Oh my God!' It was hard for me to type in English and take notes quickly, but after that lecture I got a computer and started to practice taking notes."

In Afghanistan students would sit in smaller groups, talking and getting to know each other. Raihana felt alienated by the huge lectures and the fact that as soon as they were finished everyone would get up to leave. She wondered how she would ever make friends.

At first Raihana took on a very heavy course load, piling on up to five classes with all the attendant reading, homework, and assignments. Other students told her she was crazy—they were only taking two, and they were native English-speakers.

Raihana dropped back to two classes but still found her first few months overwhelming and difficult. "I had to go to the library and sit there and study all day. I was reading and reading, and then I had to go home and do everything else, like look after my child and do the housework. I'd never been stressed by exams before in Afghanistan, but now, even though I knew the content, I had to plan for how to structure and write an essay in English within a strict time limit. It was hard."

Although she travels to the university on the bus, Raihana has also bought a small car and drives around, dropping her son off at school and going to the store. She will soon get her certificate of proficiency from the university (the equivalent of passing the bar exam in the United States) and submit her papers to the New Zealand Law Council. After completing another course of professional training, she will be able to work as a lawyer again—something she has decided she wants to do. It's a decision she knows that not all the women judges can make; only those with the best English, full financial support, and complete dedication will make it.

"I'm now certain about being a lawyer. But I'm still not sure about which part of the law. I often think about refugee law or human rights law—but when I speak to my friends some of them say, 'There is no money in humanitarian law, and in New Zealand you need to make money!'"

Unlike in Afghanistan, where a family could live very comfortably if one person had a job, Raihana says that to get by in New Zealand it feels like everyone in the family has to work every single minute. In Afghanistan, "When one person in a family worked, eight or nine people could live on that salary. You could have a proper house, pay the rent, have good food, and a good social life. The rest of the family didn't need to worry about working. But here in New Zealand if you want to have a middle-class life everyone has to work to stay at that level. As a student my father paid for everything for me, but here I see young people working to pay for their education. It's a huge pressure on people."

Although the Afghan economy was dependent upon international aid, Raihana says, "In Afghanistan everything was cheap. There were plenty of poor people, but they usually inherited land or a house from their family, and traveling around was easy—if they needed to go somewhere they'd always find a rickshaw or someone to give them a lift. My husband supported the family of his father, his mom, and his siblings, and we could still save money. Here it's impossible to save money even if you have a proper job and are a two-income family. If you're buying a house, you have to get a mortgage for your entire life."

It is as a woman, of course, that Raihana notices the most profound differences between life in Afghanistan and New Zealand.

"In Afghanistan a girl is very confined and can only do certain things. You can't do everything you want. You have to be mindful about your behavior all the time. When I was at university with my friends we would go outside to sit on the grass and talk, but we always had to speak quietly and not laugh too loudly. We couldn't lie on the grass or be free. There would be boys and men all around us, and they would always watch us. If a girl spoke too freely, they would judge her. One day we were like laughing really loudly when a boy who was a *shari'a* law student just started shouting at us and berating us, saying, 'Shut up! It is bad for a girl to laugh so loudly.' I remember exactly how that felt: we wished that we could lie on the grass, see the sky, and laugh. We could never do that in Afghanistan.

"Everywhere you went—at university, on the street, on the way to a store—men would follow you, make crude sexual jokes, and touch you and pull at your clothes. You couldn't walk when it was dark. You couldn't stop in the street. Men would drive up beside you in their cars and tell you to get in and go with them. It was normal for us. If we reacted, the situation got worse: they made more jokes or more threats. The best thing was to keep silent and not to say or do anything."

In Afghanistan women often weren't allowed to leave the house to work, but those who could were usually expected to hand over their entire salary to their husbands, who controlled all of the family money. "I knew a woman who worked for a long time, but anything they bought was in her husband's name, including their car and their house. When they separated and the divorce case went to court she had nothing."

In New Zealand, Raihana says, everything is different. "When I go to university I see girls and boys sitting together, talking. They are not afraid to be judged by anyone. You can lie down on the grass, you can sleep, you can do anything you want, you can wear what you want—and you have no fear about what others say. I am not just a girl or a woman—I am a human being. And I feel much better. I am independent, and I am free."

In Afghanistan, though, women are not free, and Raihana thinks about her friends, her family, and the sisters of her homeland every day.

"The situation has got worse for women. The Taliban is taking every opportunity to restrict their lives. Step by step, it has crept across the country. At first they let the girls go to university; then they closed the universities. At first they let women work for international NGOs; then they stopped women working for NGOs. Then they closed all the beauty shops. Then they stopped girls going to school. I'm in contact with friends who were university students or high school girls, and they have been confined to their homes for two years. They feel utterly hopeless. I can feel their deep despair because I experienced it.

"If you are in high school, thinking about your future, and suddenly they take everything from you and leave you with no choice, it is very hard. I talk with them and they just don't know what to do with their future. My sister-in-law was at medical school in Afghanistan, and when her male classmates graduated this year they all posted photos celebrating, while the girls they studied with are silent. I read the posts of those girls and they just posted crying emojis, or they replied: 'You graduated, but we are at home with nothing.' Now I hear of more and more girls being forced into childhood marriage again because their parents see no future for them outside the home."

The people of Afghanistan are tired, and they are afraid, Raihana says—and they see no support from the outside world. "There is no meaningful international support to stop the Taliban from doing whatever they want. There is nothing to hold them to account. Who will support the people of Afghanistan in bringing about change. The U.S.? Other countries? There is no clear path."

In New Zealand it sometimes feels like year zero, Raihana says. "It is hard to begin your life again in another country from year zero, and I see the emotional burden carried by the people who moved here. In New Zealand we have support from the government and the ordinary people. This is a very good country, but there are people here who were army generals and doctors and judges in Afghanistan and can't even get a job in a shop or a restaurant. They had everything at home, and now they struggle to communicate with a single word of English. They are waiting for change to come so that they can go back to Afghanistan, but when?"

Raihana says she is tired of politics, as politics has divided and destroyed her country. But she would like to see one politician from each of the countries that occupied Afghanistan for so long to stand in support of Afghan girls. "We need to stand up and advocate for those girls in Afghanistan, the millions of girls sitting in their houses with no support and no future. We need to fight for the right of those girls who were in universities to finish their education—and keep girls in schools. It will be worth it because if we can keep one girl in school, we can change a single life.

"I am worried about the new generation in Afghanistan who grow up under the Taliban regime. Those who see their moms and sisters sitting at home not participating in social activities and schools. I worry about those children whose teachers are the Taliban, with their fundamentalist ideas. Those who must read the Taliban curriculum at schools or attend madrasa or religious schools, they will grow up and think and behave as the Taliban do. Just imagining Afghanistan in the future, I see only darkness.

"One question that always comes to my mind is, why did those countries who were involved in Afghanistan for the past twenty years leave Afghanistan the way they did? They could have done better if they wanted. Why did they hand the country to the Taliban and destroy our lives?"

17.

Buddies

MORE THAN TWO HUNDRED AFGHAN WOMEN JUDGES HAVE been able to leave their homeland and are now embarking upon their new lives in exile. For Anisa, Nafisa, and Tayeba that means working and studying in the United States, while Raihana is settling down and retraining in New Zealand. Other judges are dispersed around the world with their families. As of June 2024, fifty-two are in the United States, thirty-eight are in Canada, thirty-two are in Germany, nineteen are in Australia, seventeen are in the United Kingdom, ten are in Ireland, nine are in Pakistan, nine are in Spain, six are in New Zealand, four are in France, and two are in Poland, while Austria, Belgium, Greece, Iceland, Iran, Luxembourg, and Turkey each have one judge.

In each of those very different countries the IAWJ has paired up the Afghan women with local partner judges in relationships that have become long-lasting, sometimes challenging, and often life-affirming for both women.

When a group of Australian judges first met their Afghan counterparts who had decided to settle in Melbourne, they were amused to hear that they had chosen the city for the weather. "Yes, we got that wrong," Afghan judge Mirman Dil'Aram Abid admits wryly. Nine of the Afghan women judges in Australia chose to relocate to Melbourne, in the state of Victoria, famous for its changeable and often cold and wet weather, while the others moved to the more balmy city of Sydney, in neighboring New South Wales.

Inclement weather notwithstanding, the Australian Association of Women Judges quickly abandoned the term "partner judges" for the friendlier and more relaxed idea of "buddies"—even if those buddies were all long-standing and distinguished former lawyers and judges themselves.

The Afghan women judges and their families met their Melbourne buddies for the first time on a sunny day in December 2021 in the gardens of the Royal Exhibition Building, a dazzling white nineteenth-century landmark testifying to Melbourne's desire to propel itself from a sleepy backwater into a global metropolis with the Melbourne International Exhibition of 1880. That exhibition had boasted tea from India, beer from Austria, tinplate from Birmingham, England, and agricultural machinery from the United States. Now brought into service as a COVID vaccine hub, it seemed a suitable backdrop for a group of Afghan women judges who were themselves only too familiar with the rise and fall of empires, colonies, and ideas.

After some time in COVID quarantine, the Afghan women had been in the city for about a week when they met for a picnic in the park. Retired judge Sue Cohen, one of the Australian buddies, says, "We turned up and saw people dressed in Afghan clothes and gravitated toward them—and introduced ourselves and met our buddies. We knew their names, and I think I had a list of who my buddy judge's relatives with her were—but we really only had minimal information about them." Her colleague Frances Millane, also a retired judge, adds, "And we only had one interpreter for everybody."

The Australian judge Robyn Tupman, in Sydney, had been part of the core group of IAWJ women organizing the evacuation, but now other women judges across the nation were picking up the baton to help the women settle into their new homes. Sue Cohen says, "In many ways we were ill-prepared, but there was an immediate feeling of two-way empathy, and those of us who were there with those first women have really stayed involved, and we feel that we're part of all of the family groups that have come—and we've got to know more and more of them."

Frances Millane and her colleague Diana Bryant were both active and long-standing members of the Australian Association of Women Judges (AAWJ) and were instrumental in establishing the buddy program in Victoria, as well as a model for distributing funds raised by the AAWJ to assist in the resettlement of judges and their families across Australia. Retired judge Pamela Tate was part of the group, too, and worked with Frances to arrange speaking events and dinners to keep the judges' stories alive. Within months of the judges' arrival Frances organized a planning day on a Saturday to which she invited a firm of solicitors who are specialists in immigration law. As a result, the Afghan women judges in Victoria received pro bono assistance for immigration matters.

The Australian women had all known each other for a long time, and while none of them had ever been threatened in the way the Afghan women were, or had experienced the horrors faced by the Afghans, they had all experienced the inherent sexism of working in a male-dominated profession. Pamela Tate says, "Part of my involvement in this stemmed from a general commitment to feminism. I've been involved in other feminist organizations, including Women's Legal Resource Group—a national network of women's legal services dedicated to providing better outcomes for women under the law—and other non-legal feminist organizations, so, for me, it was inevitable that I would try and help. I was motivated by trying to assist women who had sought to uphold the rule of law in dire situations where they understood that they were under threat."

Sue Cohen's experience growing up in a Jewish family also motivated her to help. "Both of my parents were born in Australia, but I was brought up by my family to recognize and appreciate the experience of migrants. I think this reflected a Jewish perspective that none of us were far from those experiences. My grandmother was born in Siberia and had come to Australia as a child with her family at a time when there were pogroms against Jews in Russia. She was widowed very young, at only thirty-seven, and went to work in factories to support herself and her children—but she always talked of those less fortunate than her, and offered food and shelter to those she could. Two of my uncles' wives were refugees who had fled Berlin and Vienna in the late 1930s, and I heard some of their stories of escape, loss, and the challenges of coming to such a different environment, including having to learn English. I grew up knowing that migrants to Australia faced the challenges of adapting to a country and culture often very different from their origins, many of them needing to learn a new language, and recognizing that Australia offered opportunities for a safe future but also regarded them as cultural minorities."

While the group of Melbourne judges had been given some advice from the Australian Association of Women Judges and were not expected to personally provide financial support or legal advice, every relationship between an Afghan judge and their buddy developed in its own way—and often became much deeper than anyone had expected. Pamela Tate says, "I followed the news on what was happening to women judges in Afghanistan, but I wasn't involved in any of the committees. All of a sudden, I got an email saying these women judges were coming to Australia and asking if we were prepared to be their buddies—and I said yes. I have to say, there was really no understanding of the scope of what that meant. It was just an open-ended kind of concept, but the word 'buddy' was used because that's an Australian term of affection for a friend."

Diana Bryant's buddy was Shakila Abawi Shigarf, who arrived with an extended family of ten. "That was a different group from many of the others. They wanted advice about practical things, like accommodation, but they also really wanted to know about Australia, and I was able to help with that." Diana took the family on a trip to the beach, where they ate fish and chips and swam in the sea for the first time. They went to Australian-rules football games (a sport with a near-religious following in Melbourne) and visited a friend of Diana's who lived out on a farm in the country. "When we met it was quite near Christmastime, so I asked them if they wanted to celebrate Christmas in a secular way, and they did—so I organized a Christmas tree and Christmas presents for the kids."

Sue Cohen's relationship with her buddy, Najiba Taj, also incorporates their religious differences. "They have been at my house when I've lit the Hanukkah candles, and they have invited me to eat with them at iftar dinners [marking the end of a day's fast during Ramadan] and Eid [marking the end of] Ramadan. This year they were here with me and my family in December, and I lit the Hanukkah candles and Najiba was nodding at me with understanding. Ten minutes later she quietly went off into another room at my house to pray, which she still does regularly five times a day. It gives me great satisfaction that we've built a relationship that encompasses all of that, and respects and appreciates each other's customs."

Sue also took Najiba to see art exhibitions at the National Gallery of Victoria. "The first time we went, I was surprised that Najiba and her daughter weren't aware of the kind of famous European artists that we learn about. I said I would show them our Picasso painting and a Monet—and they did not react. They were absolutely enthralled by our good collection of Dutch Masters, though, and they loved the seventeenth-century clothing in the pictures. I've taken them back to see other exhibitions and Aboriginal art, which they enjoyed. They are very open to learning more about all of our culture."

Just as the Afghan women have embraced the multiculturalism of Melbourne, the Australian women have also learned more about and enjoyed Afghan culture. "I think we went to eight iftar dinners for Ramadan in the first year that they were here," Frances Millane says.

Alongside these happy events, however, are the more difficult adjustments of leaving Afghanistan for a new life in Australia. Most of the judges fear desperately for the family they have left behind. In the case of at least one judge, those family members have been persecuted by the Taliban after the judge's departure.

Judge Mirman Dil'Aram Abid had been working as a judge for more than thirty years when she fled Kabul with three of her five daughters. In her work she had been head of the Court for the Elimination of Violence Against Women in Takhar province, in the north of the country, bordering Tajikistan. One day a case came before her involving a defendant called Mohammed Asif, who was charged with murdering his wife.

Dil'Aram says that Asif was a professional criminal whose life started to unravel when he was incarcerated and on trial for sexually assaulting a girl. As he was not at home to care for his children, his three young sons, ages thirteen, nine, and six, were sent to their grandparents' house, where their grandmother started to quiz them about their mother's whereabouts. She hadn't seen her daughter Fawzia for a long time. One of the boys told her, "One day my dad and mom were arguing. Then my father took a brick and hit her on her head—and all of my mom's brains splattered all over the curtains. Dad took us to someone else's house and we had to stay there for hours. He told us never to tell anyone what had happened." Eventually the children returned home, and by that time Asif had buried their mother under a toilet hole in the backyard.

Fawzia's mother reported the crime, and the police arrested Asif, who denied that he had murdered his wife and claimed that perhaps her own mother had killed her. As the case progressed, the police went to the family home and discovered Fawzia's body in the backyard. Then the children also told the police that someone else was living in the house: "There is a girl living in our house too, but she is not our sister." The police searched the house and could find no sign of the girl, but then the boys told them that Asif had hidden her at a friend's home.

When the police visited the friend's home, they found thirteen-year-old Aziza, who told them she had been abducted by Asif from beside a well when she was only six years old, held prisoner, and raped. She was so young when she was abducted that she no longer remembered who her own family were. Aziza also told them she had been sent to the friend's house with a baby Asif's wife Fawzia had given birth to before her murder—but the baby had died from neglect and malnutrition. As Asif's trial progressed, even more crimes came to light when he confessed to also having murdered three of his friends in a dispute about a motorbike.

As the head of the Court for the Elimination of Violence Against Women, Dil'Aram oversaw the sentencing hearing with two other senior judges. Asif was sentenced to twenty years' imprisonment for kidnapping and raping Aziza, and was given the death penalty for the murder of his wife. Before his execution could take place, however, the Taliban regained control of the country in the summer of 2021 and released Asif and thousands of other dangerous prisoners from jail.

After getting her number from his lawyer, the first thing Asif did upon his release was to ring Dil'Aram and demand to have thirteen-year-old Aziza returned to him, saying, "She is my wife now. I want my wife back!" Dil'Aram replied, "She is not your wife. She is a child. You kidnapped her and you were raping her."

Asif continued to call and demand Aziza back for three days before Dil'Aram's son-in-law Masoud took the phone from her and told Asif, "Under the new Taliban regime Dil'Aram is not a judge anymore, and she doesn't know where Aziza is." Then he took the SIM card out of the phone and destroyed it.

Soon afterward, Dil'Aram left the country, traveling first to Greece with some of the other evacuated women judges. When she arrived in Australia she discovered that Asif had been searching her old neighborhood looking for her. One of the neighbors had told him where her daughter Sajida lived, and he went there, demanding to "marry" one of Dil'Aram's daughters in exchange for Aziza. When he discovered that none of Dil'Aram's daughters was single, Asif demanded to "marry" her eight-year-old granddaughter Mohsena instead.

Dil'Aram's daughter and son-in-law refused to hand over Mohsena, so Asif took his case to the local imam. When the imam also denied Asif's claim, he took his case to the Taliban's Ministry for the Propagation of Virtue and the Prevention of Vice. After Asif explained his problem, the Taliban supported Asif's case, issuing orders for the arrest of Dil'Aram for taking Aziza away from Asif and for the seizure of her granddaughter Mohsena. Luckily, one of the officials in that ministry knew Dil'Aram and her family, and tipped off Sajida and Masoud that the Taliban were coming to get Mohsena. Terrified, they fled into hiding, and after many fraught months of evading capture were eventually able to slip across the border and make their way to Australia, too.

Dil'Aram's relief and delight at their reunion is palpable, but the case highlights the long arm of terror that the Taliban exercise in Afghanistan and beyond. Like the other judges, Dil'Aram deals not only with the life-threatening risks faced by her family members still in Afghanistan but also with the day-to-day challenges of life in a new country. Furthermore, in her relatively short time in

Australia Dil'Aram has already undergone major surgery for two brain aneurysms.

"This was obviously an existential crisis," Pamela Tate says. "Dil'Aram sent us an urgent request, and we had to deal with it immediately." Dil'Aram's buddy judges, Pamela and Frances Millane, were shocked to suddenly get a message saying she'd been to her family doctor, who told her to go to the hospital immediately and have an MRI scan. "The message asked us what were we going to do about it—and I seem to remember that was the end of the post!"

Pamela got Dil'Aram's consent to call the doctor and discuss her condition, and then met her at the hospital later that day. "I got to the hospital at about three o'clock in the afternoon and stayed until about eleven o'clock at night after she had the MRI. Dil'Aram did not speak very much English, so we did a lot of smiling, gesturing, and showing each other photos on our phones. She was seen by a radiologist, who also was wearing a hijab, and she told Dil'Aram that she did not have to remove her clothes."

Pamela then went back to Dil'Aram's room and waited there with her. Some weeks later Dil'Aram visited a specialist, who said that she could have a highly invasive brain surgery that would treat both aneurysms at once, or she could choose to have a less invasive vascular procedure done that would treat the larger aneurysm but not the smaller one. "I said, 'Look, you might want to take a day or two to think about this, this is a very significant operation,' but she said, 'No, I want both blocked.' She immediately chose full brain surgery. Again, I admired her courage."

Dil'Aram had her operation within a few months and was incredibly thankful to the Australian medical system, and to Pamela and Frances for supporting her. Pamela says her strongest memory of the time is sitting in the emergency room at the hospital, surrounded by people from all backgrounds and ethnicities.

"Dil'Aram said to me, in faltering English, 'This is one of the most marvelous things about Australia. It doesn't matter what ethnicity you are, nobody judges you, whereas in Afghanistan everybody judges you.'"

Pamela adds that having Frances as a co-buddy has made helping Dil'Aram a more manageable proposition. "We have had to pace the interaction a bit, because obviously it would be overwhelming if you had to be completely accessible to a new person in your life when you already have an incredibly busy life with a whole other range of commitments to other people and other organizations. I think it's varied from judge to judge, and I'm so grateful that Frances is a co-buddy with me, because having the two of us means we can at least talk through things and discuss what her current needs are. We've been buddies with Dil'Aram for more than two years now and we want to keep going because we have a very strong relationship with her—but we can't always help at the pace we set in the early days, which was very frenetic."

Sue Cohen adds that she was retired when she started helping as a buddy and that has certainly given her more time. Equally, not all of the Afghan women judges wanted to form long-term relationships with their Australian counterparts; some just wanted to settle in and get on with their lives.

Life for the Afghan judges in Australia has followed the same pattern of successes and challenges as elsewhere. All of the women miss their families and worry about those they left behind in Afghanistan. While younger members of the families have learned English quickly and found jobs, some of the older women have struggled to learn English, and an early determination to restart their lives as lawyers and judges has given way to a sense of acceptance—and sometimes depression—that this is not likely to happen. Life at home can also be difficult, as husbands discover that restarting their lives is far from easy, too.

Diana Bryant says, "The older judges have a slightly different perspective from the younger ones and that may be partly because the older ones went through a similar exile in the 1990s. Most of them were judges when the Taliban took over the first time. Most of them, if not all, went to Pakistan and worked in different jobs. Shakila was a teacher. So, they've seen their careers change in these circumstances, and lived through it."

Pamela Tate agrees: "There's a generational change of sorts, because one of the things I was surprised by was that Dil'Aram's emails come with an insignia of a woman's fist punching through a flower and the words 'Women's Rights' written underneath. I was quite amazed that someone from her background would be like that, but it's become clearer and clearer, I think, to Frances and me over time that her heart lies in women's activism. She is very interested in the advancement of women generally. I think some of the younger women judges have a stronger need to focus on their careers. That's not to say that they don't share the same beliefs about women's rights, but that they also see much more of a future in the workforce. And that has its own set of challenges."

"There was a sense at the beginning with all of them that they had suffered a great loss of identity and debasement, and that was something we talked about a lot," Frances adds. "We wanted to help them find their identity again by supporting them in reeducation, but also trying to help them through what we knew was a traumatic experience. It wasn't as though they had just caught a plane to Australia; the prelude to that was very traumatic. And I'm still amazed at how they seem to have coped."

Expectations around reeducation and career have been difficult, Pamela says. "The Australian legal system is that you graduate with a full law degree, then you become a practitioner, a solicitor, or barrister, then, if you're fortunate, you may become a judge when you're quite senior in the profession. I was appointed in my mid-fifties and that's a fairly standard age, whereas under the civil system in Afghanistan you choose at university whether to become a practitioner or a judge and start young. So Dil'Aram and Shakila had been judges for more than thirty years, but some of the younger women had been judges for eight to ten years and yet they're only in their thirties. We had to try and think, was there any way that they could have a role in our legal system, either formal or informal? I was very concerned about what expectations we induced, because it would be a challenge for the senior ones to have a formal role in the Australian legal profession. Some of the younger ones may be able to retrain, but it's going to be a long road for them."

Diana agrees, and echoes that when the women first arrived they all had a sense of urgency about reestablishing their careers. But for some, like Shakila, that agitation has given way to more a realistic dedication to learning English first—a language very few of the judges had mastered in Afghanistan. "She's hardly missed a day in her English class. She's worked assiduously at learning English, and you can have a conversation with her, chat with her and laugh with her and joke with her. I think they've now realized that their initial thoughts of being able to go straight back into the law were probably ill-conceived. Education is expensive, and getting onto courses is difficult."

"There's been a lot of goodwill expressed to try to help the women judges," Frances Millane says. "And yet turning that into something tangible and practical in their lives is more difficult."

One judge who is determined to retrain in law is thirty-three-year-old Mahtab Fazl, a former prosecutor and judge in the Court for the Elimination of Violence Against Women in Herat. Mahtab arrived in Melbourne with her husband, brother, and two sons. When the Taliban reached Kabul in 2021, Mahtab went into hiding, but on the first night her neighbor called to say that the Taliban had found her house, broken into it, and vandalized it, before stealing all the family's money and gold. A few days later the Taliban went out into the countryside to a garden that belonged to Mahtab, and shot her dog. They turned to her gardener and said, "You are associated with the woman who owns this garden—and one day we will come back and kill you, too."

In Melbourne, Mahtab juggles learning English and studying with looking after her two very young sons and trying to help other members of her family escape from Afghanistan. Mahtab's buddy judges are Wendy Wilmoth and Fiona Todd, who marvel at her ability to enroll in a local college to learn English and discuss university courses.

Wendy Wilmoth says, "I don't know how Mahtab manages to do so much with so little support. There's English classes and her diploma classes as well as looking after her family with only very limited daycare for the little boys. She is amazing."

Mahtab interjects to say she is very lucky to have Wendy and Fiona as her sisters.

"Thank you for calling me your sister. I'm old enough to be your mother, Mahtab," Wendy says.

"Yes, yes, that's true!" Mahtab laughs.

"I'm more like a grandma!" Wendy adds.

"It fills my heart to have such a kind mom," Mahtab tells her. "In fact, I am also going to call you Mom. That's a good idea!"

Mahtab says she still holds on to her dreams and goals. "Despite lots of challenges in my country, I still have hope. I am studying English, and I am now studying for a diploma in justice. After that, if possible, I want to continue my education and become a lawyer in Australia. This takes time, especially as looking after my children is challenging, and I am trying to help my family in

Afghanistan—they are in danger, and their life is very difficult. But I want to make a positive contribution to my new community and I want to be a lawyer again—and I believe in myself. We must never give up."

18.
A Tree Transplanted Takes Time to Grow

ON THE DAY IN AUGUST 2021 THAT HAMIDA FROOZANFAR heard that the Taliban were at the gates of Kabul, she ran to her university to get the certificate for her master's degree in criminal law. "I didn't anticipate that Kabul would fall so quickly. If I had known that, I would have moved my valuable belongings, including my books and judicial robe, from my office to my home earlier—but I was caught off guard."

Passing the local music school she saw a terrible sight—the boys and girls from the school were standing outside in the street, smashing their instruments in the gutter. "The streets were packed, and the roads were blocked. Everyone was scared and fleeing. The students knew they couldn't carry their instruments with them—the Taliban outlawed music and it was too dangerous. But they were crying as they broke them up, because they were literally destroying their dreams."

Hamida began her career working as a TV news anchor, but as an idealistic young woman she had retrained as a judge so that she could correct injustices and play a role in educating people about women's rights.

As the Taliban swept across the country in the summer of 2021, Hamida saw her colleagues from different cities returning to Kabul one after the other, seeking refuge. A friend who was a judge in Herat called and asked if she could stay with Hamida and her family in Kabul. "I said, 'Yes, come and we can live together,'" Hamida says. Yet, despite the ominous drumbeat of one city and province falling after the other, the arrival of the Taliban in Kabul was an enormous shock.

By now Hamida knew that her only chance was to flee, but she believed that if she left without proof of her degree it would be nearly impossible to prove her qualifications in the future.

When she reached the university she received the first of many frantic phone calls from her mother.

"Are you at work?" her mother asked her.

Hamida said, "No, why?"

"The people say the Taliban are at the doors of Kabul, come home!" her mother told her.

Hamida told her mother she was at the university.

Her mother asked, "Where are your children?"

Hamida replied that her two small children were with her mother-in-law, so her mother told her to call her husband and have him bring the children to her house. When Hamida spoke to her husband he said he was on his way to get the children, but the streets of Kabul were jammed and it was nearly impossible to get anywhere.

As Hamida waited at the university she got another call from her mother, who sounded more and more terrified. "My mother said, "I saw the Taliban in the street with my own eyes—so come quickly. Come as fast as you can, or they will kill you."

Hamida reassured her mother that she would come as soon as she got her degree.

"Then my mother phoned again and said that she was following social media. People were talking about the Taliban coming to kill the judges and the prosecutors."

In her last call Hamida's mother said, "What is more important: your degree or your life? If they find you, they are saying, they will cut your head off!"

Hamida got her certificate and ran home through the streets of the city, worried that she was not wearing a burqa and the Taliban might stop her. For the next forty days she moved from house to house in Kabul, hiding with her husband and children. To make the situation even more perilous, Hamida was also nearly nine months pregnant with her third child and needed a cesarean section. Thanks to the efforts of the IAWJ, she learned after nearly five weeks that she would be included in the group of women judges who would be taken to Mazar-i-Sharif and then hopefully flown to Greece. As she waited in the hotel room in Mazar for one final week, she wept constantly but joked with her mother on the phone, who was holding back her own tears. "My sister was also trying to leave Afghanistan, but every time they managed to reach the airport in Kabul they had to turn back. Each time they set off my mother would weep uncontrollably, and then they would come back again. Finally my sister said to her as a joke, 'Please don't cry because when you cry we get turned back.' Now they said to her, 'Don't cry for Hamida or she will never be able to leave.'" Her mother told Hamida, "I will not cry because I want you to go and be safe—but when your plane takes off the tears I shed for you are going to be huge."

After all their terror and waiting, Hamida arrived in Greece, and her third child was safely delivered by a doctor who told her he was proud to deliver the son of a woman judge from Afghanistan. Hamida found the Greek people generous, warm, and welcoming, but she understood that the country was only a temporary refuge for them as they sought visas for a country that could be their permanent home. "First we thought we were going with some of the other women judges to Brazil, so my husband started learning Portuguese," Hamida says. "Then we thought we were going to Germany, so he started listening to German on YouTube. When we found out we weren't going to Germany, either, he said, 'I am tired, and I am not learning any more languages until I know where we are definitely going.'"

Hamida's final destination was Canada, where she would join a growing group of Afghan women judges and their families in Toronto.

One of the Canadian judges who has played an active role in helping the Afghan women judges settle in the city is Anne Molloy, a justice on the Ontario Superior Court.

"We were expecting about forty judges to come to Canada," Anne says, "and we've got twenty-four of them in Toronto, with their families. Accommodating so many people has been an incredible struggle, but I understand why they want to come here because this is where the largest Afghan community is in Canada. One of the judges got sent to St. John's, Newfoundland, which is where I'm from and is—as far as I'm concerned—one of the most beautiful places on the entire planet. But the Afghan judge that got sent there took one look, saw no Afghan population, and came straight back to Toronto, too."

Trying to navigate the Canadian immigration and housing system has been shocking and chaotic, Anne says. "It's been extremely difficult and discouraging. Having committed to bring these forty women here, they just languished in Greece, or wherever they were, for months and even years in some cases. Then, inexplicably, they were given a ticket and told to leave tomorrow."

When they arrived the judges were housed out near the sprawl of highways and industrial buildings near the airport in the kind of hotels meant for a night's stopover, rather than a prolonged stay that lasted for as long as nine months for some families.

"When we arrived in Canada we were very happy, but living in one hotel room with my husband and our three small children was very difficult," Hamida says. "My youngest son was just a baby and there wasn't even anywhere to put him down. I had to sit on the bed and hold him in my arms all day long. I was exhausted, and my mental health was suffering."

Rising rents and a lack of affordable housing stock meant that finding permanent homes for the judges was incredibly difficult. Every day Hamida's husband hunted for an apartment for the family, and with the help of Hamida's Canadian partner judges, the family finally found a one-bedroom apartment at a rent that they could afford. "He called me and asked if I wanted to move into a one-bedroom apartment. I told him, 'Yes. I would rather move into a tent than stay in this hotel any longer.'" The family moved in but discovered that the rent on their new home would be going up after only one week. "We were hoping to move into a two-bedroom apartment eventually, but now that seems impossible. I think we will have to live here for a long time," Hamida says.

"We have a terrible housing crisis in Toronto," Anne Molloy says. "The Afghan women judges have been amazingly resilient, and their partner judges have helped enormously, going on the internet, pounding the pavement, and helping find them places to live, and then helping to furnish their homes with pots and pans and all the things they need. It hasn't been for the fainthearted. We are often their first and only point of contact, and sometimes the Afghan women have asked for things that their partners can't provide, like buying them a phone, or co-signing their lease, or getting the rest of their family out of Afghanistan. As judges and former judges, there are things that we are not allowed to do."

It's not possible to force friendships upon people, Anne says, but many of the relationships have become deep and life-affirming. One family arrived with a little girl who was deaf but had not received any help with her condition. "It's not easy to get a family doctor and access the medical system in Canada when you don't have a permanent address, but we got her into the main children's hospital in Toronto, where she got hearing aids, and she is now scheduled to get a cochlear ear implant. She was almost completely deaf, and now she chatters away. That family is extremely grateful."

Hamida says her partner judge not only helped her find accommodation but also showed her how to get a bank account, and visits her home now like a member of the family. "She is almost like an Afghan woman now, and my children call her aunty!"

As in Australia, the United States, and elsewhere, the Afghan women judges in Canada face perhaps their biggest struggle in restarting their careers.

Hamida is currently a researcher at the University of Toronto working on a comparative study of the parole systems in Canada and Afghanistan, which was the focus of her master's degree in Kabul. She says she hopes that she can become a lawyer again, but the difference in the legal systems and the need for excellent English make this extremely difficult.

Another judge who is pursuing a new career in Canada is Wahida Rahimi, who was a judge in the Court for the Elimination of Violence Against Women in Panjshir province before escaping from Afghanistan and resettling with her husband and children in Vancouver.

Wahida was born in Pakistan while her parents were in exile from the Taliban during the 1990s, and at first she believed she might follow her father into science and engineering—but eventually she ended up being accepted into law school. "I didn't really choose it," she says, quoting the poet Rumi, who says that what you are seeking is seeking you. "It was my destiny."

Wahida's main interest in Afghanistan was working with families and trying to address some deep-rooted problems. "The foundation of family is very important for me," Wahida says. "In Afghanistan family is the foundation of everything. Boys and girls have to learn from an early age how to be a good part of their family. If you are a woman you have to learn to be a good mother or a good sister. You have responsibilities in your family, and family always comes first. Boys' responsibilities become much heavier cultural and religious responsibilities as they grow into men. In many ways it's very beautiful, and when it's perfectly built it turns a home into a haven. But when it's not, it becomes a hell, and that's why problems occur. That is what really interests me. As a judge in Afghanistan, I could not expect an Afghan family to act like a family in Western countries because it's not built that way. You cannot make a ruling based on what the international community thinks, because the foundation for generations of Afghan families is very different."

Wahida says these differences often made her feel like there could be no good resolution for her cases. "Sometimes it was unresolved, and we were unable to understand why a husband behaved in the way that he did, and it was because he was taught to be that way. And sometimes it was hard to understand why a woman could not speak up, but it was because she had to obey, and obeying kept the family together. When that situation became violent, they didn't know where to go and how to solve it. This work was very interesting, but also very hard most of the time. Sometimes the choice was between a bad decision and a worse decision."

Wahida says that she was pleased if a case that came before her court was a woman who was not suffering from a terrible atrocity but was asking for her rights. "There were huge problems for women, and sometimes they weren't even able to be brought to court—but it signaled progress when women came to court for much smaller things. It meant that that woman was able to come; she wasn't dead, she still had hands and feet, but she was asking for freedom, she was asking for human rights. She was asking for dignity. That showed an awareness that was growing, generation by generation."

Not all Afghan women judges are the same or have the same beliefs. Family life in Afghanistan, and Afghan culture generally, is nuanced and not black and white, as it is sometimes portrayed. For Wahida, getting permission and agreement from her father and then her husband to work was very important, as they wanted to ensure she had the right and safe work space.

Women exercise soft power over men, Wahida says, and can exercise it through discussion and persuasion that don't need to be harsh. "But in many regions of Afghanistan societal expectations and reactions have jeopardized women's rights and freedom. Which is deeply rooted in culture, making it nearly impossible to ignore societal judgments when examining violence against women. Without a concerted effort to tackle the root causes of gender-based violence and discrimination, progress toward gender equality and women's empowerment in Afghanistan will remain elusive. Due to a lack of security, some provinces never had women judges and proper court systems. Kabul and major cities were improving, and women attained governmental positions and achieved the highest positions. But with all due effort, change was not fundamental, and mindsets were still patriarchal."

In Canada, Wahida joined the University of British Columbia and began work on a research project about Afghan women judges and justice. She was delighted to take up a scholarship to study for a master's degree at the University of Notre Dame in Indiana, and after she received her degree she returned to Vancouver. Even so, she often thinks of home and misses the food, the songs, and the time she spent with her family. Like a tree that has been transplanted, she says, it takes time to settle and grow.

What grieves her most is seeing the generation of girls and women who are being shut out of education. "When women are educated, they know their rights, their obligations, and they don't need anyone else telling them what to do," Wahida says, adding that "a society without education is toxic."

Her pain is shared by Hamida, who cried when she saw a photo that her young sister in Afghanistan sent her. Told that she could no longer go to school, Hamida's twelve-year-old sister finished grade six and celebrated in a homemade graduation gown and cap. She was smiling in the photo, Hamida says. "She said, 'Your sister has graduated!' I'm so proud about what she has achieved, but so sad about what she will not be able to go on to do. I found that photo very hard to bear."

In the face of so much hardship and heartbreak, Toronto judge Anne Molloy says she believes it is the children who perhaps hold the most hope for the future.

"Whenever I talk to the women judges, we usually talk about how difficult things are: their home is too small, learning English is difficult, their husbands can only find jobs working in coffee shops or as Uber drivers. Then I say, 'How are the kids?' And they say, 'Oh, fabulous!' They're just so happy, and this one's doing that in school, and another one is doing something else that is really good. The women just change completely when you talk to them about their children."

Anne Molloy says that after the women had been in Toronto for two months she rented two buses and took them and their families on a tour of the city. "We went to all the landmark places. They met the mayor, and they went to where the Toronto Raptors play, and we went to the CN Tower. And even then the little kids were speaking English. It was astounding. If there is such a thing as a happy ending, it lies with the children."

19.
The Conscience of the Nation

IN THE UNITED STATES, TAYEBA PARSA LOOKS TO THE FUTURE, too. In May 2023 she arrived in North Carolina with her husband and her newborn daughter to begin a one-year fellowship at Duke University. The family settled into a small apartment complex near the campus, surrounded by the tall trees, dense foliage, and spread-out suburbia of the American South. "Sometimes I feel like I am living in the jungle," Tayeba says one hot afternoon six months later as she struggled to juggle her studies toward a master's degree and the latter stages of her second pregnancy.

Tayeba learned English in Afghanistan and was often the spokeswoman for the women judges in their final, desperate media interviews with U.K. and U.S. broadcasters in the summer of 2021. Standing in her first class at Duke, however, she felt bewildered by the fast conversations and American drawl.

"It seemed very strange. I wasn't happy. I was sad, depressed, and everything seemed very difficult. I felt like I could not do any of the things that I needed to do on a daily basis to get by. Every day I had to communicate in English and reply to many emails in English. I would get so many letters in the mail, and wonder what they were and how to respond. I wasn't sure if I had made the right decision in coming here."

Part of her anxiety was whether she could stay in the United States and continue her studies. After months of uncertainty and complicated negotiations, Tayeba was awarded a full scholarship at Duke, but then she had to meet the requirements for a scholarship from the American Bar Association to cover her living costs. Her parents continue to live in Europe; she worries for them and, like all the Afghan women judges, for her family back home in Afghanistan.

"I struggled. I gave birth to my first baby, but then I was really worried about whether my English would be good enough to qualify for studying in the U.S. I was hardly sleeping because of the baby waking up in the night, and then I was trying to study all day. Even though my husband is very supportive, it was hard—and I didn't want anyone to regret giving me these opportunities, or to think I couldn't live up to them because I had small children."

One year into her stay in America, however, she no longer struggles with understanding the English spoken in classes, and is learning to navigate the bureaucratic and cultural differences of a foreign country. Her friends at Duke have supported her and celebrated with her. First they held a celebration for the birth of her second child, and then they held a belated wedding party.

"At first I wanted to celebrate my son's birth, because I thought that as a family we were missing everything. We were missing all these big moments. I didn't celebrate my wedding party because we were fleeing from Afghanistan. My daughter was born in Poland and I took her to visit some members of my family in Denmark, but we didn't celebrate because my mother and sister were depressed and stressed about leaving Afghanistan, and waiting for the outcome of different asylum and immigration applications in Sweden. Then when my son was born I delayed celebrating for a month because I was studying for my TOEFL [Test of English as a Foreign Language] exam and entrance to the LLM [program]. So eventually I thought we should celebrate, and in Afghanistan you celebrate the birth of a boy in the most luxurious way."

Tayeba says that in her culture they celebrate the birth of a boy by sacrificing a sheep, so she sent money back to her in-laws in Afghanistan to do that. But she also wanted to have a party in her new hometown. She reserved a small local venue, but then realized that the party would coincide with her wedding anniversary—and she wondered if she should celebrate that, too. Tayeba had two months to prepare for the party, but as she did so, buying special clothes from Afghan stores and ordering food, she realized that she was in fact preparing for the wedding celebration she had never had.

"Gradually it became a real wedding. We have many Afghan friends here now, especially in our neighborhood, and they encouraged me to do it. They had all missed a real Afghan party. I felt embarrassed about inviting my American friends, but when I asked my friends from Duke, Melinda and Jennifer, for advice about hiring a venue and a photographer, they asked if they could come, too.

"Melinda and Jennifer were so kind to me—they helped me in every aspect of my daily life as I settled in. They helped me understand how to get a bus to the grocery store, how to buy food and clothes, open a bank account, and get a driver's license—and they helped with very complicated things like how to navigate health insurance issues and apply for an LLM scholarship. No one assigned them to help with all of those things, but they did it all anyway."

Even so, Tayeba was still unsure about the wedding party because, she says, in Afghanistan it is embarrassing to get married without your family present. "When I tried on a big white wedding dress I said, 'No, I can't go through with it. I'm going to change the event back to a birth celebration for my son.' But my Afghan friends encouraged me to go ahead. I'd been so sad about the fact that I hadn't been able to have a traditional big Afghan wedding, or even wedding photos, when I got married—and now I could."

Tayeba ordered three dresses for her wedding celebration. "I ordered a green dress, a white wedding dress, and an Afghan dress. In Afghanistan people, brides wear a green dress and then the bride and groom put henna on each other hands. It's a special ceremony and we bring that henna in a special container. For our wedding we designed the containers. Girls dance with those containers and then bring them and we do the henna, and then we change into our traditional costumes. We bought those costumes from an Afghan store and we found an Afghan chef to cook very delicious traditional food. Everyone was so happy that they were at a real Afghan party. We ended up with ninety guests, which was too many! I wasn't expecting so many people to come but our American friends were surprised and delighted to be part of our Afghan customs."

The kindness and hospitality of her American friends have been a constant source of surprise and happiness to Tayeba. "When I needed a babysitter so that I could run around and make the preparations, they came to my house and looked after my son. One friend made my wedding background—a huge display hung with curtains and flowers—and she helped me find my wedding dress, too."

Her American guests were surprised, Tayeba says, that she did not wear her hijab, and that there was music and dancing. "We do a special dance with a knife before we cut the wedding cake. Someone will dance with the knife and will pretend that they will not give you the knife unless you pay money for it. The groom has to pay more and more money until she's satisfied. It was so funny for our American friends to see that. And we have special group dances, and a ceremony where we drive into the city and make a lot of noise. The men at our wedding wanted to do that and asked us to direct them to a highway so that they could dance on the road, but I sent them to our parking spot instead—I really didn't want them to get arrested! They danced and they played music—and everyone was watching them from their windows, wondering what was going on. Then we came home—to our new home—and they accompanied us to the door."

Tayeba had welcomed in her new life with a glorious celebration, but she remains painfully aware of the dire circumstances facing the women of Afghanistan. "The situation is getting worse and worse. For girls the situation is terrible; they cannot study, they cannot even work. Hazara people, and Hazara girls, face even greater discrimination. Hazara people cannot work for government organizations, and even international NGOs won't employ them because they have to meet Taliban demands to operate in the country. So they have to be laborers forever. The Hazara people struggle with poverty and the huge discrimination they face within their own country."

Tayeba says her dream is to help the Afghan people, even from exile. "I need a degree to be able to work in international organizations that have the authority to help Afghanistan in practical ways. Working for Afghans gives meaning to my life, and it makes me feel I am still alive. It makes me feel I did not lose my job, my life, and my personality. It connects me to the country that I will always belong to. For now all I can do is study hard to get my degree, and then I will start working for Afghanistan."

As Anisa Rasooli and Nafisa Kabuli settle into their new lives in America, the fate of Afghan women remains at the forefront of their concerns, too. In 2022 both took up two-year fellowships at Yale University, sharing their experiences as senior figures who shaped the Afghan judiciary, and at the same time they are considering how they can build a movement in exile—and, on top of all that, navigating the challenges of rebuilding a life in a foreign country. As Nafisa explains, that can be as mundane—and as complicated—as figuring out how public transport works, taking a long walk to find the bus stop, and then an even longer bus ride to her English class, and back again.

American and allied forces have now pulled out of Afghanistan, and the grip of the Taliban, with its merciless persecution of women, appears to be getting tighter. In the face of what sometimes seems to be global indifference, Anisa and Nafisa have often discussed what they, and the world, can work toward now.

Anisa says, "I am very worried about the judges who are still in Afghanistan and Pakistan. Obviously, my first wish is that they can safely leave Afghanistan and start their new life somewhere safe. I have three brothers and two sisters and all of their children still in Afghanistan. I'm always worried that my interviews might bring attention and harm to them.

"Despite this, I'm not going to stop talking about the situation of women, and women judges, in Afghanistan because their situation is desperate. They have nothing to eat. They have no safety or security. They cannot earn a living and they are finding it increasingly difficult to even stay alive.

"The IAWJ has worked so hard, but one organization cannot do it all.

"I would like to ask world leaders and international organizations to consider what the Universal Declaration of Human Rights says. Does it say that Afghans are not human? It says anybody of any skin color, any man or woman, is a human being. But the world does not see Afghans as human beings, and they don't pay attention to what is happening to us.

"The women of Afghanistan are, in effect, under house arrest. Young people are being killed, schools are closed, universities are barred to women. Women can't even go to the park, they can't even go to the hairdresser. They can't exercise or play sports.

"Men are now marrying three or four wives again. We have a lot of educated girls who now have no other choice but to become the second and third wives of these men. Often they marry an illiterate man who hasn't even gone to school. With no education or work opportunities for these girls, families are forced to marry them off just to ensure that they can eat and have a place to live.

"Where is the United Nations in acknowledging these women and their needs? The United Nations legitimizes the Taliban by giving them $40 million a week—and the Taliban tells their countrymen, and the world, that this means that they are recognized as a legitimate government.

"The United Nations says that they are giving this money so that it can alleviate poverty, but the Taliban doesn't give any funds to the people. They don't even pay people's pensions. I would like to ask them which schools they have opened and whose lives they have improved.

"My other disappointment is that the international community thinks that the closing of schools for girls is 'worrisome.' I see that word a lot. This is not 'worrisome.' This is suppressing women; this is persecuting women and depriving them of their most basic human rights. This is one of the worst things that any government can do. Does anyone know how long it will take to get back to having educated mothers raising their children in safe and healthy homes? What life does an illiterate mother have, and what kind of children can they raise?

"The Taliban are now taking the women who got divorced over the last twenty years and, one by one, forcing them to go back to their previous husbands. This is against Islamic practice, because in Islam a woman is allowed to get a divorce, and that divorce is final. What kind of Islam is the Taliban practicing?

"Another myth I hear these days is that the Taliban have brought security to Afghanistan. But they were the cause of the insecurity in the first place. Right now Afghanistan is like a big prison, for both men and women.

"To the international community I say: As a judge in Afghanistan, I worked for many years to pass all the human rights conventions that you created. Now I would like to ask you to follow your own conventions with regard to the people of Afghanistan. Afghans are also human beings, and they deserve the same rights and protections as everyone else."

Epilogue

AS OF SEPTEMBER 2024, APPROXIMATELY FORTY WOMEN JUDGes still remain trapped in Afghanistan. Their cases are complex, and the bureaucratic hurdles of getting them visas to final destinations, like the United States, seem insurmountable at times. The women will not travel without their families also moving to safety, making the evacuation infinitely more difficult. Meanwhile, the attention of the world has long moved on to other crises, such as Ukraine. After more than three years of late nights, endless Zoom calls, intense negotiations, and the responsibility of so many lives depending upon their actions, the international women of the IAWJ are tired, truly tired, sometimes putting their own health at risk in order to continue with their mission. "I think we actually all have some post-traumatic shock disorder from the things we've heard and seen," says Susan Glazebrook in New Zealand. "It has changed us," Robyn Tupman in Sydney agrees. "Getting the remaining women judges out of Afghanistan is not easy. Sometimes it seems impossible. But we are still committed to what we pledged at the beginning: we won't stop until every woman judge in Afghanistan is safe." As Susan Glazebrook told them: "We will leave no one behind."

As international negotiations with the Taliban continue, Mahfuza Folad is one former Afghan woman judge who is continuing the struggle on the ground. Now living in Toronto, Mahfuza was a judge in a Kabul primary court for four years before stepping down to found Justice for All—Afghanistan's first legal aid organization, set up to give all Afghan women access to justice. Starting in a tiny office in Kabul and with one small legal awareness program for schoolchildren, Justice for All spread across eleven provinces of Afghanistan, mainly aimed at women and girls, but also at all poor people who could not pay for a defense lawyer. Mahfuza says, "It was not easy work. One of our lawyers was murdered by the ex-husband of one of the women who had come to us for help. In some provinces we were the only organization attempting to give women access to justice and raise awareness about women's rights and human rights. We ran programs to raise awareness about women's rights with men, too, because if women know about their rights but men do not respect them, they are useless."

After the Taliban took over the country again in 2021, Mahfuza and her family fled, but even in exile her work continues. "No one can go into the office in Afghanistan, but we have started working again to support journalists, doctors, human rights activists, and people who are at risk. We also offer psychological counseling, and in two provinces we offer legal advice and legal aid."

Mahfuza says part of their work is observing and reporting what the Taliban have done to the Afghan justice system. "Someone needs to report what is going on. The Taliban have dismantled everything. They make decisions themselves based upon their own interpretations of *shari'a*, which do not respect the law."

Working with other women and human rights groups, Mahfuza and Justice for All are agreeing on a set of recommendations for the international community in negotiations with the Taliban. Mahfuza says she is nervous about what could be considered any small steps forward when the government itself is illegitimate. "I don't want the international community to get the Taliban to agree to keep girls in school for longer, for example, if those are just Taliban schools that teach extremism. The very foundation is wrong, because the Taliban government is illegitimate. The Taliban took

Afghanistan by force, and it is not serving the will of the people. The change we need is fundamental. We need to correct the foundation." Mahfuza smiles and shrugs a little. "I'm not saying this is going to be easy to achieve. I know it takes time, but I will not keep quiet. I will advocate, and fight for our rights for as long as I am alive."

The women judges of Afghanistan in this book are also continuing to advocate for women and the future of their country, with Nafisa Kabuli, Anisa Rasooli, and others working toward reforming the Afghan Association of Women Judges in Exile as a global nonprofit organization, registered in the United States.

Anisa Rasooli says: "Despite all of this suffering, I want to end my story on a good note. I want to say that despite all the problems and all of the bad news and the hardship, as a Muslim woman, I am hopeful for the future. I believe that the future will be good—but to ensure that, please don't leave the women of Afghanistan alone. Be with them. Speak for them and support them. Help them to rise up."

In the United Kingdom, IAWJ judge Anisa Dhanji says that as a former immigrant herself she understands the struggle of restarting your life in a new country, but "these are brilliant women, and I am excited to see how they are going to change the world and what they are going to do with the rest of their lives."

For twenty years the women judges of Afghanistan served as the conscience of their nation. As they continue in their struggle they remain united in one endeavor: keeping the story alive.

Notes

1. Nadia Sonnevelt and Monika Lindbekk, eds., *Women Judges in the Muslim World: A Comparative Study of Discourse and Practice* (Leiden, The Netherlands: Brill, 2017).

2. Ibid., xiii.

3. Bureau of Democracy, Human Rights, and Labor, "Report on the Taliban's War Against Women," U.S. State Department report, November 17, 2001, https://2001-2009.state.gov/g/drl/rls/6185.htm.

4. "Women in Afghanistan: The Back Story," Amnesty International report, https://www.amnesty.org.uk/womens-rights-afghanistan-history (accessed November 11, 2024).

5. Amita Parashar Kelly, "A Legal Trailblazer's Journey: Vanessa Ruiz '72," *Wellesley Magazine*, Summer 2023, https://magazine.wellesley.edu/summer-2023/legal-trailblazer%E2%80%99s-journey.

6. "How We Protect Children's Rights with the UN Convention on the Rights of the Child," UNICEF, https://www.unicef.org.uk/what-we-do/un-convention-child-rights/ (accessed November 11, 2024).

7. Special Inspector General for Afghan Reconstruction, "Private Sector Development and Economic Growth: Lessons from the U.S. Experience in Afghanistan," April 2018, https://www.sigar.mil/pdf/lessonslearned/SIGAR-18-38-LL.pdf.

Acknowledgments

AS A WRITER LIVING IN LONDON, COMPLETING THIS BOOK REQUIRED ENORmous help from many people, none more so than the judges themselves, Afghan and international, who facilitated so many meetings, patiently answered questions, clarified misunderstandings, and each devoted hour upon hour of their time to telling their stories and allowing the world to share their experience of building justice in Afghanistan, and having that taken away in the cruelest and most terrifying circumstances.

In addition, their longtime translator and friend, Farah, did all of this and more—spending hours translating in person, and in writing, and showing incredible commitment to resolving every single issue and question. Without Farah, I'm not sure this book could exist at all.

A huge acknowledgement too to Gaia Banks, Lucy Fawcett and colleagues at Sheil Land, and Valerie Borchardt at Georges Borchardt, for sharing a belief that the story of the women judges of Afghanistan should be told, and to zakia henderson-brown, Diane Wachtell, and the team at The New Press, and Hannah MacDonald at Duckworth, for bringing it into reality.